Software Design and

Software Design and Prototyping using *me too*

Heather Alexander

Systems Engineering Division, STC Technology Ltd

Val Jones

Department of Computing Science, University of Stirling

Prentice Hall

New York London Toronto Sydney Tokyo

First published 1990 by
Prentice Hall International (UK) Ltd,
66 Wood Lane End, Hemel Hempstead,
Hertfordshire, HP2 4RG
A division of
Simon & Schuster International Group

Printed and bound in Great Britain by
BPCC Wheatons Ltd, Exeter

Library of Congress Cataloging-in-Publication Data
are available from the publisher

British Library Cataloguing in Publication Data

Alexander, Heather, *1955–*
Software design and prototyping using me too.
1. Computer systems. Software. Development.
Prototyping
I. Title II. Jones, Valerie, *1952–*
005.1

ISBN 0-13-820259-1

1 2 3 4 5 93 92 91 90 89

ISBN 0-13-820259-1

What's a book? Everything or nothing. The eye that sees it is all.

Ralph Waldo Emerson

Contents

PART II THE *me too* NOTATION

5 *me too* notation – the basics

6 *me too* notation – sets

7 *me too* notation – binary relations and maps

8 *me too* notation – sequences and records

PART III EXAMPLES AND CASE STUDIES

9 Example 1 – a design for a simple frames system

10 Example 2 – a simple concordance package

Preface

Introduction

This book describes a design method and tool named *me too*, the result of bringing together the fields of functional programming and software engineering. When the *me too* project began in the early 1980s, such a combination was unusual, because functional languages were then seen as impractical and inefficient, with little to offer the software engineer facing all the difficulties of software development. Since then, implementations of functional languages have become more efficient and functional programming is being applied to larger-scale industrial developments.

In *me too*, the properties of functional languages have been exploited to provide a practical design tool for software engineers. This tool takes the form of an executable formal specification language for describing and prototyping system designs at an early stage of development. The language is drawn from the mathematics of functions and set theory, taking some relatively simple but powerful constructs which are capable of execution on a computer. As the early chapters of the book show, this approach turns out to be highly relevant to the issues of software reliability and quality.

The major objectives of this book are to demonstrate that formal design methods need not be daunting but can be mastered by programmers and designers, and that, combined with a prototyping environment, such methods have much to contribute to the tasks facing systems and software engineers.

The scope of the book

This book is intended both for academic researchers and students, and for software engineers, designers and programmers. Despite being built on the possibly unfamiliar foundations of functional programming and formal methods, the book assumes no knowledge of these areas, introducing and explaining concepts as they are required. The reader who wishes to pursue such areas further will find appropriate references throughout the text.

This book does not attempt to convey the subtler intricacies or delights of functional programming, leaving this to such texts as Henderson (1980), Glaser *et al.* (1984) or Bird and Wadler (1988). Nor does it attempt more than a brief survey of the spectrum of formal methods in software engineering. Instead, it focuses on a practical and useful means of improving the business of software and systems design. The book is a self-contained tutorial for the *me too* language and method. Study of the book is sufficient to enable readers to begin using *me too* as part of their work where appropriate. Moreover, readers who wish to explore other uses of formal methods will find here a solid foundation from which to proceed.

The structure of the book

The book is divided into three major parts. Part I explains the main influences and concepts in the development of *me too*. This part of the book sets *me too* in the context of related approaches and within the framework of the software development process. We discuss how software is developed and the rôle that both formal methods and prototyping can play in that process. A brief description is given of how *me too* results from combining these techniques, followed by an explanation of the *me too* method.

Part II describes the language of *me too*, covering the mathematical notation for such data types as sets, maps and sequences. We would emphasize that mastering this language has been demonstrated to be well within the capabilities of any competent software practitioner – even self-styled 'mathematical failures' have been successfully trained in the use of *me too*! Little mathematical knowledge is assumed on the part of the reader. These chapters include exercises for the reader which may be tackled either on paper or using the *me too* shell. All the exercises, examples and case studies have been validated using the tools. The reader who wishes to make use of *me too* will find it helpful to type in the specifications given in the text and to experiment with the prototypes thus created.

Part III presents a series of extended examples and case studies, several of which are the result of collaborative work with project groups from International Computers Limited (ICL).

The *me too* tools

Enquiries about *me too* should be addressed to

STC Technology Ltd (*me too*)
Copthall House
Nelson Place
Newcastle-under-Lyme
Staffs, ST5 1EZ
England

Acknowledgements

The *me too* method is the product of a four-year collaborative project between STC Technology Ltd (STL), Newcastle-under-Lyme, England, and the Department of Computing Science, University of Stirling, Stirling, Scotland. The method and notation are based on work by Professor Peter Henderson, now at the University of Southampton, England. His main collaborator in this work was Cydney Minkowitz.

The project was funded through the UK Alvey programme as part of its Software Engineering theme.* Those who have worked on the project, and on whose collective effort this book is based, were (in alphabetical order):

University of Stirling	**STC Technology Ltd**	
Keri Davies	Heather Alexander	Anne Jones
Peter Henderson	Stephen Bennett	Cydney Minkowitz
Simon Jones	Eleanor Bruce	Jonathan Rowles
Val Jones	Nick Capon	

The personal contribution of each member of the project team is acknowledged.

The case studies in Part III involved collaboration with various project teams from ICL. The NTU team referred to in Chapter 12 consisted of Ben Potter, Parmjeet Pandha, Ari Gershuni and Vince Wood. The specifications and descriptions of PARIS, as discussed in Chapter 13, were made available by ICL Group Information Systems. The specifications described in that chapter are based on those developed by David Wigglesworth, with assistance from Richard Tesh. The FAM architecture and security mechanisms described in Chapter 14 are the work of David McVitie, ICL, and we would like to thank him for his long and patient explanations of the architecture. Together with the ICL, STL, BT, NCR and other staff who have attended the *me too* courses run by the project team, the workers mentioned above have influenced the development of *me too* as a result of their practical experience and by their penetrating questions.

In writing this book, we have been given constructive and incisive criticism from Bob Clark, Simon Jones and Chic Rattray (University of Stirling), from Stephen Bennett, Cydney Minkowitz and Jonathan Rowles (STL) and from several anonymous reviewers, all of which has resulted in considerable improvements over our original efforts.

* ALV/PRJ/SE/029 'Use of functional programming as a design and prototyping methodology for intelligent business systems'.

Our thanks go to Rena and to Andrew for all their encouragement and support.

The authors and publishers gratefully acknowledge permission from the following owners and controllers of copyright to reprint extracts from published material:

G.L. Alexanderson: George Polya, *How to Solve It: a new aspect of mathematical method*. Doubleday & Co. Inc.;
Cambridge University Press: Gordon L. Glegg, *The Design of Design*;
Constable & Co. Ltd.: George Santayana;
The Daily Telegraph: Walter Sickert, *Artist and Public*;
Grafton Books, A Division of the Collins Publishing Group: Flann O'Brien, *At Swim-Two-Birds*;
Hamish Hamilton Ltd.: Cyril Connolly, *The Unquiet Grave: a word cycle by Palinurus*;
The Harvester Press Ltd.: Douglas R. Hofstadter, *Gödel, Escher, Bach: An Eternal Golden Braid*;
A.M. Heath and Company Ltd, and the estate of the late Flann O'Brien: Flann O'Brien, *At Swim-Two-Birds*;
Macmillan Publishers Ltd.: Lewis Carroll, *The Hunting of the Snark: an agony in eight fits*; Osbert Sitwell (ed.) *A Free House! The Writings of Walter Richard Sickert*;
Macmillan Publishing Company: W.B. Yeats, *Collected Poems of W.B. Yeats*, © 1933 by Macmillan Publishing Company, renewed 1961 by Bertha Georgie Yeats, lines from 'Lullaby';
Oxford University Press: A.N. Whitehead, *An Introduction to Mathematics*; William Wordsworth, *Wordsworth: Poetical Works*, lines from 'The River Duddon';
Simon & Schuster Ltd.: Douglas R. Hofstadter, *Gödel, Escher, Bach: An Eternal Golden Braid*;
Unwin Hyman Ltd.: Tobias Danzig, *Number: The Language of Science*; Bertrand Russell;
A.P. Watt Ltd., on behalf of Michael B. Yeats and Macmillan London Ltd.: *Collected Poems of W.B. Yeats*, lines from 'Lullaby'.

Heather Alexander
Val Jones
July 1989

PART I

INTRODUCTION TO *me too*

The chapters in this part of the book are intended to show why techniques such as *me too* are of value in software development. They also introduce the concepts associated with *me too*. Chapter 1 discusses the difficulties surrounding the production of reliable software and identifies areas which may yield improvements, given appropriate tools and techniques. Chapter 2 presents two software engineering techniques that have been suggested as ways of overcoming some of the problems already described, while Chapter 3 shows how they complement each other when combined in *me too*. Finally, the *me too* method is described and exemplified in Chapter 4.

Chapter 1

Producing reliable software

The last thing one discovers in composing a work is what to put first.

Blaise Pascal

Despite decades of constructing software systems, their development remains an expensive, unreliable and unpredictable business. Tools and techniques have been introduced, many of which have a valuable rôle to play, yet the production of software, and of systems with software subcomponents, is still no easy task.

Why should this be? Even a cursory examination of the history of software development indicates that significant progress has been made over the years. We have moved to high-level programming languages, sophisticated debugging tools and fourth-generation application builders, with the prospect of programming environments that earlier generations of programmers could never have imagined. And yet, in spite of this, there are few software developers who will guarantee the reliability of their products and fewer still who expect to achieve 'zero-defect' code. This chapter looks at some of the obstacles to achieving reliable systems and how they might be overcome.

1.1 Problems in systems and software development

One reason for the difficulty of producing reliable software is the nature of software itself. Software is abstract rather than physical in nature. We might think that the lack of physical constraints would make software production easier – there is no deterioration with use, no friction, no variation of performance under different environmental conditions – but the lack of physical attributes also makes software production the complex and difficult task that it is. Software deals with quantities that take discrete values, not the continuously varying quantities like temperature which concern other types of engineer. Consequently, testing a software product at its limits of permissible values does not guarantee its behavior between those limits. For example, showing that a database enquiry produces a correctly formatted reply when there are no entries in the database and when the database is full is no guarantee of the results when there is only one entry. Nor can a satisfactory reply with one entry give any guarantee of a correct reply when there are two entries, and so on. In contrast, in other types of engineering, engineers are able to test their products at the limits of performance and environment, and infer their behavior for intermediate values.

Another reason for the difficulties we find in software development is that the computer hardware on which software products run has become cheaper and more sophisticated, giving rise to greatly increased expectations about what computer systems can achieve. As a result, the size, capabilities and complexity of software systems are also increasing, putting further demands on our ability to produce reliable software.

A further reason lies in the way in which software is developed. Despite the use of the term 'engineering', very often the process of creating software systems is far removed from the well-established engineering practices of other fields. The emphasis is on coding, debugging and testing as the means of software building, with insufficient time given to requirements analysis or design. The attitude to faults in the product is illuminating – fixing errors in a released product is normal practice for software producers, but is rare and highly embarrassing for, say, car manufacturers.

The question that arises concerns how we are to overcome these obstacles to the production of reliable and effective software. In constructing any complex artefact, the process by which that construction is effected is crucial. It is no different with software artefacts. The process for constructing software systems contributes a great deal to the reliability and effectiveness of the end product. It is important, therefore, to look at how software production is organized, what activities are undertaken, what priorities are set and where costs are incurred. The following sections examine this process in more detail.

1.2 The software development process

A common way of proceeding in systems and software development is to adopt a phased lifecycle, where the development process consists of a series of phases. There is much debate about what those phases are and what they deliver, but the details are not particularly relevant here, since we wish to make a more general point about how the phases are related.

Presentation of this phased process can take a number of forms, one of the earliest and most persistent views being that of the **waterfall model**, arising from the expectation that the products of the phases 'cascade' from one phase to the next. A waterfall model of the process is shown in Fig. 1.1 (with some feedback between phases to allow for corrections and modifications).

However, it is recognized that there are deficiencies in this view, e.g. Birrell and Ould (1985). A major criticism is that it does not show clearly the relationships that exist between the early development phases and the later validation phases, despite the importance of these relationships in determining activities, priorities and costs. An alternative way of presenting the phased process has been offered which does show these links – the **V-diagram**, shown in Fig. 1.2.

This view is based on an approach described in Ould and Unwin (1986) and the *STARTS Guide* (NCC, 1987). In the 'V', the left side shows the development phases while the right side shows the validation phases. This diagram explicitly

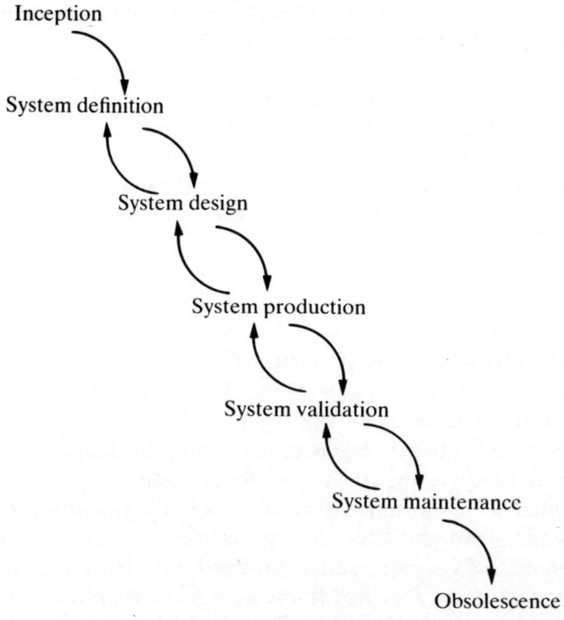

Figure 1.1 A waterfall view of the phased process.

relates the later validation activities to the earlier development phases, stating that there is a direct relationship between those which appear on the same level, such as 'system design' and 'system testing', for example. Note that, in order to show these relationships across the 'V', it has been necessary to expand the single validation phase shown in Fig. 1.1 into module testing, system testing and system acceptance.

As the process moves down the development side of the V-diagram, each phase

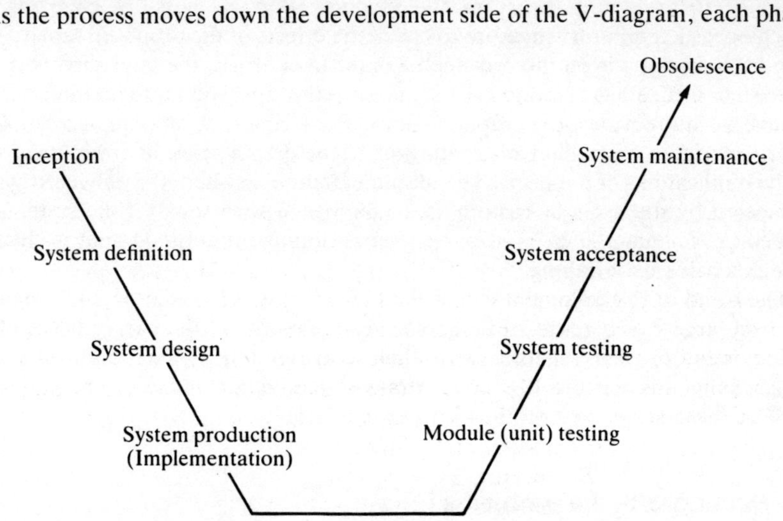

Figure 1.2 A V-diagram view of the phased process.

yields a further decomposition of the system, giving a more detailed view of that system. Each phase in the validation side validates the view of the system created at its level. Thus, 'system testing' validates the high-level view of the system described in the 'system design' phase while 'module (unit) testing' validates the detailed code level of the 'implementation' phase.

By making these relationships explicit, the V-diagram aids our analysis of some of the shortcomings of software development, where our concern is both the prevention and the discovery of errors in software systems. In the next section, we examine where errors are made, when they are found and the costs associated with them.

1.3 The cost of modification and repair

As mentioned above, one result of this view of software development is the recognition that there are different levels of validation. Further, it gives credence to the observation that in practice errors tend to be discovered at the level at which they were made. Thus, the majority of simple coding errors made during the implementation phase are detected during unit testing. On the other hand, the overall structure of the system created during the design phase cannot be fully validated until modules are available to create a version of the system for testing. Similarly, misunderstandings about the requirements and abilities of customers and users are incorporated during the definition of the system, but are unlikely to emerge until acceptance testing or user trials, when the system is released to users for testing.

A serious consequence of this late discovery of errors is the high cost of remedying them. It is not surprising to find that the later any faults are discovered, the more expensive they are to rectify (Boehm, 1981). A coding error results in a change to the source program and recompilation, or possibly some form of 'patching' as a temporary measure to check the effects of the proposed repair. Very little back-tracking is required in such a case. In contrast, the later discovery that the system design has failed to take some aspect of operation into account is likely to have far more widespread repercussions. Repairing such an omission can affect several modules, and will involve returning to the design phase in order to consider all the implications of the error. The ultimate 'failure' is where the delivered system is rejected by the users or customers, as happened with some of the systems described in Neumann *et al.* (1987a, b). Redeveloping an entire system is clearly a very expensive undertaking.

The trend of this argument is that the highest costs of validation and repair are incurred largely as a result of inadequacies or failures in the early phases of the development process together with their correspondingly late discovery. This indicates that it is reasonable to concentrate both on reducing the numbers of errors made at these stages and on their earlier detection.

1.4 Dealing with the problems

One conclusion which has been drawn from the above discussion is that the relationships across the 'V' should be made explicit in the process itself. That is, each validation phase should be planned as part of the corresponding development phase, in order to provide a more comprehensive, more objective and better managed validation strategy (Ould and Unwin, 1986). Thus, for example, acceptance criteria would be defined during the definition of the system, whereas system tests would be specified when the system itself was being designed.

In addition, there is an emphasis on 'testing' the products of all the development phases, rather than just the implemented code. Such testing is usually achieved by reviewing designs, specifications and code against the relevant products of the previous phase. Thus, the system specification is verified against the requirements specification, say, while the code is compared with the detailed module specifications.

Structuring a project in this way has two aims. The first is to prevent errors from being carried through the development phases by detecting them 'at source', that is, in the phase where they occur. The second aim is to ensure that the validation phases are as comprehensive as possible, thus trapping errors which find their way into the implemented code.

An extension to this approach is to incorporate techniques such as prototyping, which make the early detection of errors even more likely than reviews, inspections or walk-throughs. However, this is still concerned with finding (and 'curing') errors rather than preventing them from being made in the first place. A more fundamental issue is how to reduce the number of errors which occur in these early phases.

1.5 Engineering software

The discussion so far has indicated that many of the problems we have identified arise in the early phases in the process, implying that most benefit will be gained by investing time and resources there. This conclusion is strengthened when we consider the development process in other fields of engineering. There, production is often a short (and increasingly automated) phase, with the bulk of the effort being given to design and early experimentation.

In the other engineering disciplines, too, there is considerable emphasis on models (both theoretical and concrete) or prototypes during the design phase. Electrical engineers produce a 'bread-board', that is, a rough version of their product, with only those components essential to its functionality present. Civil engineers may construct a model of a proposed bridge design and use a wind tunnel to evaluate its performance under extreme conditions. Prototype cars are subjected to desert and arctic conditions, as well as being driven in trials. Alternatively, the experimentation and analysis may be theoretical in nature. Stress analysis, flow analysis and simulations which model the behavior of a system are among the many techniques available in the different fields.

Gradually it is being recognized that software engineers will have to develop and use analogous techniques if they are to overcome the problems of reliability described above (Hoare, 1982). Software engineers need techniques with a sound theoretical basis which, by their precision and demand for accuracy, reduce the number of errors made. They also need techniques enabling them to check and review their designs during the requirements and design phases, rather than waiting until system validation, when it is more difficult and more expensive to make changes.

Such techniques are now emerging and are being given a place in the development process. Formal specification methods and prototyping are two of these techniques. Formal specification methods use mathematical language to describe software designs, so that the designs can then be analyzed, reasoned about and shown to possess (or avoid) certain properties. Prototyping involves the rapid production of a version of the system, perhaps to evaluate likely performance, or to assess the feasibility of proposed designs, or to allow early user trials.

Formal specification and prototyping are not the only means of addressing the problems of software development, but there is increasing evidence that they both have a contribution to make (Boehm *et al.*, 1984). Together they form the basis of the design tool described in this book.

1.6 Summary

In attempting to analyze some of the difficulties encountered in producing software systems and subsystems, we have acknowledged the relationships that exist between the different development and validation phases. In particular, the high costs incurred when errors and omissions are discovered in a late phase are an encouragement to invest more time and effort in the corresponding early phase. This leads to a consideration of techniques that can be applied early in the development process, with the aim of both detecting and preventing errors in the eventual system.

Chapter 2

Formal specification and rapid prototyping

We all know how difficult it is, in drawing up the simplest communication, not to say the contrary of what we mean.

Walter Sickert

This chapter introduces two software engineering techniques which are intended to aid the prevention and detection of errors in the early phases of software development. The techniques are formal specification and rapid prototyping. The objective of formal specification is to produce a precise and concise description of a system whilst rapid prototyping provides a means of modeling a proposed system in order to explore its characteristics and to experiment with alternative ideas.

2.1 Formal specification methods

. . . it is a sound tendency to seek meaning and facts behind the words.

George Polya

2.1.1 What are formal methods?

Formality, as defined by Naur (1982), means expressing some concept 'purely by means of symbols given a specialized meaning', the main benefit being that there is then no room for argument about the meaning of the concept being described. Other engineering disciplines use formal notations of various kinds (graphical, symbolic, mathematical and so on) as a matter of course when specifying their designs. The resulting specifications can be checked, reviewed and endorsed by other designers in the field. They then offer a precise basis for production of the product.

In software engineering, too, there are various kinds of formal notations, ranging from state transition diagrams and decision tables through regular expressions to algebraic and set-theoretic languages. For software engineering, though, the term 'formal specification' is usually reserved for notations whose symbols are mathematical rather than, say, diagrammatic, and this is the sense in which it is used in this book. Formal specification in software engineering, then, involves using some form of mathematical notation to describe the structure and/or properties of a proposed system.

2.1.2 Why formal specification is advocated

The primary benefit of mathematics is that the meaning of a mathematical expression is defined. It may be abstruse and complex, it may be elegant in its simplicity, but it has a single, unambiguous meaning. Traditionally specifications and designs at all levels for software systems rarely display this essential quality, leaving much of their interpretation to their readers. When the readers are the system implementors, this freedom of interpretation can lead to errors and omissions in the code, resulting in high costs for support and repair.

A major benefit of formal specification methods is that a formal specification has a precise interpretation, determined by the mathematical language in which it is written. Designers may wish to argue about what *should* be specified in a design, but using a mathematical language means that they cannot argue about what *has* been specified. A further advantage is that, by adhering to the discipline of a formal language, the production of a formal specification clarifies the concepts of the design at an early stage.

Abstraction is a powerful aid to mastering the complexity of a system, because it allows us to draw back from details and consider higher-level issues of overall structure, organization or functionality. Mathematical notation enables systems to be described in abstract terms, yet with a precision and succinctness not found in diagrams or natural language specifications. In particular, specifications can consider only *what* the system is to do, rather than the details of *how* the system is to do it.

Producing a formal specification has immediate benefits. It brings comprehension of the system at an abstract level, demands attention to issues of completeness and consistency, and results in a documented and precise record of agreement between the designers (Guttag *et al.*, 1982). However, there are further uses for the specification. Mathematical expression brings the potential for formal reasoning about the specification, so that the designers can prove that it possesses certain desirable properties (or avoids undesirable ones). For example, one important property might be that the specification is equivalent to a more abstract version created earlier in the development process. The use of mathematics allows the possibility of transforming the specification repeatedly towards more and more detailed versions, until it contains sufficient information to be executed as a program. This leads to the prospect of automatic generation of programs from formal specifications.

2.1.3 Varieties of formal specification methods

There are many approaches to formal specification, employing widely different notations and styles. For convenience, we consider them here in two groups, although there is some overlap between them since some methods draw on techniques from both groups. The first group is **axiomatic** specification, alternatively known as property-based specification. The second is **model-based** specification, also known as abstract model or operational specification. In both groups, the methods can be used to specify abstractions of both the data and the operations which make up the system being described.

The categories of formal specification are expanded upon in Liskov and Zilles (1975), while the application of the more popular methods to a non-trivial system can be found in Cohen *et al.* (1986).

Axiomatic methods

Axiomatic methods make statements about the properties of a system by means of axioms, that is, rules governing how the system is to operate. Consider first specifying an operation. In this case, the axioms state the conditions on the input to the operation (the **precondition**) and on the relationship between that input and the output from the operation (the **postcondition**). The axioms do not specify how the transformation from input to output will take place. This style of axiomatic specification is also known as input/output or implicit specification, because it states the relationship between input and output but is not explicit about how that relationship is achieved.

In specifying a class of data objects, the axioms state relationships between operations which can be performed on those objects. Such a class of objects is often referred to as an **abstract data type**. An oft-quoted example is the stack, of which a simple version might be

```
Operations:
  new_stack : -> Stack
  push : Item x Stack -> Stack
  pop : Stack -> Stack
  top : Stack -> Item

Axioms:
  pop(new_stack()) = error_stack
  pop(push(i,s)) = s
  top(new_stack()) = error_item
  top(push(i,s)) = i
```

new_stack and push are constructors of the stack object (or type), and are considered primitive. new_stack creates an empty stack while push adds an item to the stack. The operations pop and top, which manipulate stacks of items, can then be defined in terms of the constructors. The operation pop removes the top item from its supplied stack and returns the shortened stack, while top returns the top item of the supplied stack.

Where, as here, the axioms are stated as equations, this style of specification is known as **algebraic specification** (Guttag and Horning, 1978; Ehrig and Mahr, 1985). This is because the specification identifies a class of algebras which satisfy the axioms for the system being described, where an algebra identifies a collection of objects, together with rules for manipulating and combining them.

There are other forms of axiomatic specification. For example, some methods employ formal logic, such as first-order predicate logic (Kowalski, 1985) or temporal logic (Manna and Pneuli, 1981).

The most widely practiced axiomatic method is that of algebraic specification, of which one example is OBJ (Goguen and Meseguer, 1982). OBJ allows designers to describe abstract objects or, more rarely, algorithms. Objects can import existing objects, creating a hierarchy of objects, and can be parameterized in order to allow generic objects to be created and then later specialized. For example, the object Stack could be defined for items of any sort, allowing it to be instantiated later as Stack_Of_Boolean, Stack_Of_Integer, Stack_Of_Real, and so on. OBJ is unusual among axiomatic methods in that specifications written in OBJ can be executed.

Model-based methods

Rather than basing the meaning of a specification on axioms, model-based methods rely on the existence of an underlying model whose meaning is predefined. That model may be an operational model, based on operations provided by a well-defined but possibly hypothetical machine, or it may be a data model, based on mathematical data types.

When specifying an operation, the transformation between input and output is stated explicitly in terms of the operations available in the language for the underlying machine. One possibility, for example, is to use purely functional constructs in the Lisp language.

When specifying an object, the object is modeled on an existing mathematical object and the operations on that object are specified in terms of existing operations for the underlying object. For example, the stack object might be based on the mathematical object of the sequence. A model-based specification for the stack could then be written as

```
Stack = sequence(Item)

new_stack : -> Stack
new_stack() ≡ []

push : Stack x Item -> Stack
push(s,i) ≡ [i]^s

pop : Stack -> Stack
pop(s) ≡
  if s ≠ [] then tl(s) else error_stack()

top : Stack -> Item
top(s) ≡
  if s ≠ [] then hd(s) else error_item()
```

This is not written in any particular specification language, but simply relies on the existence of some predefined notation for sequences. In this case, we assume that there is a means of denoting the empty sequence (shown as []) and of enumerating sequences by giving their constituent elements (as in [a,c,b]), together with operations on sequences such as concatenation (^) for joining two sequences, hd for extracting the first item of the sequence, and tl to remove the first item from the sequence.

Both the Vienna Development Method (VDM) (Jones, 1986) and Z (Hayes, 1986) are model-based methods, where data objects are modeled on underlying mathematical entities, with operations on the objects being defined in terms of operations associated with those underlying entities. However, both VDM and Z also draw on axiomatic styles of specification. In VDM, operations are specified using preconditions and postconditions, which state the conditions to be satisfied before an operation is invoked and the conditions which hold after it has been invoked. In Z, operations are also specified using predicates to relate the before and after state of the objects. Tools are being developed to support both these methods, and both are being applied in industrial software development.

As subsequent chapters show, *me too* is related to VDM and Z since it takes a model-based approach to specification. However, with its absence of state and emphasis on designing abstract data types, it also shares some common ground with algebraic methods.

2.2 Rapid software prototyping

> *Nothing ever becomes real till it is experienced.*
>
> John Keats

2.2.1 What is prototyping?

According to the *Shorter Oxford English Dictionary*, a prototype is 'the first or primary type of anything; a pattern, model, standard, exemplar, archetype', being derived from the Greek words *protos* meaning 'first' and *typos* meaning 'a type'. For Brooks (1975), this first-of-its-type is a 'pilot system', so that prototyping is the initial attempt to produce the system, purely with the intention of learning how to do the job properly.

The inclusion of the term *model* in the dictionary definition shows us another aspect of prototyping, namely the building of models. Models are preliminary representations of the system, often on a smaller scale than the final product. Some elements or aspects of the full-scale system may be omitted from the models if they are not important to the design issues being investigated. This view has been succinctly expressed by Peters:

> *... a prototype is a working model in which only some of the features of the final system are supported.*
>
> *Peters, 1981, p. 34*

These approaches are complementary, leading us to view prototyping as the creation of preliminary representations of a system, perhaps on a smaller scale than the final version, in order to explore characteristics of that system before committing to a particular design. There are other views of prototyping which have extended this definition beyond the preliminary phases, considering development to be an evolutionary process involving successive 'prototypes' (Ince and Hekmatpour, 1987). These and other variations on the theme of prototyping are discussed in Section 2.2.3.

2.2.2 Why prototyping is advocated

As with formal methods, we can look at other fields of engineering to discover how and why they use prototyping. We find that prototyping is used amongst other things for exploring ideas, for assessing potential markets, for estimating costs, and for establishing feasibility and performance limits. All of these objectives apply also to software engineering when new systems are being considered or existing systems are to be enhanced.

A benefit arising from prototypes which are genuinely rapid in construction is that designers have the time to explore alternative designs. For example, they may wish to assess the relative merits of various algorithms or data structures, or to offer different versions of a proposed user interface.

The V-diagram description of the development process highlights the cost of early design errors by showing that they are often discovered in the later phases when correction becomes both difficult and expensive. Prototyping is one way of reducing these costs, because it allows testing of designs at an early stage of development, well before implementation begins. Errors and omissions detected at this stage can be remedied since there is still the opportunity to make changes, even radical changes if they are deemed necessary.

A major underlying reason for considering prototyping as a valid use of development resources is encapsulated by Brooks' dictum

> *... plan to throw one away; you will, anyhow*

which indicates his view that rarely, if ever, is the system right first time in any case. The only question, says Brooks, is whether the pilot system is thrown away or sold to customers. The argument is that, until a first version or prototype has been developed, the designers do not know how to set about the system design properly. Based on feedback from a prototype, a full-scale system can then be constructed, with the confidence that it will meet the requirements set for it.

It might be said, too, that prototyping also allows designers to experience what they inflict on the users of their systems. Although designers are no substitute for users (since the two groups usually have little in common, either in experience or in expectations), making them users of their own system is at least a first step towards considering how the system is to function in practice and may avoid some of the worst excesses of 'user unfriendliness'.

Having described some of the advantages of prototyping as an activity in the development process, we now examine some of the different types of prototyping.

2.2.3 Varieties of prototypes

There are many different forms of prototyping available to the designer (Carey and Mason, 1983; Ince and Hekmatpour, 1987) and a great deal of discussion about the rôle and content of a software prototype (e.g. Squires, 1982; Floyd, 1984). One common feature is that a prototype is intended to explore some area of uncertainty or some critical aspect of a design. Where there is no doubt concerning how to proceed, or where the facilities of the system are well understood, there is little justification for any prototyping activity. Where there are still questions to be answered, prototyping can be a way of providing those answers. The details of how a prototype is constructed and then used are largely dependent on the particular objectives it is intended to achieve.

There is a further element in common between the various kinds of prototypes, namely that they should be cheaper and quicker to produce than the intended system. In general, this means restricting the system in some way, omitting those aspects of the final product which are familiar or less important and selecting those which still need to be investigated. This could mean, amongst other things, limiting the amount of data handled, considering only a subset of the required facilities or disregarding performance characteristics.

These two strands of exploration and cost-effectiveness, though, can still give rise to a wide variety of prototypes. For example, the designers may choose to concentrate on the user interface. Here they provide only a surface presentation of the product with little or no functionality behind it (what industrial designers call an *appearance model*). For a system which has to meet stringent performance criteria, they are more likely to investigate different ways of achieving the required high performance. In an entirely novel system, it may be necessary to experiment with its structure, the algorithms it uses, or the supporting hardware facilities. Where user requirements are not clear or are difficult to ascertain, it can be worthwhile using quite detailed prototypes with potential and/or typical users in order to establish and refine those requirements.

Questions also arise about the fate of the prototype once the investigations have been completed. Should it be thrown away, as advocated by Brooks (1975), or developed into the final product (Blum, 1983)? Not surprisingly, much depends on the reasons for building the prototype and the methods of its construction. A prototype which models the core functionality of a system can be quickly written in a powerful high-level language which is not intended for the target implementation. However, this choice of language means that it may well have to be discarded, whereas, say, screen formats created for user trials can be incorporated into a final product. A prototype which is simply a subset of the intended facilities, written in the target programming language, may take longer to produce but could well be incorporated into the eventual system.

It is crucial to establish the objectives of the prototyping exercise. Defining these objectives relies on identifying the aspects of the system which need to be explored. Allied with this, there has to be some means of deciding when those objectives have been met (or when they should be abandoned). These objectives, along with the development environment, will determine the way in which the prototype is constructed and used.

Prototyping is increasingly being accepted and encouraged as part of software development. In some cases, prototyping is formally incorporated into the process; in other cases, it is simply one of several techniques used by designers wishing to determine characteristics of the system.

2.3 Summary

This chapter has introduced formal specification and rapid prototyping. These are both advocated as techniques to be used in designing software systems. Formal specification enables designers to communicate their intentions accurately and at an abstract level. Rapid prototyping allows an experimental approach to design which aims to explore areas of uncertainty in the proposed system. Both techniques are intended to reduce the number of errors and omissions which originate during system design.

Chapter 3

me too in context – introduction

In this chapter, we see how the use of functional languages allows the two techniques of formal specification and rapid prototyping to be brought together, yielding the design method called *me too* which is the subject of this book. *me too* provides a way of precisely describing a proposed system which allows that system to be prototyped early in its development.

3.1 Formal specification + executability = rapid prototyping

This section outlines the development of programming languages from binary code to high-level languages, and shows how this can lead to the idea of executable mathematical languages.

3.1.1 From low-level to high-level languages

If we consider the development of languages for programming computers over the years, we see them moving away from the intricacies of binary coding to machine code and assembly languages, from there to early high-level languages such as FORTRAN, and then to higher-level languages with facilities for more complex data handling and structured flow of control, such as Algol-68 or Pascal.

With each of these steps, the programmer has been given a greater variety of data structures and control mechanisms, which provide a way of abstracting away from the details of the underlying computer architecture. These make it possible to define complex structures, organizations and algorithms more concisely and with less scope for error. Consider, for example, writing a procedure to search a text array for an entry containing a particular word; the effort needed for a Pascal implementation is considerably less than for a hexadecimal or machine-code version, because the language itself takes care of many of the details which would have to be written explicitly in machine code.

Languages such as Ada* and Smalltalk (Goldberg and Robson, 1983) add facilities for creating programmer-defined objects. These objects hide their internal

* Ada is a trademark of the US Government – Ada Joint Program Office.

details from external users and thus allow programmers to create even higher-level abstractions for their own use.

One discernible trend in language development has been the provision of more powerful data structures together with the means to manipulate them. The mathematical 'data structures' of sets, sequences, and so on, offer another step higher in terms of abstraction, and already have well-defined means of manipulating them. So if a way can be found to implement mathematical constructs on a computer, such a language could be considered a 'very high-level' programming language.

At this point, the distinction between programming languages and specification notations begins to become blurred. This is evident in the fact that a programming language with mathematical data types is advocated for specification (Turner, 1985) and the mathematical language of logic is advocated for high-level programming (Kowalski, 1985). This overlap of rôles is further underlined by designers' current practice of using variants of programming languages (pseudocode) to specify their designs.

So is an executable mathematical notation a specification language or a programming language? Critics of executable specifications might reply that it is a compromise between the two. Advocates of executable specifications, however, might counter with the argument that they combine the best of both worlds. It is true that a design expressed in an executable specification language cannot be entirely divorced from operational considerations since the specifications have to be capable of being executed; this implies that it is a programming language. On the other hand, the language *is* mathematical. It therefore offers many of the benefits of a formal specification language – it is precise, succinct and powerful, it allows a greater degree of abstraction than most programming languages and it admits the possibility of employing formal proof techniques.

3.1.2 Executable formal specifications

A formal specification language which is executable offers a means of achieving rapid prototyping of software designs. A specification can be typed into the computer and executed as if it were a program. This allows experimentation with alternative designs without going to the detail of implementation normally required.

Prototyping with specifications also aids the specification process. Mathematicians are not immune from making errors, and formal specifications can still contain mistakes (Alexander, 1988; Cottam, 1984) or omit essential information. Formally, a specification is checked by reasoning, by stating and proving theorems about its properties. However, an executable specification language leads to the idea of testing the specification as an alternative approach.

Testing and proof are complementary approaches to determining whether or not a system meets the requirements set for it. Testing is usually performed to demonstrate that a system can perform intended tasks or take appropriate action in the range of test cases supplied. Proofs are usually undertaken to demonstrate that the system behaves in a particular way for classes of circumstances, or that it possesses or avoids certain properties.

Although proof techniques have much to offer in assuring software reliability, the practical demands and timescales of system development mean that few designers devote the time to go through the formal steps of stating and proving theorems.

On the other hand, testing is a familiar strategy and executable specifications give designers the opportunity to carry out testing at an earlier stage in development.

3.1.3 Using declarative languages for specification

How is a mathematical specification language to be made executable, and still retain the mathematical properties necessary to allow precision, succinctness and clarity in the executable specification?

To answer this question, we examine another strand in the development of powerful high-level languages. Traditional programming languages conform to the general architecture of computer systems, with its provision of assignment to variables whose values may change while the program is running. This means that programs written in these languages must specify exactly the order in which those changes may occur. This style of programming is **imperative**, that is, it explicitly states the order in which events must occur.

An alternative is to consider languages which are **declarative** rather than imperative in style. That is, they dispense with variables and the assignment of values to them so that there is no longer any need to order changes to the values of variables. Declarative programs are constructed from expressions rather than ordered statements. Expressions in a declarative language have a value, which may or may not have been computed yet, but that value does not change during program execution. All that matters about an expression is its value and any (sub)expression can be replaced by any other which is equal in value. This is a mathematical property known as **referential transparency** and it has several effects in a language. Firstly, it makes it easier to reason mathematically about the program or parts of it. Secondly, control structures such as 'if' statements or 'while' loops are no longer necessary to sequence the order of value changes to a variable since there are no variables or changes of value. These features of declarative languages have various important ramifications, including the appropriateness of declarative languages for formal specification and the possibility of parallel execution of functional programs.

Declarative languages currently fall into two categories: functional (or applicative) languages and logic languages. Examples of modern functional languages are ML (Wikström, 1987), Miranda* (Turner, 1986) and Hope (Bailey, 1987). Prolog (Clocksin and Mellish, 1985) and Tempura (Moszkowski, 1986) are examples of logic programming languages.

Because of their mathematical foundations, there have been several attempts to use declarative languages as a notation for executable formal specifications. For example, Tavendale (1985) reports on the addition of the set construct and its associated operations to Prolog. Miranda includes sets and sequences as basic data structures, and is advocated as being suitable for specification as a result (Turner, 1985). Although VDM was not originally intended to be used in conjunction with prototyping, researchers are investigating how specifications produced using VDM can form the basis of a prototyping method (Hekmatpour and Ince, 1986; Ince and Hekmatpour, 1988). *me too* was one of the early ventures in this area, combining functional languages with the mathematics of set theory.

* Miranda is a trademark of Research Software Limited.

3.2 How *me too* evolved

This section gives a brief description of how *me too* has developed from its origins in a research environment to a method which is being increasingly used in an industrial environment.

me too emerged from research into the uses of functional programming languages. The first such language was Lisp, dating from the 1960s (McCarthy, 1960). Lisp was based on mathematical foundations and was designed to handle symbolic data. However, important though Lisp is in both the history and current practice of functional programming, most of the many versions of Lisp include imperative features, such as assignment, jumps and labels, thus sacrificing the benefits and 'purity' of declarative languages. As part of research into functional languages, a purely functional dialect of Lisp called LispKit was developed (Henderson, 1980; Henderson *et al.*, 1983).

LispKit became a vehicle for exploring applications of functional languages, one of which borrowed the idea from KRC (Turner, 1982) of implementing set operations. Specifications could then be written in this language of sets. Because set operations were implemented as LispKit functions, the specifications could be executed as prototypes using the ProtoKit prototyping shell developed by Peter Henderson and Simon Jones at Stirling University. Similar techniques were used to model other mathematical types, such as relations and maps.

ProtoKit was the precursor of the *me too* tools and was the starting point for the Alvey project, which was concerned with development of the method, the notation and the tools. Early versions of the *me too* notation appear in Henderson (1985, 1986a) and in Henderson and Minkowitz (1986). Since then, *me too* has been applied to a wide variety of different problems, some of which are described in later chapters of this book. As a result, the notation has developed. An early compiler was written by Simon Finn. For reasons of portability, it was recognized that implementing *me too* in LispKit was not adequate for the needs of industry. Accordingly, the *me too* system has been reimplemented using proprietary versions of Lisp, whilst ensuring that the implementations retain the sound mathematical basis derived from the functional programming paradigm.

The *me too* notation is executed by a tool known as the '*me too* shell'. This makes available the language described in this book, together with some shell commands (for example, for loading and saving files containing *me too* specifications). The shell is implemented in a variety of commercially available Lisp systems. The *me too* notation is uniform across the various host environments.

3.3 A rôle for *me too* in system development

So far, we have seen both the motivation behind the development of *me too* and the technical background from which it emerged. The impetus came from the recognized need to invest greater resources in overcoming deficiencies in the early phases of system development. *me too* is an attempt to meet this need by a style of executable formal specification based on functional programming. Before presenting the *me too* notation and method, it is important to see how *me too* fits into the development process. This section raises some questions about how *me too* is used.

First we need to define some of the terminology we use in describing the development process, taking as our basis the phases identified in Chapter 2. It is important to note that there is no 'system specification' phase. This is because the process produces not one but many specifications of the system – of different kinds, at different levels of detail and in different phases of development. Indeed, the process can be seen as producing ever more detailed system specifications until they are sufficiently detailed to form the basis of the implementation.

System definition is the phase in which the system requirements are established. These are documented in the requirements specification, which acts as the top-level reference for the rest of the process. In **system design**, an implementable means of meeting those requirements is devised. In practice, this is likely to involve several levels of design, from overall system architecture to detailed module design. Each level produces a design which in turn acts as the specification for the next level of the design activity. At some point, this yields a set of designs which can be implemented in the **system implementation** phase.

In which phase or phases is *me too* most appropriate? The title of the book indicates that its primary rôle is as an aid to design. In other words, based on a set of requirements for a system, *me too* can help the system designers to understand the system, to make unambiguous statements about its design and to test their designs at an early stage of development. That understanding evolves as a result of several aspects of *me too*. Firstly, the designers are forced to think through the concepts being described in order to write their definitions in the formal language of *me too*. Secondly, use of a prototype allows exploration of the consequences of the design. Thirdly, the speed with which new specifications can be created and validated encourages investigation of alternative designs.

In this rôle, *me too* is most readily understood as a tool for *modeling* systems. The model is abstract, in that the power of the mathematical notation allows us to omit implementation-level detail. The model is formal and can be reasoned about, because it is specified using mathematics, but it is also a 'working' model, because its specification can be executed. In engineering terms, models are for trying out ideas, for examining consequences of decisions, for seeing how an artefact behaves – so it is with *me too* models of software systems.

This view of *me too* leads to the next question – what do we model? *me too* is more suited to describe some aspects of a system than others. Put simply, *me too* models are created to explore what the system should do rather than what it should look like or how fast it will run. This conclusion is based on the experience gained by exposing *me too* to non-academic, non-research problems in industrial project teams. It became clear that *me too* is best seen as a modeling tool to be applied to the **functionality** of a system – that is, the functions it performs: what it does and what it provides – rather than to its performance or the details of its user interface. Used in this way, the application of *me too* by industrial groups has repeatedly demonstrated its value in practice, as may be seen from the case studies given in Part III.

me too can be used in a rather broader context than just the system design phase. We can build models of existing systems in order to understand them better. We can model the high-level architectural aspects of a system, or even its low-level detail if we so choose. We can move away from 'systems' and model complex standards definitions, such as those produced by the networks community. All these different kinds of project have been successfully tackled by groups using *me too*.

Once we have a model, though, what do we do with it? The answer is dictated by the purpose of the model-building exercise. If it is regarded purely as a means of gaining an understanding of a system, then the model has served its purpose and can be discarded. The understanding, rather than the specification itself, is the basis for proceeding with system development. This was the situation, for example, in the case study described in Chapter 14 which took an informal description of a proposed system architecture and produced a clearer, simpler and more consistent version.

Often, however, one of the purposes of producing a formally specified design is to provide a means of communicating that design accurately to its implementors. The specification indicates the structure of the system, identifying the objects and operations in the system. The required properties of these objects and operations are defined by their mathematical specifications. There may well be parts of the specification which can be used directly in the implementation, where the specification contains data structures and/or operations which can be expressed in the implementation language. If the implementation is in a Lisp-like or functional language, then it is straightforward to develop the specification into an implementation. Transformation to other target languages requires rather more effort but is equally possible. Clark (1986) shows how *me too* specifications can be automatically transformed into outline Ada programs.

The final question we shall raise here is – how are *me too* models built? The answer to this is the subject of this book and is covered in the remaining chapters. The method for constructing models is introduced in Chapter 4 and expanded upon in Chapter 11. The *me too* notation, the constructs of which provide the 'materials' for construction, is presented in Part II. In Part III, we see how some *me too* models have been built in practice.

3.4 Summary

Formal specification and rapid prototyping are complementary techniques for improving the design of software systems. This chapter has shown how they can be combined by providing an executable formal specification notation. One means of achieving this has been introduced, namely by implementing the notation in a functional programming language. *me too*, a modeling tool for system designers, results from this combination.

Chapter 4

The *me too* method of software design

> *"What is the difference between method and device? A method is a device which you use twice."*
>
> George Polya

Like VDM, *me too* is a language and an associated design method. This chapter describes that method. A detailed example of the application of the method is deferred until Chapter 11 after the *me too* notation has been presented.

By 'method' we mean, with *Chambers' Twentieth Century Dictionary*, an

orderly procedure; a mode or rule for accomplishing an end.

The *me too* method is an orderly procedure for using the *me too* language which accomplishes our ends: the derivation of precise, succinct descriptions of a proposed design which have been tested and debugged by executing those descriptions.

4.1 The design approach

The *me too* method introduces formality into a systematic design approach which already underlies much of the existing practice of designers. This section illustrates that approach by describing the steps in current practice. Subsequent sections describe how using the *me too* notation affects that underlying systematic approach.

In the description below, it is assumed that there is some element of team responsibility for the design. This is because the design of systems is very often undertaken by groups of designers, who have to communicate their ideas to one another and reach a common agreement about the design. However, the *me too* method can be applied by a single designer as well.

In the first step, system designers begin by discussing concepts informally. They sketch out their ideas about what makes up the proposed system, the types of object to be manipulated and the tasks or activities required. As they do so, they find that they are beginning to define their 'vocabulary' for the design, through identifying the essential parts of the system and the way that they will talk about them.

Proceeding from this informal debate, the designers capture their ideas in a written or diagrammatic description. This often involves informal notation such as natural language, or semi-formal notation such as data-flow diagrams (Gane and Sarson, 1979) or Jackson diagrams (Jackson, 1983). Whatever technique is used, the main aims of this second step are to ensure that misunderstandings are detected and resolved, and that the designers' decisions are accurately recorded in a specification of some form.

Designers are fallible, though, and may make mistakes or leave out essential or useful parts of the system, so there is normally a third step. This involves some attempt at experimenting with and/or checking the specifications. This may be by means of reviews and inspections which check, for example, that local quality standards have been adhered to, or that the design meets the requirements set for it. The designers may also invest effort in producing a prototype version of the designed system, in order to test it and to understand its capabilities.

Given sufficient time, the designers can improve their design on the basis of lessons learned in these steps, both from the specification and the validation, by iterating upon the design. In this way, mistakes are corrected, ambiguities are resolved, misunderstandings are clarified and the design is respecified appropriately. This process should be repeated until the designers are satisfied with what they have produced, but often time constraints do not permit this.

This outline of design practice indicates three basic stages. In the first stage, tasks and data are analyzed, discussed and explored until the essential ingredients of the system begin to emerge. Once these have been identified, they can be specified more concretely and in more detail in the second design stage. The third stage is to validate the specified design in some manner appropriate to the techniques employed in the first two stages.

These three stages may be reflected in change control procedures. The informal first stage corresponds to the time before the design specification is placed under change control. The second stage corresponds to the issue of a controlled specification document. The validation stage corresponds to the reviews or inspections that follow.

The *me too* method follows this pattern of design, specialized to take account of the nature of its mathematical language.

4.2 The *me too* method

Given the outline above, it should come as no surprise to find that there are three basic steps in the *me too* method. These are called the Model, Specify and Validate steps, and are shown in Fig. 4.1.

In the Model step, the designers establish the structure of the design. To do this, they identify what *me too* calls the 'objects' and the 'operations' of the system under consideration. That is, they decide upon the entities or pieces of information in the system, the **abstract objects**, and the activities required to manipulate them, the **abstract operations**.

Abstract objects can be thought of as types. Simple examples would be 'integer' or 'string', but *me too* also allows definition of complex mathematical types to describe objects in a system. Instances of the abstract objects thus identified are created during the Validate step. Abstract operations can be thought of as procedure or function headings, together with a brief informal description of their

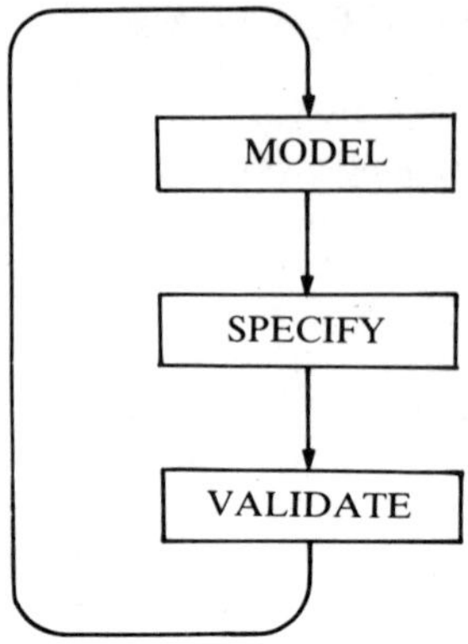

Figure 4.1 The *me too* method.

meaning and purpose. The definitions of the operations are left unspecified until the Specify step.

Consider, for example, a computer-based diary system. One abstract object might be Diary, another might be Appointment, others might be Reminder, Day, Task or Slot. Operations could include ScheduleTask, FindFreeSlot, and so on. Alternatively, in a supermarket system, objects could be Store, Shelf, Product, BarCode, with operations such as RestockShelves being identified at this stage. All operations are represented in this step in terms of the objects to which they are applied and the objects which they return as a result. This is recorded for each operation by its **functionality**, which can be thought of in programming terms as a procedure heading. For example, the operation FindFreeSlot might have the functionality

```
FindFreeSlot : Diary -> Slot
```

which says that *the operation* FindFreeSlot *is supplied with an object of type* Diary *and returns an object of type* Slot (the details of this notation are explained in Chapter 5). Naming and documenting the parts of the system in this way gives the designers a written outline model of the system, which they elaborate in the next step.

In the Specify step, the designers express their intentions about the abstract objects and operations by formally specifying them in the *me too* notation. That is, they decide upon representations for the objects, drawing on the basic mathematical types available in *me too*, such as sets and sequences. Based on these decisions, the rest of the specification can be written.

Firstly, the designers can specify **invariants** on the data types. That is, they can make mathematical statements about the properties of the object types. An invariant takes the form of a boolean-valued operation on the object type in question, returning true if the object supplied to it meets the condition specified in the invariant. For example, there might be an invariant defined for the Diary object above; this invariant would have the functionality

```
inv_Diary : Diary -> Boolean
```

In the specification, an invariant can be read as an assertion concerning the unchanging properties of an object type. When the specification is executed in the Validate step, the invariant is applied to instances of the type to ensure that they do not violate the properties specified for that type.

Secondly, the definitions of the operations are given. *me too* allows considerable flexibility in how this is achieved. An operation can be specified as a single operation, exactly as indicated by its functionality. Alternatively, designers who prefer to work with pre- and postconditions may specify each operation by a pair of operations, one defining its precondition, the other its postcondition. Another approach is to consider preconditions explicitly and then incorporate them into the operation itself, either directly or by a call on a precondition operation; Chapter 11 illustrates this approach. Irrespective of the style adopted, though, the result is a formally specified description of the system under consideration.

During this process, any misunderstandings about the objects and operations appear, because different ideas about the meaning of an object or operation result in different mathematical statements about them. When this occurs, the precision of the notation allows the group to express and decide between the options available to them. Thus the Specify step should result in the delivery of an unambiguous description of the design.

The design can be modularized if appropriate, both for ease of understanding and to indicate a structure for the system being designed. Examples of one style suitable for modular specifications can be found in this and other chapters, as well as in Appendix 2. However, the layout shown is advisory only. It is not enforced by the *me too* shell, which expects to interpret only record declarations and definitions of operations in the SPECIFY section of the module, nor does the shell suppress the names of hidden operations.

The specification document is amenable to inspection and review, but it is also executable in the *me too* shell. In the Validate step, the design is tested by executing the specification. That is, the operations are used to create and manipulate instances of the objects in order to examine the behavior of the specification. At this stage, errors or omissions are usually detected. It should be understood that the usual principles of testing apply, including devising appropriate test cases and following a well-designed test schedule.

Experimenting with the prototype has an additional advantage as it will often suggest new ideas or simplifications of the design, not least because it is easier to criticize an existing artefact than to create a new one. Once a prototype is available, executing it tends to generate ideas for alternative or additional facilities in the design or alternative means of achieving the intended results.

It can be seen that there are two primary rôles for the prototyping aspect of *me too*: verifying the specification by testing it, and experimenting with the prototype in order to understand the properties of the specification. Both activities may well require the designers to return to earlier steps in the method in order to make changes to the specification.

It may have been noticed that mathematical reasoning about the specification has not figured in the description of the method. Should designers wish to state and prove theorems about the specification, they do so in the Validate step. Such activity may either replace testing or complement it. The established practice in *me too*, however, is to concentrate on testing and demonstration as the means of verification and validation, since it demands less mathematical skill on the part of the designer. Readers who wish to pursue the subject of verification by proof will find an excellent description and further references in Jones (1986).

Figure 4.2 illustrates the method showing the breakdown and product of each step. The Model step identifies and documents the objects and operations of the system at an abstract level. The objects and operations are named, with the relationships between them shown formally by the functionalities of the operations. An informal description may also be given. The Specify step adds mathematical representations for the objects and definitions for the operations. The descriptions arising from the Model and Specify steps together constitute the specification of the system. That specification is then executed in the Validate step, allowing interactive use and testing of the system by means of a prototype.

Design is an iterative activity, so the *me too* method encourages iteration in its application. The figure shows the obvious iterative cycle: having progressed through the three steps, the designers have learned more about the system and use their new knowledge to improve its design in a further iteration. Examples and case studies in later chapters show that iteration is equally possible at other points, for example, the result of the Specify step may be to discard the model and start again.

Because proceeding from specification to prototype is automatic, simply requiring that the *me too* notation be typed into the shell and executed, the iterative cycle is not a long one. Even radical changes to the nature of the design can be made within a short space of time, with an iteration being measured in hours or days, rather than weeks.

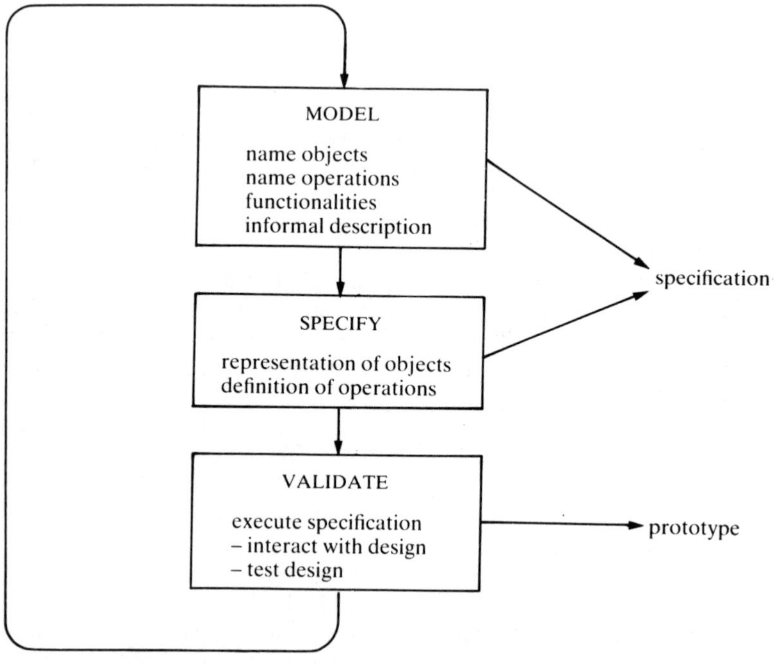

Figure 4.2 The *me too* method (detailed).

4.3 An illustrative example

In order to highlight some of the benefits of employing such a method, we consider a small example. This example is extremely simple, since it is intended purely as an illustration of some of the benefits of a design method like *me too*. In the next section, the method is presented in more detail.

A design team, consisting of two designers, has been asked to specify a new product. They both agree that what they need to produce is, for want of a better name, a 'widget'. Unfortunately, as Fig. 4.3 shows, in the Model step, they don't realize that they both have completely different ideas about what constitutes a widget. They are using the same language, the same terminology, to describe what they want, but their underlying ideas are very different, as represented by the different shapes of widget.

In the Specify step, when they come to write down the formal definitions, they discover these differences, because using a formal language means that they are bound to produce two different definitions. After some negotiation, they agree on what a widget really is and complete their specification. Thus, progress has been made and potential errors have been avoided. Perhaps design inspections would have picked up these errors as well, although the use of a formal notation does enforce a precision of description that makes it more likely. What design inspections cannot do, though, is to help designers modify their original ideas in the light of experience. In the normal course of events, the specification would be handed on to the implementation team, and the designers would move on to some other task.

In *me too*, the designers *can* gain some experience with their design. In this example, when the two designers experiment with the prototype they discover that a widget would be much more useful 'the other way up'. Fortunately, because they

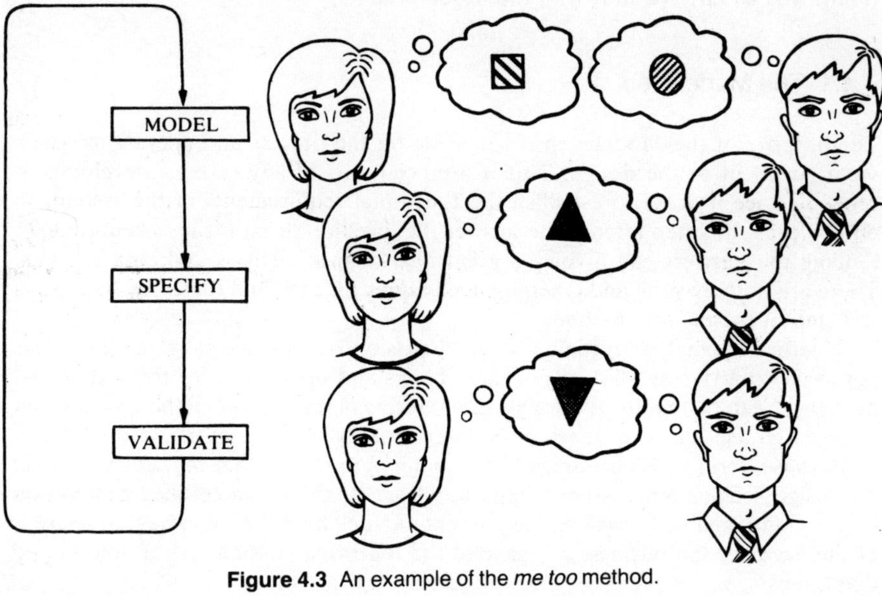

Figure 4.3 An example of the *me too* method.

are still at an early design stage and have committed nothing to implemented code yet, they have invested very little in the development process so far and changing their minds is not a major or costly undertaking.

Although a trivial example, this serves to point out some of the ways in which the *me too* method helps designers to arrive at an agreed, unambiguous and succinct description of the system with which they are concerned. Moreover, the speed with which systems can be specified and prototyped enables an explorative approach that would not be feasible with more traditional methods or tools.

It should be noted that the method is equally applicable when the task involves enhancements to or redevelopment of an existing system. Using *me too*, the designers can analyze and describe the system before going on to consider new features. The case study in Chapter 13 describes such a development.

4.4 Using the *me too* method

In this section, we present a small example to show the steps of the method in more detail. The exercise is *not* intended to teach *me too* notation, since this is the purpose of Part II of the book. Inevitably, though, some notation has to be used in the presentation; where this happens, the notation is explained briefly. It should also be noted that the errors and omissions 'discovered' during the application of the method are both trivial and obvious, and are included solely to illustrate the method.

The example tackles some of the problems of stock control which are faced by a small retail business. How does the manager know how much stock is left? At what point should a line be reordered? Where is a particular item stored in the stock room? and so on. We start with the Model step.

4.4.1 The Model step

The purpose of the Model step is to decide on the objects and operations which seem pertinent to the design. This is a crucial part of any systems development process, since it seeks to establish the functional requirements of the system. In other words, this step attempts to answer the question 'what is the system to do?'. Finding the answers can involve a great deal of task analysis and data analysis. There are both existing and emerging techniques for this, and these can be used in this step of the *me too* method.

Whether by analysis techniques, by discussion or by some other method, it is necessary to arrive at a list of possible objects and operations for the system. At first, these can be tentative, because the iterative nature of the method means that these early decisions can be reviewed later, usually several times.

Because iteration is encouraged, it is common to start with some central issue in the design, leaving other issues to later iterations. In this example, the first iteration is only concerned with tracking the amount of stock held. We assume that analysis of the needs of the business has yielded the following possible list of objects and operations:

StockItem	items stocked in the shop
StockBook	record of all items stocked
Quantity	number of items
NewStockBook	creates an empty stock book
AddItem	adds a quantity of an item to the stock book
SellItem	the sale of an item in the stock book
InStock	returns the quantity held for an item

The operation NewStockBook may seem unusual, in that we have used an operation to construct a constant data value whereas the other operations correspond to actions. However, it should be remembered that in the functional paradigm *all* expressions represent a value. Thus, for example, AddItem(s,i,q) represents the value of a stock book, given that s is the original value of the stock book to which a quantity q of an item i has been added.

The next part of the Model step is to decide what kinds of parameters each operation will take and what kind of result each will return. These decisions are recorded by writing the functionality of each operation. For example,

AddItem : StockBook x StockItem x Quantity -> StockBook

This reads AddItem *takes parameters of type* StockBook, StockItem *and* Quantity, *and returns a result of type* StockBook. The details of this notation, and the notation which follows, are left to later chapters, since the intention here is simply to demonstrate the method in action. However, it is worth noting that this discipline of considering what each operation needs to be given and what each will return is the first step towards the formal description of the design. Consequently, writing the functionalities may mean that ideas about suitable objects are revised.

The results of the Model step are presented below.

MODEL

Objects

StockItem	items stocked in the shop
StockBook	record of all items stocked
Quantity	number of items

Operations

NewStockBook : -> StockBook
AddItem : StockBook x StockItem x Quantity -> StockBook
SellItem : StockBook x StockItem -> StockBook
InStock : StockBook x StockItem -> Quantity

where

NewStockBook() creates an empty stock book

AddItem(s,i,q) adds the quantity q of the item i to the stock book s

SellItem(s,i) returns the stock book resulting from the sale of item i

InStock(s,i) returns the quantity held for item i in stock book s

---

4.4.2 The Specify step

Once the objects and operations are settled, at least for the current iteration, they are specified. The first stage is to decide which mathematical types will represent the objects in the model. This depends on the properties of the objects, such as whether they occur individually or in groups, whether a group of objects is ordered or not, whether a group can contain duplicates or not, whether some form of look-up table is required or not, and so on. The chapters which present the *me too* language elaborate on the properties of the various mathematical types available.

Here, the stock information is held in a look-up table (it can be thought of as an array, but is more properly called a **map**) indexed by the name of a stock item:

```
StockBook = map(StockItem,Quantity)
StockItem = String
Quantity = Nat
```

where a stock item is represented by its name (a string) and a quantity is a non-negative integer (a natural number). Finding the quantity of an item in stock, then, is just a matter of looking up its entry in the stock book.

Having decided on the representation of the objects, the operations can be defined, making use of the natural mathematical operations for the types chosen. For example, there is a *me too* operation called map application which looks up a value in a map. Its syntax is

```
map[index,default]
```

allowing a default value to be given in case the index is missing. Values can be added to a map by the overwrite operation, overwr:

```
map overwr {index -> value}
```

If the index already appears in the map, its corresponding value is overwritten by value. Otherwise a new entry linking index and value is added to the map. These constructs are explained in Chapter 7.

The operations in this model can be specified by

```
NewStockBook() == {} ;
AddItem(s,i,q) == s overwr { i -> q } ;
SellItem(s,i) == s overwr { i -> s[i,0] - 1 } ;
InStock(s,i) == s[i,0] ;
```

The details are not important here. It is sufficient to note that

- NewStockBook creates an empty look-up table
- AddItem creates a table entry for the item in question, overwriting any existing entry
- SellItem looks up the quantity for the item and subtracts one before replacing the entry in the table
- InStock looks up the entry for the item, supplying a default of zero in case there is no entry for the item.

Upon review, some improvements may be obvious immediately. For example, what happens when a quantity of an existing item is added to the stock? The specification of AddItem shows that no account is taken of the current quantity on hand. Remedying this deficiency produces a new definition for AddItem:

AddItem(s,i,q) == s overwr { i -> s[i,0] + q } ;

This differs from the previous version in that the quantity q is added to the existing stock level rather than overwriting it. Lastly we can substitute a call on the operation InStock wherever the expression s[i,0] is used to look up a quantity in the stock book. The final version of the specification is given below:

SPECIFICATION OF STOCK

MODEL

Objects

StockItem	items stocked in the shop
StockBook	record of all items stocked
Quantity	number of items

Operations

NewStockBook : -> StockBook
AddItem : StockBook x StockItem x Quantity -> StockBook
SellItem : StockBook x StockItem -> StockBook
InStock : StockBook x StockItem -> Quantity

where

NewStockBook() creates an empty stock book
AddItem(s,i,q) adds the quantity q of the item i to the stock book s
SellItem(s,i) returns the stock book resulting from the sale of item i
InStock(s,i) returns the quantity held for item i in stock book s

SPECIFY

Objects

StockBook = map(StockItem,Quantity)
StockItem = String
Quantity = Nat

Operations

NewStockBook() == {} ;
AddItem(s,i,q) == s overwr { i -> InStock(s,i) + q } ;
SellItem(s,i) == s overwr { i -> InStock(s,i) - 1 } ;
InStock(s,i) == s[i,0] ;

Once the specification is written, we can move on to the validation step.

4.4.3 The Validate step

The operations above are supplied to the *me too* shell, either by typing them in directly or by reading them in from a file. They are then available for testing the specification.

For testing, we need to create instances of the objects in the specification so first we check the operation NewStockBook. A new data object of type StockBook is created and given the name st:

```
st == NewStockBook() ;
```

This notation shows how a data object may be associated with a name. It is only used in the shell when executing the specification; it is not part of the specification itself.

Next we wish to test AddItem. There are two cases to consider: when the item already exists in the stock book and when it does not. We make repeated calls on AddItem to test these two cases. These may be made by a series of individual calls:

```
st == AddItem(st,"crystal vase",2) ;
st == AddItem(st,"melamine tray",3) ;
st == AddItem(st,"leather purse",10) ;
st == AddItem(st,"crystal vase",5) ;
```

or alternatively in one step:

```
st == AddItem(AddItem(AddItem(AddItem(st,"crystal vase",2),
          "melamine tray",3),"leather purse",10), "crystal vase",5) ;
```

Either way, the resulting value of st is the same and is shown in tabular form in Fig. 4.4, showing that AddItem is behaving as required.

crystal vase	7
leather purse	10
melamine tray	3

Figure 4.4 Stock book table (version 1).

Now we wish to check the enquiry operation InStock, both for items which are present in the stock book and for those which are not.

```
InStock(st,"crystal vase") ;
```

returns the value 7,

```
InStock(st,"melamine tray") ;
```

returns the value 3 and

```
InStock(st,"leather handbag") ;
```

returns the value 0, because there are no handbags in stock.

We use further changes in stock level to test SellItem, again covering the two cases when items are present in the stock book and when they are not. The calls are

```
st == SellItem(st,"crystal vase") ;
st == AddItem(st,"leather wallet",12) ;
st == SellItem(st,"leather handbag") ;
```

crystal vase	6
leather purse	10
melamine tray	3
leather wallet	12
leather handbag	−1

Figure 4.5 Stock book table (version 2).

They result in the new table shown in Fig. 4.5.

The attempted sale of a handbag has had an unfortunate effect as there are none in stock. With the hindsight afforded by this failure, it is clear that SellItem should check that an item is available before trying to sell it. Accordingly, the Specify step is revisited and the operation is respecified as

```
SellItem(s,i) ==
  let current == InStock(s,i)
  in if    current = 0
     then s
     else s overwr { i -> current - 1 } ;
```

which makes no change to the stock book when there is no stock of the item to sell.

Now, starting from the original table of Fig. 4.4, the calls given above result in the table shown in Fig. 4.6, which is as intended.

crystal vase	6
leather purse	10
melamine tray	3
leather wallet	12

Figure 4.6 Stock book table (version 3).

4.4.4 Iteration

With these basic stock control operations in place, the method can be employed in further iterations. The next step might be to add the concept of reorder levels, or to consider physical placement in the stock room, or to extend the item details to include cost and retail prices, or to add cross-references to alternative items which could be offered to a customer.

Such changes can affect one or both of the Model and Specify steps. They may require extensions to the model or may demand a fresh start altogether. Alternatively, the model may remain unchanged, but the object representations may change. Operations may need to be respecified. However, because *me too* is used at an early stage in system development, there is still time to make changes and to experiment with alternative designs.

In conclusion, it is worth noting that, as with any design process, it can be valuable to retain a record of early iterations and the reasons for any changes made. Later in the development process, such information can help to resolve problems or arguments about these design decisions.

4.5 Summary

me too encompasses both a method and a notation, giving a framework for design that is based on many years' experience of applying the method to a variety of systems. This chapter has presented the three steps of the *me too* method, both in general terms and by giving a more detailed example of its use. The method is simple, flexible and iterative, prescribing an 'orderly procedure' for delivering system designs written in *me too*.

PART II
THE *me too* NOTATION

The notation of *me too* is covered by this part of the book. Beginning with basic concepts and constructs, the chapters progress through sets, relations, maps, sequences and records. Each chapter illustrates the notation and its use with examples, as well as setting exercises for the reader.

Chapter 5

me too notation – the basics

How then shall mathematical concepts be judged? They shall not be judged. *Mathematics is the supreme arbiter. From its decisions there is no appeal.*

Tobias Dantzig

The *me too* language is a notation for system specification based on the mathematics of functions and set theory. The language is similar to the constructive part of the VDM (Vienna Development Method) notation, that is, the executable subset of the VDM language. Indeed, an important feature of the *me too* notation is that it is executable. The *me too* notation is summarized in Appendix 1.

In the previous chapter the *me too* method was discussed, with its three stages: Model, Specify and Validate. In this and the following chapters we present the notation used in these three steps.

To recap briefly, in the Model step abstract objects are named and the collection of operations needed to manipulate those objects is determined. The abstract objects can be thought of as user-defined **types**. An operation is specified in the Model step in terms of the types of its arguments and of its result, that is, in terms of the abstract objects which are input to, and output by, the operation. Informal descriptions of the objects and operations are also given at this point.

In the Specify step each abstract object is given a particular mathematical representation; this can be thought of as a **type specification**. Then the operations are defined. Operations are all defined as functions.

In this chapter we cover the simple parts of the *me too* notation. First we deal with the primitive object types, namely **numbers**, **strings** and **booleans**, and the operations on them. Next we discuss **functions**. The **conditional** construct and **local definitions** follow, before we examine the use of **tuples** in *me too*. Many of the concepts treated in this chapter will be familiar to software engineers and programmers; we therefore deal with these briefly. More time is spent on establishing the fundamental concepts behind the mathematics of functions, since these may not be as familiar to software professionals as some of the other features covered in this chapter.

5.1 Primitive object types in *me too*

Numbers, strings and booleans are primitive types in *me too*.

5.1.1 Numbers

Very unlike a divine man would he be, who is unable to count one, two, three, or to distinguish odd and even numbers.

Plato

The type Number is subdivided into types Integer and Real. Examples of integers are

```
1938
-12
```

and examples of real numbers are

```
-10.1
10.94
```

The positive integers together with zero form a subtype of Integer known as Nat (natural numbers). The standard arithmetic and relational operators are provided for numbers:

```
+ - * / truncate mod < > = /= <= >=
```

(truncate and mod give the result of integer division, and the remainder on integer division, respectively; /= denotes 'not equal to'). In *me too* these are all used as **binary infix** operators; that is, they take two parameters, and the operator is written between the parameters. Expressions involving more than one operator must be bracketed explicitly. The following are examples of arithmetic expressions:

```
10.94 + 2
(10 * 2) + 3
14 * -10.1
```

Relational operators return a boolean result. The following are *me too* expressions involving relational operators:

```
3 /= 4
10.1 >= 3.2
(x mod y) > 5
```

These are valid expressions, provided x and y are of type Number. The equality operator and its negation (= and /=) are generic operators in *me too*: they may be applied to any *me too* data types, including tuples, sequences, sets, sets of sets etc. The other relational operators are defined for strings as well as numbers.

Infix operators are simply a syntactic convenience in *me too*. Expressions involving infix operators have the same denotation as the underlying functional notation. For example,

```
(1 + 12) - 7
```

can be thought of as a convenient shorthand for the functional notation

```
-(+(1,12),7)
```

The infix forms must be used with the *me too* shell.

There is a predicate is_number:

```
is_number(x)
```

which returns true if the argument supplied is a number. is_number is a **unary** operator (i.e. takes one argument) and therefore is written in **prefix** notation.

5.1.2 Strings

> *Achilles:* *Jeepers creepers! I'll have to try out your method myself. I have never seen a string like this!*
> *Tortoise:* *I hope it is well-formed.*
> *Achilles:* *I see it's got a knot at one end.*
> Douglas Hofstadter

String constants in *me too* are enclosed in double quotes, for example:

```
"a"
"Goodbye"
"007"
"1958 was a good year"
"FK15 3DG"
```

Strings are treated as literals, so case differences within a string constant are preserved. In all other respects, the *me too* shell is case-insensitive, and defaults to either upper or lower case depending on the host Lisp environment. In this book we assume upper-case working throughout.

The default on output is that the shell does not print the quotes. For example, if the user enters the string constant "Goodbye" to the *me too* shell, the shell will read, evaluate and print the value thus:

```
? "Goodbye" ;
= Goodbye ;
```

The prompt '?' appears when the shell is ready to accept an expression for evaluation. Expressions entered into the shell must be terminated by a semicolon. Values returned by the shell are preceded by '=' and followed by a semicolon.

A predicate is_string is provided in *me too* to test whether a data object is a string:

```
is_string("FK15 3DG")
```

will have the value true, and

```
is_string(10)
```

will evaluate to false.

The relational operators = /= < > <= >= may be applied to strings, as the following examples show:

```
"BbC" = "BbC"
"a" /= "A"
"a" < "b"
"zzz" >= "y"
```

Each of the above expressions evaluates to true.

5.1.3 Boolean values and logical operators

Logic and consistency are luxuries for the gods and the lower animals.
Samuel Butler (II)

We have noticed a disposition on the part of the human race always to take its logic with a chaser.
Don Marquis

The boolean constants are true and false, and the logical operators and, or and not can be used to combine boolean values in the usual way. The relational operators have already been mentioned in Section 5.1.1. Operations are provided for **implication**, **equivalence** and **quantification**. Quantification is dealt with in Section 6.2.1.

The operators and, or and not should be familiar to programmers, and do not require detailed explanation here, beyond furnishing some examples:

```
true or false
true and (false and true)
(x > y) or (y > x)
not(true)
("black" = "white") and (10 = 20)
```

and and or are binary operators; not is a unary operator. Like arithmetic expressions, boolean expressions involving more than one binary operator must have explicit bracketing, as the examples above show.

The predicate is_boolean can be applied to any data object, and returns true if the object has a boolean value.

Implication and equivalence may be less familiar concepts. Logical implication is sometimes called 'material implication'. The implies operator, =>, takes two boolean values and returns a boolean. Here we simply present the truth table for implication (Table 5.1). The interested reader is referred to any introductory text on logic (such as Hodges 1977) for further illumination.

Equivalence (sometimes called 'iff', short for 'if and only if') means two boolean expressions are equal in value. If two expressions both evaluate to true then they are equivalent. Similarly, if they both evaluate to false they are equivalent. Otherwise they are not equivalent. Since the equality operation = is a generic operation in *me too*, it has exactly the same meaning as equivalence when applied to boolean values. This operation is therefore used in *me too* for logical equivalence. Table 5.2 shows the truth table for equivalence.

Table 5.1 Truth table for implication

b1	b2	b1 => b2
true	true	true
true	false	false
false	true	true
false	false	true

Table 5.2 Truth table for equivalence

b1	b2	b1 = b2
true	true	true
true	false	false
false	true	false
false	false	true

Table 5.3 shows the conventional symbols used for logical operators and the corresponding *me too* notation.

Table 5.3 Logical operators

Symbol	*me too* operator
$\wedge$	and
$\vee$	or
$\neg$	not
$\Rightarrow$	=>
$\Leftrightarrow$	=

5.1.4 Abstract objects and data objects

With a knowledge of the name comes a distincter recognition and knowledge of the thing.

Henry David Thoreau

In the Model step, abstract objects, or types, are named. For example, it may be decided that there are three object types needed in a particular application: names of people, addresses and ages. Names for these object types are listed in the Model part of the specification document:

```
Name
Address
Age
```

In the Specify step, these object types are given a representation:

```
Name = String
Address = String
Age = Nat
```

This means that data objects of type Name or of type Address belong to the type String, and data objects of type Age belong to type Nat.

In the Validate step, the specification is tested by executing the operations which have been defined in the Specify step. When validating a specification using the *me too* shell, data objects must be supplied as actual parameters to the operations being tested. The objects may be simple constants or complex structures, perhaps whole databases. Data objects are most conveniently dealt with by having named objects within the environment of the shell. The construct for defining a data object is as follows:

```
a == e ;
```

where a is an identifier and e is a *me too* expression. The == symbol is read *is defined to be*. The expression e is evaluated, and its value is associated with the name a.

```
name1 == "Arthur" ;
```

defines a data object whose identifier is name1 and whose value is the string "Arthur". Here name1 is a data object of type Name. Some more examples of definitions follow:

```
address1 == "The Lock Up" ;
age1 == 56;
```

When a definition is typed in, the shell responds with the name of the variable. The shell prints the name in upper case:

```
? x == 1 + 2 ;
= X ;
```

An identifier which has been assigned a value may be passed as an actual parameter to a function, as in

```
is_number(age1)
```

which, given the prior definition of age1 above, will return true.

The data object denoted by an identifier may be inspected. If the identifier is entered, followed by a semicolon, the *me too* shell will print the value of the expression assigned to the identifier, as in the following interaction:

```
? x == 1 + 2 ;
= X ;
? x ;
= 3 ;
? y == is_number(x) ;
= Y ;
? y ;
= TRUE ;
```

Variable identifiers may be entered in mixed case, but case is ignored. Identifiers y and Y, for instance, are indistinguishable to the system.

5.2 Functions

Still glides the Stream, and shall forever glide;
The Form remains, the Function never dies.
William Wordsworth

The use of functions is a familiar concept in programming. Most programming languages offer the programmer a range of predefined functions, such as *square root* and *cosine*. In addition, many languages offer the user a facility for defining his or her own functions.

In *me too*, all user-defined operations are defined as functions. A *me too* specification, then, is written in a purely functional style, and so can be executed as a program in a purely functional language. More importantly, the specification inherits a number of desirable mathematical properties, such as *referential transparency* and *freedom from side effects*, which are not found in non-mathematically based notations. These properties make the problems of formal verification much more tractable.

Although the use of functions may be familiar to the reader, the mathematics of functions may not be. In mathematical terms, a function is a correspondence, or *mapping*, between one set of entities, the **domain** of the function, and another set of entities, the **range** of the function. Applying a function to a certain entity from its domain uniquely determines an entity from its range. A function returns a single result. That result, however, may be arbitrarily complex; it could be a whole database, or even a collection of databases.

5.2.1 Functionality

In the Model step, each operation (function) is named. It is also given a **functionality**, that is, the types of its parameters and the type of the result it returns are specified. In other words, the functionality of an operation is specified by giving its domain and range types. For example, we may design an operation even, which takes an integer argument, returning true if the integer is even, and false if it is odd. The functionality of even is written as

```
even : Integer -> Boolean
```

The name of the operation is followed by a colon, the type of the argument is then given, and the type of the result follows the arrow. even is a unary operation, that is, it takes one argument. The domain of this operation is the set of integers; its range is the set of boolean values. Another unary operation is abs, which gives the absolute value of an integer:

```
abs : Integer -> Nat
```

Operations may take any number of arguments. An operation ave which returns the average of two real numbers would have the functionality

```
ave : Real x Real -> Real
```

This is a binary operation, that is, it takes two arguments. The types of the arguments appear in the functionality separated by the cross symbol. The domain of an operation which takes more than one argument can be thought of as the **cartesian product** of the types of its arguments: in this case, the product of the set of real numbers with itself.

An operation may take no arguments; in this case it always returns the same value. For example, we might have a number of operations which return error messages, such as this one:

```
errmsg1 : -> String
```

Another binary operation which we may choose to define is an exponentiation function, power, which raises an integer to a non-negative exponent:

```
power : Integer x Nat -> Integer
```

The general form for specifying a functionality is

$$f : T_1 \times T_2 \times \ldots \times T_k \rightarrow T$$

where the arguments of function f are of type T_1 to T_k, and the result is of type T. Here and throughout the remainder of the book we use T and subscripted T to stand for type variables.

The functionality of an operation is sometimes called its **signature**, as in VDM for example. Functionalities appear in the Model part of the specification document as commentary.

5.2.2 Function definition

Nothing requires a rarer intellectual heroism than willingness to see one's equation written out.

George Santayana

In the Specify step each operation is defined as a function. In *me too*, a function definition looks like this:

```
even(n) == (n mod 2) = 0 ;
```

The whole definition is terminated by a semicolon. The name of the function is followed by a list of formal parameters enclosed in parentheses. If there is more than one, the parameters are separated by commas. The == symbol stands for *is defined to be*, and is followed by the function body. The function body is a *me too* expression, in this case (n mod 2) = 0.

The general form of a function definition is

$$f(p_1, \ldots, p_k) == e \; ;$$

where f is the name of the function, p_1 to p_k are formal parameter names and the function body e is a *me too* expression. The function body is a rule for computing the result of a function application from the values of the arguments supplied.

The function abs is simply defined as

```
abs(n) == if   n < 0
          then -n
          else n ;
```

The average function would be defined as

```
ave(n,m) == (n + m)/2 ;
```

The error message function takes no parameters; it is not surprising, therefore, that this function always returns the same result. A definition of the error message function might be

```
errmsg1() == "invalid response : please type a number" ;
```

The power function could be defined as a recursive function:

```
power(n,m) == if    m = 0
              then 1
              else n * power(n,m - 1) ;
```

This version of the power function is defined for non-negative values of m only.

Much use is made of recursion in functional programming. However, we will discover that there are constructs available in *me too* which enable the designer to avoid using recursion equations in many cases. In Section 8.1.1, for example, an alternative definition of power is given, which makes use of the sequence constructor and does not involve any explicit recursive calls. This is true in *me too* for many operations which would traditionally involve recursion or iteration.

Higher order functions and **lambda expressions** may be defined in *me too* (see Section 6.2.2 for an example of a higher order function). A higher order function takes another function as one of its arguments, or returns a function as its result. A lambda expression is an expression whose value is a function. The function is not named, hence the alternative term *anonymous* functions. Details of the syntax and use of lambda expressions may be found in the *me too Reference Manual* (Bennett *et al.*, 1989).

The predicate is_lambda returns true if applied to an expression whose value is a function (either a named function or a lambda expression).

5.2.3 Function application

When a function has been defined, it may be called, that is, it may be applied to arguments of the appropriate types. If f is a function, and x is an element from the domain of f, then f(x) (f *applied to* x, or f *of* x) denotes an element from the range of f.

In the Validate step, the function definitions shown above would be typed into the *me too* shell. They might then be applied to suitable values, as shown in the following interaction:

```
? even(3) ;
= FALSE ;
? errmsg1() ;
= invalid response : please type a number ;
? ave(10,11) ;
= 10.5 ;
? power(-2,3) ;
= -8 ;
```

The general form of function application is

$$f(e_1,e_2,\ldots,e_k)$$

for a function f with k parameters. All user-defined functions are applied using this prefix notation. The actual parameters supplied must be of the correct types as specified in the functionality of the operation, otherwise the result will not be defined. The result is computed by evaluating the body of the function f with the values of the actual parameters e_1 to e_k bound to the formal parameter names.

The arguments supplied to a function may themselves be expressions which involve operators or function applications. These expressions must return values of the required types for their respective parameter positions. For example, the power function requires two arguments, the first an integer and the second a natural number, so

```
power(abs(3 - 10),2 * x)
```

is a well-defined expression if and only if x is a natural number. If so, then the second argument, 2 * x, evaluates to a natural number. The first argument is type-wise correct, since abs expects an integer argument and returns an natural number, and Nat is a sub-type of Integer.

The *me too* shell incorporates a limited form of type checking. The interpreter checks that the arguments supplied to any predefined *me too* operation are of the correct type. If not, an error is raised.

5.3 Conditionals and local definitions

The conditional construct and the local definition are *me too* expressions which appear frequently in function definitions.

5.3.1 Conditionals

IF statements should be familiar to the reader, being a common device providing branching control structures in high-level programming languages. In *me too*, the conditional construct is an expression, rather than a statement, and returns a value. The *me too* conditional has three parts: an if clause with a predicate, a then clause which is evaluated if the predicate is true and an else clause which is evaluated if the predicate is false. The else clause is obligatory – otherwise the whole expression would be undefined if the predicate evaluated to false.

We have already met the conditional construct in the definition of power:

```
power(n,m) == if   m = 0
              then 1
              else n * power(n,m - 1) ;
```

Here the if clause provides a terminating condition; otherwise the function would recurse infinitely. The function power calls itself recursively, decrementing the value of m each time, until the predicate in the if clause is satisfied.

The general form of the conditional construct is

$$\text{if } b \text{ then } e_1 \text{ else } e_2$$

where b is a boolean expression, and e_1 and e_2 are expressions which evaluate to the same type.

Another use of the conditional, this time not in conjunction with recursion, is found in the function abs, which gives the absolute value of an integer:

```
abs(n) == if   n < 0
          then -n
          else n ;
```

Conditionals may be nested.

5.3.2 Local definitions

Where the same subexpression, and therefore the same value, appears more than once in an expression, it is sometimes convenient to give a name to the value of the subexpression. The let construct permits this by the definition of local identifiers, which may then be used within the body of the let expression. The general form of the let expression is

```
let a1 == e1, a2 == e2,...,ak == ek in e
```

where the local identifiers a_1 to a_k are in scope within the expression e where they have the values of the expressions e_1 to e_k respectively. The value of the whole let expression is the value of the body e.

The following example illustrates the use of a local definition. Suppose that students in a class are required to sit two examination papers. In order to gain an overall pass, their average mark across the two papers must be at least 50%. Otherwise, a mark of 40% or above means resitting the examinations. Students with an average mark of less than 40% fail the examination. The following function could be used in printing a report on examination results:

```
exam : Nat x Nat -> String
exam(result1,result2) ==
  if   ave(result1,result2) >= 50
  then "pass"
  else if   ave(result1,result2) >= 40
       then "resit"
       else "fail" ;
```

Here the subexpression ave(result1,result2) appears twice. We can rewrite this definition with an equivalent one which uses a let expression to assign a local identifier to the value of this subexpression. This identifier is then substituted for the subexpression wherever it appears:

```
exam(result1,result2) ==
  let avemark == ave(result1,result2)
  in if   avemark >= 50
     then "pass"
     else if   avemark >= 40
          then "resit"
          else "fail" ;
```

let expressions may be nested; for example, the body of the let expression may itself be another let expression. This is used where the local identifiers are themselves to be used in the right-hand side of a further local definition, as in

```
let x == 10
in let y == x * x
   in .....
```

Here x is defined as a local variable, and is then used in the definition of another local variable, y. In such cases, the inner let is obligatory.

In the context of executable specifications, the choice of whether or not to use local definitions is a stylistic one, and is not primarily related to efficiency of computation. It is true that using let expressions will generally speed up the execution of a prototype, since the same expression will not have to be evaluated twice or more. However, a more important goal of specification is to produce a clear and readable record of the design. The use of let, then, is recommended when it clarifies the definition of an operation.

5.4 Tuples

A *tuple* is a composite object which has a fixed number of (ordered) components. The components of a tuple are not necessarily of the same type. A tuple of length two is usually referred to as a *pair*, and sometimes as an *ordered pair* or *two-tuple*:

```
("Arthur",56)
```

is an example of a pair; its type is tuple(String,Nat). Another tuple of the same type is

```
("Terry",38)
```

The type of these tuples can be written alternatively as pair(String,Nat). Tuples of any length may be defined in *me too*. For example, we can define a tuple of length three, tpl:

```
tpl == ("Arthur","The Lock Up",56) ;
```

and write its type as

```
tuple(String,String,Nat)
```

Alternatively, we could first define types Name, Address and Age:

```
Name, Address = String
Age = Nat
```

and then give the type of tpl as

```
tuple(Name,Address,Age)
```

The general form of the tuple constructor is

$$(e_1,e_2,\ldots,e_k)$$

and the associated type specification would be

$$tuple(T_1,T_2,\ldots,T_k)$$

where each expression e_i is of type T_i.

The *me too* predicate is_tuple may be applied to an object of any type; if the object is a tuple, the value true will be returned. For example,

```
is_tuple("Arthur")
```

and

```
is_tuple(tpl)
```

have the values false and true respectively.

An element of a tuple may be selected using the operation nth, which takes as arguments a natural number and a tuple. For example,

```
nth(2,tpl)
```

will select the second element of tpl, namely "The Lock Up". The result of an application of nth to a tuple is defined only where the first argument is greater than zero and less than or equal to the number of elements in the tuple. As an alternative to nth, the selectors first, second, third, fourth and fifth have been provided in *me too* for convenience. So, the second element of tpl could have been extracted just as well by

```
second(tpl)
```

first(tpl) will evaluate to "Arthur" and third(tpl) will evaluate to 56.

Much of the material in later sections makes use of tuples, in particular, of pairs.

5.5 Summary

In this chapter we have seen how to define and manipulate objects using the primitive types of *me too*. To begin with we looked at numbers and the arithmetic operators, and at strings and booleans.

All user-defined *me too* operations are realized as functions; we have therefore spent some time examining how to specify operations as functions, and how to use operations through the mechanism of function application.

The conditional construct and local definitions were described, and finally we introduced the mathematical objects known as tuples.

When choosing representations for objects, it is important to consider the mathematical properties of the data types available. For example, a tuple would be an appropriate representation for a fixed number of related items, possibly of different types.

The simpler parts of the *me too* notation have now been presented. From this basis we can go on to examine the more sophisticated data types of *me too*, and the operations on those types. In the next chapter we shall make a start by discussing set theory and the use of sets in *me too*.

5.6 Exercises

(i) If x=−29.3, n=12 and m=3, which of the following are *not* valid *me too* expressions, and why?
   (a) 10 − x
   (b) 3 + 2 + n
   (c) m mod n
   (d) "1812 Overture"
   (e) "Hamlet
   (f) "x" + 1

(ii) Using the same values as above for x, n and m, which of the following are *not* valid boolean expressions in *me too*, and why?
   (a) true and false
   (b) n = m

(c) not(m)
(d) (n > m) and (x = 2)
(e) true and false or true

(iii) Still using the values for x, m and n, and given that b1 = true and b2 = false, which of the following are *not* valid definitions of data objects and why?
(a) k == 10 ;
(b) fred == 3 + m ;
(c) a == (5 + 4)/n
(d) b = 24 ;
(e) "queen" == "mary" ;
(f) flag == b1 and not(b2) ;

(iv) Give *me too* specifications (functionality and definition) of the following operations:
(a) a function square, which takes an integer argument, and returns the square of the argument (make use of the power function from Section 5.2);
(b) an alternative definition of square, this time without using the power function;
(c) a function odd, which, when applied to an integer, returns true if it is an odd number, otherwise false (use the even function from Section 5.2);
(d) an alternative definition of odd, which does not refer to even;
(e) a function oddoreven, which takes an integer and returns the string "odd" if it is an odd number, otherwise "even";
(f) modify oddoreven to test that the argument is a number, and, if not, to return an appropriate message.

(v) (a) The following operation takes a non-negative real number and rounds it to the nearest integer. The type Real+ in the functionality indicates that the operation is defined for *non-negative* real numbers only:

```
rnd : Real+ -> Integer
rnd(x) ==
   if      (x mod 1) = 0 then x
   else if (x mod 1) < 0.5 then x truncate 1
        else (x truncate 1) + 1 ;
```

We expect rnd(3.3) to evaluate to 3, and rnd(3.5) to evaluate to 4. Rewrite the definition of rnd to make use of a local definition (a let expression).

(b) Objects of type bank account are represented as a tuple:

```
BankAcc = tuple(Name,AccNo,Balance)
```

where Name is of type String, AccNo is of type Nat and Balance is of type Integer. Construct a tuple which records Terry's bank account details. Show how his balance can be selected from this tuple.

Chapter 6

me too notation – sets

It can be shown that a mathematical web of some kind can be woven about any universe containing several objects. The fact that our universe lends itself to mathematical treatment is not a fact of any great philosophical significance.

Bertrand Russell

In the first section we discuss the basics of set theory, using conventional set notation. The second section gives the *me too* notation for set expressions, and introduces some of the more advanced constructs of set theory which are available in *me too*.

6.1 Basic set theory

The Pooka MacPhellimey, a member of the devil class, sat in his hut in the middle of a firwood meditating on the nature of the numerals and segregating in his mind the odd ones from the even.

Flann O'Brien

A **set** is a collection of items. Those items in a particular set are known as the **elements** or **members** of that set. For a set with a finite number of elements, we can represent that set by listing or **enumerating** its elements. For instance, the vowels in the English alphabet can be represented as a set thus:

{a,e,i,o,u}

The elements of the set are enclosed in braces and separated by commas. Sets are sometimes illustrated by means of **Venn diagrams**, wherein the members of a set are shown enclosed by a circle. Figure 6.1 is a Venn diagram showing the set of vowels in the English alphabet.

There is no ordering on the elements of a set, so that the set

{u,o,a,e,i}

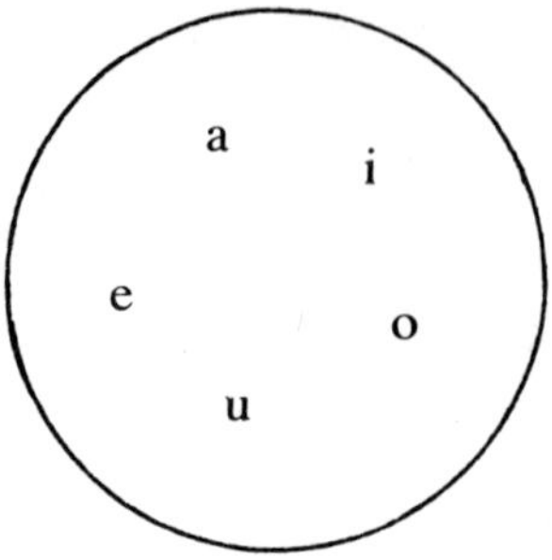

Figure 6.1 Venn diagram showing the set of vowels in the English alphabet.

is identical to (*is the same set as*) the one shown above. Set equality means that two sets have exactly the same members, so

$$\{a,e,i,o,u\} = \{u,o,a,e,i\}$$

but

$$\{1,2,3\} \neq \{2,3\}$$

Elements are never repeated in a set: an item is either a member of a set, or not. The value of the expression

$$\{a,a,e,i,o,u\}$$

is therefore not distinct from the set of English vowels.

Set enumeration is only one way of denoting sets with a finite number of elements; later we shall make use of other methods for specifying finite sets. Clearly it is not possible to enumerate sets with an infinite number of elements; however, the concept of infinite sets is far from unfamiliar. The set of integers is one example. There are ways of denoting infinite sets, although only the infinitely patient should attempt to compute their values... In *me too* we will sometimes refer to infinite sets such as the integers and the reals in type specifications. Many of the *me too* operations we define will construct finite sets of objects.

Sets may be named. For example the set of decimal digits can be defined as follows:

$$\text{digits} = \{0,1,2,3,4,5,6,7,8,9\}$$

and the set of odd numbered digits as

$$\text{odddigits} = \{1,3,5,7,9\}$$

We can test whether an entity is a member of a set. The membership symbol is $\in$:

$$133 \in \text{digits}$$

will evaluate to false, whilst

$$5 \in \text{odddigits}$$

has the value true.

The number of elements in a set is known as its **cardinality**:

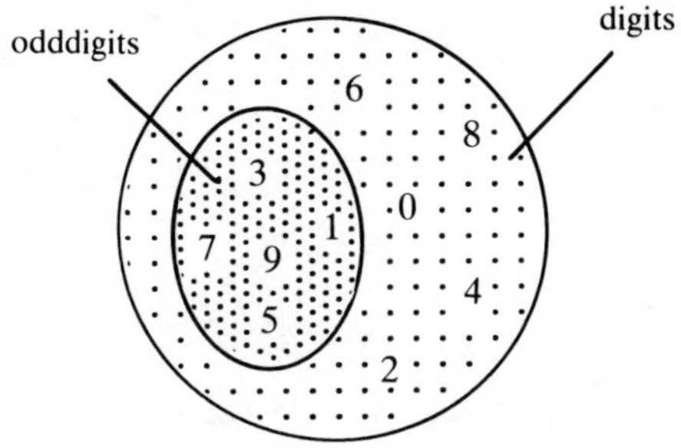

Figure 6.2 Venn diagram illustrating subset.

card(digits) = 10

and

card(odddigits) = 5

There is one set with a cardinality of zero – this is the set with no members, known as the **empty set**. The empty set is sometimes represented by a symbol resembling the Greek letter *phi* – ϕ or by set brackets with no elements between them – {}.

A set s1 may be a **subset** of (or *included in*) another set s2. That is, each of the members of s1 is a member of s2. If we draw a Venn diagram of the sets digits and odddigits (Fig. 6.2) we have a graphic representation of set inclusion.

By inspecting the Venn diagram, we can easily verify that

odddigits ⊆ digits

where the ⊆ symbol means subset.

We now define a set smallprimes, which contains all the prime numbers smaller than 10:

smallprimes = {2,3,5,7}

and use the sets smallprimes and odddigits to illustrate the set operations **union**, **intersection** and **difference**.

The union of two sets s1 and s2 gives the set whose elements are members of s1 or s2; it merges the two sets together. Some elements may be shared by both sets; however, they will not appear twice in the union of s1 and s2 since there is no repetition of elements in sets. The set union symbol is ∪, and the union of s1 and s2 is written

s1 ∪ s2

So, the union of our example sets odddigits and smallprimes is written as

odddigits ∪ smallprimes

and has the value

{1,2,3,5,7,9}

which can be verified informally by inspecting Fig. 6.3. Here we can see that the

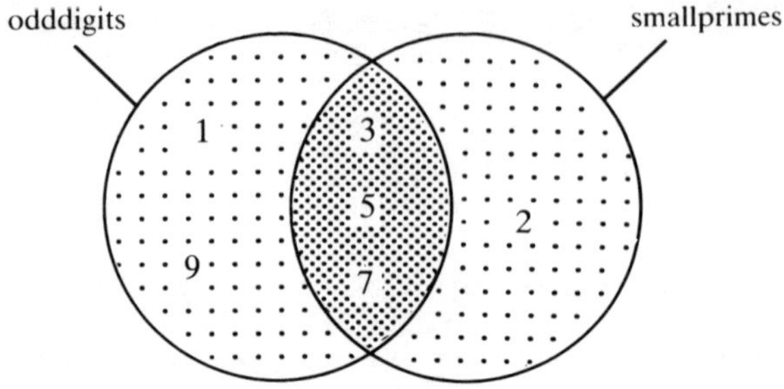

Figure 6.3 Venn diagram illustrating union, intersection and difference.

union of the two sets gives the set of elements enclosed within the outer boundary of the two circles.

The intersection of two sets gives the set of elements common to both sets. The intersection symbol is written ∩, and

    s1 ∩ s2

gives the set of elements which are both a member of s1 and a member of s2. So

    odddigits ∩ smallprimes = {3,5,7}

and appears on the Venn diagram as the central area where the two circles overlap.

Union and intersection are both **commutative** operations, that is, for any sets s1 and s2,

    s1 ∪ s2 = s2 ∪ s1

and

    s1 ∩ s2 = s2 ∩ s1

and **associative**, that is

    s1 ∪ (s2 ∪ s3) = (s1 ∪ s2) ∪ s3

and

    s1 ∩ (s2 ∩ s3) = (s1 ∩ s2) ∩ s3

The **set difference** operation is written as a minus sign:

    s1 − s2

and removes from s1 any elements which are included in s2. Looking back to Fig. 6.3 we can confirm that

    odddigits − smallprimes = {1,9}

and that set difference is not commutative, since

    smallprimes − odddigits = {2}

Set difference is not associative.

In the next section we examine the *me too* notation for these set expressions, and introduce some more complex operations on sets.

6.2 Sets in *me too*

Here we give the machine-readable *me too* notation for the basic set expressions seen in the previous section. From there we proceed to some more powerful notation for constructing sets. Finally we deal with **quantification** and **reduction** over sets.

Set enumeration in *me too* uses the same syntax as we have seen in the previous section, where sets are enclosed in braces, and elements are separated by commas:

```
{2,3,5,7}
```

If the elements are strings, they must be enclosed in double quotes in the usual way:

```
{"a","e","i","o","u"}
```

The empty set is always written in *me too* as

```
{}
```

To define an object which is a set, the normal rules for *me too* definitions of objects apply; namely, the *is defined to be* symbol is used, and the whole definition is terminated by a semicolon. For example,

```
smallprimes == {2,3,5,7} ;

rainbow ==
  {"red","orange","yellow","green","blue","indigo","violet"} ;
```

The elements of smallprimes are of type Integer, and the elements of rainbow are of type String. The types of these two sets then can be specified as

```
set(Integer)
```

and

```
set(String)
```

respectively. So, the type of a set object is written as set(T) where T is the type of the elements of the set. All elements of a set should be of the same type. However, this type may itself be a **constructed type**. For example, objects of type set(set(Integer)) are sets wherein each element of the set is itself a set of integers. set(Integer) and set(set(Integer)) are examples of constructed types; Integer is not.

me too provides a predicate is_set, which returns the boolean value true if the argument is a set. So

```
is_set(rainbow)
```

evaluates to true, but

```
is_set("green")
```

and

```
is_set(-49)
```

both evaluate to false.

Most of the set notation symbols are not available in machine character sets. In *me too* therefore we replace these symbols with names. Table 6.1 shows the correspondence between standard set notation and *me too* notation.

The empty set is a constant; the rest of the notation in Table 6.1 refers to operators. With the exception of card, these are binary operators, and are written in infix notation. card is a unary operator, and is therefore written in prefix (functional) notation.

Table 6.1 *me too* set notation

Symbol	*me too* notation
{} or ∅	{}
∈	member
⊆	subset
∪	union
∩	inter
−	diff
card	card
=	=
≠	/=

The following are valid *me too* expressions involving sets:

```
{} /= {1}
"blue" member rainbow
{7,3,1} subset {2,3,5,7}
{1,2} union {-10,4}
odddigits inter {1,9,11,20}
digits diff smallprimes
card(digits)
smallprimes /= digits
```

We can give functionalities for the basic set operations, such as

```
_ member _ : T x set(T) -> Boolean
```

where the underscores either side of the operator name indicate that member is an infix operator. This functionality shows that member takes an argument of any type (denoted by the type variable T), and a set whose members are of that same type, and returns a boolean value. The other set operations have the functionalities shown below.

```
_ subset _ : set(T) x set(T) -> Boolean
_ union _  : set(T) x set(T) -> set(T)
_ inter _  : set(T) x set(T) -> set(T)
_ diff _   : set(T) x set(T) -> set(T)
_ = _      : T x T -> Boolean
_ /= _     : T x T -> Boolean
card       : set(T) -> Nat
```

Recall that equality and inequality are defined in *me too* for any data types, including sets. Note also that the binary operators such as union should only be applied to arguments which are sets of the same type; they also return a result which is a set of that same type.

We now introduce some further set notation. This notation is available in *me too*. A set which contains a single element, in other words, a set with a cardinality of one, is known as a **singleton set**. Sometimes it is useful to be able to extract or select that element from the set. The operation the does just this:

```
the : set(T) -> T
```

and is only defined for singleton sets. So, if a set s has the value {129}, then the(s) has the value 129.

We can see that the functionality of the is consistent with this result. In this case, we have applied the to a (singleton) set of type set(Integer), and the result is of type Integer.

It is often useful to construct a set of integers within a particular range. Such a set is by definition finite; we therefore have a mechanism for specifying it using set enumeration, as in

```
{10,11,12,13,14}
```

This method of course becomes increasingly tedious with larger sets, so an equivalent shorthand notation is provided:

```
{10,...,14}
```

where (precisely three) dots denote the intervening integers. The general form is

$$\{e_1,...,e_2\}$$

where e_1 and e_2 are expressions denoting integers. If $e_1 > e_2$ then the result will be the empty set. We can now redefine the set digits more simply:

```
digits == {0,...,9} ;
```

Now we turn to a more powerful notation for constructing sets. Specifically, we will construct new sets from old, by selecting each element from the original set, performing some action on it and building a new set from the resulting values. This method of construction is referred to as **set comprehension**. The notation used is called **ZF notation** after the set theoreticians Ernst Zermelo and Abraham Fraenkl.

The simplest form of set constructor using set comprehension is

```
{ e | x<-s }
```

where s is an expression whose value is a set and e is some expression which will usually involve x. The meaning of the whole expression is *the set of* e *such that* x *is drawn from the set* s. Each element is taken from s and is temporarily referred to as x. For each of these values of x, the value of expression e is collected into the result set. The expression to the right-hand side of the vertical bar is called the **generator**; it generates values of x. To the left-hand side of the vertical bar is the expression from which the values of members of the new set are computed. If the cardinality of s is k, then the whole set expression denotes the set whose elements are the result of evaluating e k times, once for each binding of x to an element of s.

For example, if s1 is the set {1,2,3}, then

```
{ x * 2 | x <- sl}
```

denotes the set obtained by binding x to each of the members of sl and doubling it, thus:

```
{1 * 2, 2 * 2, 3 * 2}
```

which evaluates to

```
{2,4,6}
```

The same set could be constructed by means of the expression

```
{ x * 2 | x <- {1,2,3}}
```

where the reference set is enumerated rather than referred to by name.

This kind of construct can be used in the definition of a *me too* operation. For example, we may design an operation which takes any set of integers and returns the set which results from doubling each of the elements in the original set. We will call this function doubleset, and write its functionality and definition as

```
doubleset : set(Integer) -> set(Integer)
doubleset(s) == { x * 2 | x <- s} ;
```

We may now apply doubleset to an appropriate argument, such as the set sl defined above:

```
doubleset(sl)
```

will evaluate to

```
{2,4,6}
```

and of course

```
doubleset({1,2,3})
```

will have exactly the same effect. The empty set is a valid argument for this operation, since the set with no elements is the degenerate case of a set of any type; the *empty set of integers* is simply the empty set. So

```
doubleset({}) = {}
```

because the expression x * 2 is evaluated zero times (once for each member of the empty set) and the result returned is the empty set.

An alternative approach to designing the operation doubleset would be first to define an operation double, which takes an integer and doubles it:

```
double : Integer -> Integer
double (n) == n * 2 ;
```

and then to use this operation in the definition of doubleset:

```
doubleset(s) == {double(x) | x <- s} ;
```

Here we have changed the definition, but not the functionality or the semantics, of doubleset.

Like any other *me too* expressions, set constructors may be used in definitions of objects. For instance, the set of even digits could be constructed from the set of odd digits, which was defined previously as

```
odddigits == {1,3,5,7,9} ;
```

by associating the value of a set constructor expression with an identifier evendigits:

```
evendigits == { d − 1 | d <− odddigits} ;
```

evendigits has the value {0,2,4,6,8}.

In an expression of the form

```
{ e | x <− s }
```

the expression e may be arbitrarily complex. Here is an example where the resulting set is a set of pairs. The set rainbow, which has the value

```
{"red","orange","yellow","green","blue","indigo","violet"}
```

is used to construct a set of pairs, where the first element of each pair is the name of one of the colors of the rainbow, and the second element is the length of that color name. We assume that an operation to count the number of characters in a string has been defined, with functionality

```
stringlength : String −> Integer
```

When applied to "green", for example, stringlength will return the value 5.

We now define the set of pairs colorlengths:

```
colorlengths ==
    {(color, stringlength(color)) | color <− rainbow} ;
```

and expect it to have the value

```
{("red",3),("orange",6),("yellow",6),("green",5),("blue",4),("indigo",6),("violet",6)}
```

Each element in the set colorlengths is of type pair(String,Integer). The type of colorlengths therefore is set(pair(String,Integer)).

In all of the examples so far, constructs taking the form

```
{ e | x <− s } ;
```

have yielded a set with the same cardinality as s. This is not necessarily the case. Consider, for example, the set

```
{ x truncate 2 | x <− {2,4,5}}
```

truncate gives the result of integer division, discarding any remainder, so 4 truncate 2 and 5 truncate 2 both have the value 2. The set constructed above, then, has the value {1,2} and cardinality 2, whereas the set in the generator has cardinality 3. So, if the expression e yields the same value for two different values of x, the duplicate values disappear from the result set and it has fewer members than the original set. In no case, however, will a constructor of this form return a set with *more* members than the set in the generator; nor will it evaluate to the empty set, unless s is itself the empty set. This property may be stated formally as

```
min(1,card(s)) <= card({ e | x <- s}) <= card(s)
```

for any set s and any valid expression e.

min has its usual meaning here, as a function which returns the lesser of two numbers. This function is not predefined in *me too*, but can be simply defined by the user as

```
min : Number x Number -> Number
min(x,y) == if x < y then x else y ;
```

A further elaboration of the set comprehension notation permits us to construct more interesting sets. By introducing a **predicate**, or test, the candidates for membership of the result set may be restricted to those satisfying the test. This is known as **filtering**. The general form of the set constructor with filter is

```
{ e | x <- s; b }
```

where the filter is provided by b. Here b is a boolean expression which usually involves x, and is part of the generator. The filter is separated from the preceding part of the generator by a semicolon. The construct means *the set of* e *such that* x *is drawn from* s *and* b *is satisfied*. This notation can be used to construct the set of odd digits from the set of digits:

```
{ n | n <- digits; not(even(n))}
```

where the set digits has already been defined, and the operation even is defined as previously. Each number n is drawn from the set digits, and is put into the result set only if it satisfies the test not(even(n)).

Using the previous definitions of the set rainbow and the operation stringlength, we can construct the set of colors of the rainbow whose names are less than six characters long:

```
{ color | color <- rainbow; stringlength(color) < 6}
```

The value of this set is

```
{"red", "green", "blue"}
```

Once again the expression to the left of the vertical bar may be arbitrarily complex. Similarly, the predicate can be an arbitrarily complex boolean expression. For example,

```
{n * n | n <- digits; even(n) and ((n > 2) and (n < 6))}
```

constructs the set of integers with the values n^2 where n is an even digit greater than two and less than six. The set constructed has the value {16}.

The following example demonstrates that the set constructor with filter may in some cases construct the empty set. In the case of the set

```
{ n | n <- digits; (n > 0) and ((n * 10) member digits)}
```

there are no digits which satisfy the predicate; the result is therefore the empty set. In fact, for any set constructor with filter,

```
0 <= card({ e | x <- s; b}) <= card(s)
```

We can give further examples of the set comprehension notation by using it to specify the set intersection and difference operations:

```
s1 inter s2 == { x | x <- s1; x member s2} ;
s1 diff s2 == { x | x <- s1; not(x member s2)} ;
```

Expressions of the form x <- s and x <- s; b are generators. More than one generator may be used in a set constructor. A more general form of this construct, then, is given by

{ e | $g_1, \ldots, g_k$ }

where g_1 through g_k are generators (with or without filters). An example of a set constructor using two generators is

```
{ n * m | n <- s1, m <- s2}
```

which is read *the set of* n *multiplied by* m *such that* n *is drawn from* s1 *and* m *is drawn from* s2. The meaning is that every element is selected from s1, and, for each of these, every element is drawn from s2. The expression n * m is evaluated for every possible pairing of elements from the two sets. So, if s1 has the value {1,2} and s2 has the value {10,20} then n will be bound to 10, and the value of 1 * 10 will be collected into the result set. n will continue to be bound to 1 while m takes the value 20, and another value, 1 * 20, will be added to the result set. n * m will also be added to the set for the pairs of bindings n = 2, m = 10 and n = 2, m = 20. The set constructed will be

```
{ 1 * 10, 1 * 20, 2 * 10, 2 * 20}
```

and will evaluate to

```
{10,20,40}
```

To take another example, the set

```
{(x,y) | x <- s1, y <- s2}
```

builds a set of pairs from two sets. The first element of each pair is taken from the first set, and the second from the second set. Every possible pairing of elements from the first set with elements from the second set is used. If s1 has the value {"L","E"} and s2 has the value {3,5} then the expression above evaluates to

```
{("L",3),("L",5),("E",3),("E",5)}
```

This, as it turns out, gives a concise specification of the **cartesian product**, or cross product, of two sets.

Here is an example of a set constructor which has multiple generators and a filter:

```
{ n * m | n <- s1; n > 1, m <- s2}
```

If s1 has the value {1,2} and s2 has the value {10,20}, then the expression above will evaluate to

```
{20,40}
```

since only one element from sl is greater than one. A predicate may not refer to variables from generators to the right of it. So, in the example above, the boolean expression may refer to n but not to m. Any filter referring to m would have to appear as part of, or to the right of, the second generator.

In the exercises in the previous chapter there was an example of a tuple which represented a bank account. We can record Terry's bank account details in the tuple

```
("Terry",123,15)
```

where the three fields record the customer's name, account number and balance. This notion can be elaborated by representing a bank as a collection of such tuples, in fact as a set of tuples:

```
Bank = set(Account)
```

where

```
Account  = tuple(Name,AccNo,Balance)
Name     = String
AccNo    = Nat
Balance  = Integer
```

We can create a data object which represents a particular bank. This bank has two customers:

```
dodgybank == {("Terry",123,15),("Arthur",124,3000)} ;
```

An object of type Bank is a set of tuples. The set constructors can be applied to a set of tuples just as they can be applied to any other set. Remembering that the selectors first, second etc. can be used to extract the elements of a tuple, we can find the names of the customers by constructing the following set:

```
{first(x) | x <- dodgybank}
```

Each account is drawn from the bank and referred to as x. An account is a tuple; first(x) selects the first element from the tuple. The first element of an Account object is a name, so the result set will be a set of names. The whole set expression evaluates to

```
{"Terry", "Arthur"}
```

which is the set of names of customers of the bank.

There is a more useful form of the notation for sets of tuples, however, which permits pattern matching:

$$\{ e \mid (a_1,\ldots,a_k) <- s \}$$

This construct can be read as *the set of* e *such that each tuple is drawn from the set* s *of k-tuples, where* a_1 *through* a_k *are bound to the elements of each tuple*. Using this construct, we have an alternative way of determining the set of customer names:

```
{ n | (n,a,b) <- dodgybank}
```

In this case we have simply collected all the first elements from the tuple. More interesting sets can be constructed using this notation, however. If, for example, we wanted to deduct bank charges of $20 from each customer, the following expression specifies the new bank which results from performing this transaction:

```
{(n,a,b – 20) | (n,a,b) <– dodgybank}
```

Every account is extracted from dodgybank and a new bank is constructed which consists of the set of accounts from dodgybank, with the balance of each decremented by 20. The result is

```
{("Terry", 123, –5), ("Arthur", 124, 2980)}
```

This construct can be applied to tuples of any length. A particular set of tuples, however, should contain tuples which are all of the same length and type.

Set constructors using tuple notation may have the same combinations of multiple generators, with or without filters, as we have already seen.

6.2.1 Quantification over sets

Universal and **existential quantifiers** are provided in *me too*. The form of the universal quantifier in *me too* is

```
all x in s . b
```

which corresponds to the usual logic notation

$$\forall x \in S . b$$

s is a set and b is a predicate normally involving x. The expression means *for all elements* x *in* s, b *is true*. As with the set constructors, x takes the value of each element in s, and b is evaluated for each binding of x. The whole expression evaluates to true only if b is true for all values of x.

Returning to the set smallprimes, which has the value {2,3,5,7}, the expression

```
all x in smallprimes . not(even(x))
```

has the value false, since there is one even number in the set. The expression

```
all x in smallprimes . (x > 1) and (x < 8)
```

has the value true, since all the members of smallprimes are both greater than one and smaller than eight.

We can show the meaning of the quantifier by specifying it in *me too*. For any set s,

```
all x in s . b
```

is equivalent to

```
not(false member { b | x <– s })
```

If s is the empty set, this expression evaluates to true, since

```
{ b | x <– {} }
```

returns the empty set, and false is not a member of the empty set.

Existential quantification is written in *me too* as

```
exists x in s . b
```

which corresponds to

$$\exists\, x \in S\,.\, b$$

The expression means *there exists an* x *in* s *such that* b *is true*, that is, it evaluates to true if b is true for at least one member of s. For example,

```
exists x in smallprimes . even(x)
```

has the value true, since 2 is an even number, and

```
exists x in smallprimes . not(even(x))
```

also evaluates to true, since at least one member of the set is an odd number.

Again we can specify the quantifier in *me too*: for any set s,

```
exists x in s . b
```

is equivalent to

```
true member { b | x <- s }
```

If s is the empty set, then this expression will evaluate to false.

There is one further quantifier in *me too*, known as the **unique existential quantifier**. It is written

```
exists1 x in s . b
```

and has the value true only if there is *exactly one* member of s for which b is true. It is equivalent to

```
card({ x | x <- s; b}) = 1
```

and returns false if s is the empty set.

```
exists1 x in smallprimes . not(even(x))
```

has the value false, since the predicate is true for more than one element of smallprimes. On the other hand,

```
exists1 x in smallprimes . even(x)
```

has the value true, since exactly one member of smallprimes is an even number.

All the quantifiers may be applied to sets of tuples, using the forms

```
all     (a1,...,ak) in s . b
exists  (a1,...,ak) in s . b
exists1 (a1,...,ak) in s . b
```

as in, for example,

```
all (n,a,b) in dodgybank . b > 100
```

That is, all the accounts in this bank have balances higher than \$100. The expression has the value false, since, although Arthur has more than \$100, Terry does not.

6.2.2 Reduction over sets

The idea of **reduction** originated with the programming language APL and has been used in many functional programming languages including LispKit. Sometimes, as in APL, LispKit and *me too*, it is known as *reduce*; in other languages (such as Miranda), it is called *fold*. *reduce* is a higher order function: it takes a function as a parameter.

In *me too*, reduction can be applied to sets or sequences. Used in conjunction with sets, reduction permits the repeated application of a function over the different members of the set. The function must be binary, and the elements of the set must be of the appropriate type for the function. The result of the reduction collapses the set into a single element.

The binary operator +, for example, can be reduced over a set of integers; the effect is that all the numbers in the set are summed together.

```
+ reduce (0) {2,3,5,7}
```

reduces the function + over the set containing the prime numbers less than 10. The meaning is

```
(((0 + 2) + 3) + 5) + 7
```

and the result of the reduction is the value 17.

The general form of the reduction construct is

```
f reduce (unit) s
```

where f is a binary function and usually has functionality

```
f : T x T -> T
```

T is again being used as a type variable – the function, in other words, takes two arguments of the same type, and the result is also of this type. The set s is a set whose elements are of this same type T.

As well as the name of the function, and the set which the function is to be reduced over, a **unit** or reference value of type T must be supplied. The unit is a value which is 'injected' as the starting point for the reduction. If the function is reduced over the empty set, the unit is the value which will be returned. The unit chosen will often have the property that applying the function to the unit and any member of the set will not affect the cumulative result. In the case of addition, the unit chosen is often zero, since zero plus any number x is equal to x. The unit is written after reduce, and is surrounded by brackets.

If we were to define a function add, with the same meaning as the operator +, but using prefix notation, then

```
add reduce (0) {2,3,5,7}
```

would be equivalent to

```
add(add(add(add(0,2),3),5),7)
```

and would have the value 17. The set we have used here is the set smallprimes. The function add may be reduced over smallprimes since the functionality of add is

```
add : Number x Number -> Number
```

and smallprimes is of type set(Number), or, more precisely, set(Integer), which is a subtype of set(Number).

Care must be exercised when reducing functions over sets. The elements of a set are not ordered, therefore the order in which the function is applied to different elements of the set must be immaterial. Or, more formally,

$$\mathrm{card}(\{f(\ldots f(u,e_1)\ldots,e_k) \mid e_1 \leftarrow s,\ldots,e_k \leftarrow s; \{e_1,\ldots,e_k\} = s\}) = 1$$

where f is the function to be reduced over set s, and u is the unit. If the characteristics of the set s are not known, this reduces to the constraint that the function must be commutative and associative. So, + may be reduced, but not −.

A frequently occurring situation is where *a set of sets* needs to be collapsed into a single set. Suppose ss is a set of sets with members s1, s2, s3 and s4 which are themselves sets of type set(T). So, ss is of type set(set(T)). ss can be collapsed into a set of type set(T) by taking the union of its elements

```
((s1 union s2) union s3) union s4
```

Or, equivalently, reduction may be used

```
union reduce ({}) ss
```

Here the empty set is used as the unit, since the result of taking the union of any set s with the empty set is s. If

```
s1 = {1,2}
s2 = {10,20}
s3 = {3,5,6}
s4 = {1,9,2}
```

then

```
union reduce ({}) ss
```

expands to

```
((({} union {1,2}) union {10,20}) union {3,5,6}) union {1,9,2}
```

which evaluates to

```
{1,2,10,20,3,5,6,9}
```

So, reducing union over any set of sets s returns the set which contains all the members of the members of s.

Reducing union over a set of sets is a common occurrence. In set theory this operation is known as **distributed union**, and is sometimes written with a large union symbol. In *me too*, a special operation is provided for distributed union, called dunion, so

```
dunion(ss)
```

is equivalent to

```
union reduce ({}) ss
```

In fact, reduction is more general than we have suggested: the complete story is that operations whose functionality is

$$f : T_1 \times T_2 \to T_1$$

may be reduced over a set of type set(T_2). The unit and the result of the reduction are both of type T_1. This more subtle use of reduce, however, is rarely needed. In the simpler examples given above, T_1 and T_2 happen to be the same type.

The functionality of reduce, then, is

```
_ reduce (_) _ : (T1 x T2 -> T1) x T1 x set(T2) -> T1
```

where the brackets round the type of the first argument indicate that it is a function.

We might use reduce in this way if, for example, we wanted to find out how many numbers there are altogether in the set ss, where ss as before has the value

```
{{1,2},{10,20},{3,5,6},{1,9,2}}
```

Simply reducing + will not do the job, since

```
+ reduce (0) {card(s) | s <- ss}
```

is equivalent to

```
+ reduce (0) {2,3}
```

which evaluates to 5, rather than 10, because the duplicated cardinalities have been removed. One solution is to define a function sumcard:

```
sumcard : Integer x set(Integer) -> Integer
sumcard(x,s) == x + card(s) ;
```

and reduce this function over the set ss:

```
sumcard reduce (0) ss
```

which gives the required result of 10. The reader may care to verify that this use of reduction is consistent with the functionality given above.

6.3 Summary

The first section of this chapter furnished an introduction to elementary set theory. The remainder of the chapter covered the *me too* notation for sets and introduced some of the more advanced set-theoretic concepts such as set comprehension, and quantification and reduction over sets.

We have seen that a set is a suitable representation for a collection (of arbitrary size) of items of the same type, providing we are not concerned with any ordering relation on the items, and in a context where any duplication of items is not significant.

The material in this and the previous chapter forms the foundation from which we can proceed to examine the more complex data types available in *me too*. We shall see that these more complex data types can be built from a combination of sets and tuples.

6.4 Exercises

(i) (a) Define a set s1 whose members are the integers between 13 and 19 inclusive. Show two alternative definitions using set enumeration and integer range respectively.

Using the set s1, and given another set s2 with the value {6,9,12,15,16,18}, evaluate the following expressions:

(b) s1 union s2
(c) s1 inter s2
(d) s1 diff s2
(e) s2 diff s1
(f) (12 member s1) and (12 member s2)
(g) {13,19} subset s1
(h) card(s1) + card(s2)
(j) card(s1 union s2)
(k) the(s1)
(l) the({"aargh"})
(m) s1 = {13,. . .,19}

(ii) (a) Using the set digits, with the value {0,. . .,9}, write a set constructor which denotes the set obtained by multiplying each of the members of digits by 10.

(b) Again using digits, write a set constructor which denotes the set of digits which are multiples of 3.

(c) Using the object dodgybank, which has been defined:

```
dodgybank == {("Terry",123,15),("Arthur",124,3000)} ;
```

write a set expression which denotes the set of account numbers in dodgybank. The type of dodgybank is Bank, where

```
Bank = set(tuple(Name,AccNo,Balance))
```

(d) Define an operation robinhood, which takes an argument of type Bank, and returns an object of type Bank. Each customer's balance is altered in the following way: customers with balances of over $1000 have $100 deducted, all other customers have $100 added to their balance.

(e) What is the result of applying robinhood to dodgybank?

(iii) (a) Write an expression which uses quantification to test whether all the elements of the set s2 defined above are even numbers. Assume the function even is available, with functionality

```
even : Integer -> Boolean
```

What is the value of this expression?

(b) Using the object dodgybank, write an expression which tests whether any of the bank's customers have less than $50 in their account. What is the value of this expression?

(c) Again using dodgybank, write an expression which tests whether *exactly one* of the customers is in credit. What is the value of this expression?

(iv) Assume the definitions of max and min are

```
max, min : Number x Number -> Number
max(x,y) == if x > y then x else y ;
min(x,y) == if x < y then x else y ;
```

(a) What is the value of the following expression?

```
max reduce (0) {1,5,3,20,2}
```

(b) What is the value of

```
and reduce (true) {even(x) | x <- {2,4,20}}
```

(c) Define a function minset which takes a set of natural numbers and returns the smallest number in the set. If the empty set is supplied, zero should be returned as the result. Use reduction.

Chapter 7

me too notation – binary relations and maps

In this chapter we examine two further object types available in *me too*. **Binary relations** and **maps** are mathematical constructs which provide a useful representation for data objects, and which have associated with them a number of powerful operations. Binary relations and maps represent the next stage in the hierarchy of increasingly sophisticated mathematical constructs erected on the foundation of set theory.

7.1 Binary relations

> *In our description of nature the purpose is not to disclose the real essence of the phenomena but only to track down, so far as it is possible, relations between the manifold aspects of our experience.*
>
> Niels Bohr

A binary relation is an association between entities which records the fact that they are connected in some way. A binary relation can be thought of as a table with two columns. The entries in the left-hand column belong to a set, the **domain** of the relation, and are connected via the relation to the corresponding entries in the right-hand column – the **range** of the relation. The table is annotated with the name of the relation.

For example, Fig. 7.1 records the list of prices in a cocktail bar in a relation called pricelist. This relation records the fact that a cocktail called a Moscow Mule costs $2.75, and so on. The domain of the relation is the set of names of cocktails, and the range is the set of prices.

domain	range
moscow mule	2.75
screwdriver	2.25
mickey mouse	1.75

Figure 7.1 The relation pricelist.

moscow mule	lemon juice
moscow mule	vodka
screwdriver	vodka
screwdriver	orange juice
mickey mouse	lemon juice
mickey mouse	pineapple juice

Figure 7.2 The relation contains.

The designer of the system might decide that another relation would be useful, and record the ingredients of each cocktail in another relation contains (Fig. 7.2). The fact that a particular cocktail contains more than one ingredient means that there is more than one entry in the table for it. (In our example, it happens that all the cocktails have two ingredients.) Names of cocktails, then, may appear more than once in the left-hand column. Notice also that ingredients are repeated in the right-hand column if they are used in more than one cocktail. Lemon juice and vodka appear twice, whilst orange juice and pineapple juice appear only once.

Binary relations are a special case of relations in general. Although they resemble the familiar data structures of tables, relations are in fact well-understood mathematical constructs, and a variety of mathematical models has been developed around them. These models provide the theoretical foundations for relational database technology, namely the relational algebra and the relational calculus (Codd, 1970, 1972, 1979).

7.1.1 Binary relations in *me too*

A relation can be represented mathematically as a set of tuples, where each tuple corresponds to a row in the tabular representation of the relation. In *me too*, operations are provided for manipulating binary relations only. A binary relation is represented as a (finite) set of pairs.

Since any n-ary relation can be represented by n binary relations, any relational database could therefore be represented using only binary relations. Restricting ourselves to binary relations means that many of the complexities of the relational algebra are avoided. The cost incurred by this approach is the proliferation of relations which follows.

The standard *me too* operations on binary relations permit a wide range of queries to be addressed to a relational database.

To return to the cocktail bar example from the previous section, the relation pricelist would be represented by a set of pairs:

```
pricelist == {("moscow mule",  2.75),
              ("screwdriver",  2.25),
              ("mickey mouse", 1.75)} ;
```

Here we are using the relation constructor, which takes the form

$\{(e_1,e_2),(e_3,e_4),\ldots,(e_k,e_{k+1})\}$

The domain and range types of pricelist are Cocktail and Price, where

```
Cocktail = String
Price    = Real
```

so pricelist itself is a relation of type

```
rel(Cocktail,Price)
```

In general, the type specification for a relation takes the form

$$rel(T_1,T_2)$$

where T_1 and T_2 may be arbitrarily complex types. (They may, of course, be of the same type.)

The relation contains is also represented as a set of pairs:

```
contains == {("moscow mule", "lemon juice"),
             ("moscow mule", "vodka"),
             ("screwdriver", "vodka"),
             ("screwdriver", "orange juice"),
             ("mickey mouse", "lemon juice"),
             ("mickey mouse", "pineapple juice")} ;
```

If the range type of contains is declared as Ingredient, where

```
Ingredient = String
```

then the type of contains is

```
rel(Cocktail,Ingredient)
```

Since relations are represented as sets of pairs, all the set operations may be applied to them. So, for example, the relation contains could have been constructed in stages, using a series of union operations:

```
contains == {("moscow mule", "lemon juice")} ;
contains == contains union {("moscow mule", "vodka")} ;
```

and so on, until all the pairs had been entered. Similarly, set difference could be used to remove pairs from a relation, and the other set operations could be used to test membership, and so on.

As well as the set operations, *me too* has a number of predefined operations which are specific to binary relations. The predicate is_relation tests whether a data object is a relation:

```
is_relation(contains)
```

has the value true, but

```
is_relation("vodka")
```

returns false.

Given a relation such as contains, we might want to find out all the names of cocktails in the relation. The notions of the domain and range of a relation have already been introduced; the *me too* operations dom and rng return the set of values in the domain and range of a relation respectively.

```
dom(contains)
```

returns the set which includes each of the first elements of the pairs in contains:

```
{"moscow mule", "screwdriver", "mickey mouse"}
```

This gives the complete set of cocktail names in the relation. Notice that there are six pairs in the relation, that is

```
card(contains) = 6
```

but there are only three elements in the domain

```
card(dom(contains)) = 3
```

This is because cocktail names are repeated in the domain of contains.

A *me too* specification of dom can be given. Its functionality is

$$\text{dom} : \text{rel}(T_1,T_2) \text{ -> } \text{set}(T_1)$$

showing that dom can be applied to any relation, and that it returns a set whose members are of the same type as the domain of the relation. The definition of dom is

```
dom(r) == { x | (x,y) <- r} ;
```

Each pair is drawn from the relation r, the first and second elements of the pair are bound to x and y, and the first elements of the pairs (the x values) are collected into the result set.

The rng operation is similar to dom, except that it constructs the set of second elements from the pairs in the relation. In our example, rng can be used to discover the set of ingredients which must be stocked in order to make all of the cocktails:

```
rng(contains)
```

will return the set

```
{"lemon juice", "vodka", "orange juice", "pineapple juice"}
```

As with dom, we find that

```
card(rng(contains)) < card(contains)
```

since some of the ingredients appear in more than one cocktail. The rng operation is defined:

$$\text{rng} : \text{rel}(T_1,T_2) \text{ -> } \text{set}(T_2)$$

```
rng(r) == { y | (x,y) <- r} ;
```

Earlier we noted that pairs could be removed from a relation by using set difference. For example,

```
contains diff {("moscow mule", "vodka")}
```

returns the relation

```
{("moscow mule", "lemon juice"),
 ("screwdriver", "vodka"),
 ("screwdriver", "orange juice"),
 ("mickey mouse", "lemon juice"),
 ("mickey mouse", "pineapple juice")}
```

Another way of removing pairs from a relation is to use the **domain subtraction** operation, ds. Here we supply not a set of pairs to be removed, but a set of domain elements. All pairs whose first element is included in this set are deleted from the relation. (Strictly speaking, in the functional paradigm we should say that *a new relation is constructed from the old relation*, which differs from it in that the specified pairs are not present.) Domain subtraction could be used to remove the entries for Moscow Mule and Screwdriver from the price list:

```
pricelist ds {"moscow mule", "screwdriver"}
```

which returns a very impoverished price list as its result:

```
{("mickey mouse", 1.75)}
```

Or, ds could be used to remove from contains all those pairs which have "moscow mule" in the first position:

```
contains ds {"moscow mule"}
```

returns the relation

```
{("screwdriver", "vodka"),
 ("screwdriver", "orange juice"),
 ("mickey mouse", "lemon juice"),
 ("mickey mouse", "pineapple juice")}
```

Notice that this is not the same relation which resulted from using set difference earlier. The domain subtraction operation is defined as

```
_ ds _ : rel(T1,T2) x set(T1) -> rel(T1,T2)
r ds s == {(x,y) | (x,y) <- r; not(x member s)} ;
```

The complementary operation is known as **domain restriction**. The operator dr is applied to a relation and a set of objects from the domain of the relation, and returns a relation which contains only those pairs whose first element is a member of the set specified. Domain restriction is similar to one of the uses of the SELECT operation in the relational algebra. dr has the same functionality as ds, and is defined as follows:

```
r dr s == {(x,y) | (x,y) <- r; x member s} ;
```

The only difference in the definitions is in the filter, where the predicate is inverted. We could discover the price of a particular cocktail using dr:

```
pricelist dr {"moscow mule"}
```

which returns a relation containing only one pair:

```
{("moscow mule", 2.75)}
```

Alternatively, we could find out the ingredients of a particular cocktail:

```
contains dr {"moscow mule"}
```

which tells us which ingredients are needed to make a Moscow Mule:

```
{("moscow mule", "lemon juice"),
 ("moscow mule", "vodka")}
```

Here the relation returned has two pairs, since this cocktail has two entries in the relation contains.

We find that

```
(contains ds {"moscow mule"})
 union
(contains dr {"moscow mule"})
```

is equal to contains, that is, it reconstructs the original relation. In general, given a relation r and a set s, domain subtract and domain restrict have the effect of partitioning the relation r into two relations r_1 and r_2, where r_1 contains only those pairs whose first element is *not* a member of s, and where r_2 contains only those pairs whose first element *is* a member of s. So, if

```
r1 = r ds s
```

and

```
r2 = r dr s
```

then

```
r1 union r2 = r
```

and

```
r1 inter r2 = {}
```

This relationship can be seen in the definitions of ds and dr.

Like any other *me too* operations, the operations on binary relations can be embedded in arbitrarily complex expressions in order to frame more complicated queries. We could ask, for example, whether we have a recipe for all cocktails on the price list. If

```
(dom(pricelist) diff dom(contains)) = {}
```

evaluates to true, then we know that this is the case. Or, it might be useful to collect the ingredients of a particular cocktail into a set:

```
rng(contains dr {"moscow mule"})
```

has this effect, and evaluates to

```
{"lemon juice", "vodka"}
```

This kind of operation will frequently be useful; here we are looking up the ingredients of a particular cocktail. It is an example of a fundamental operation on relations, which mathematicians refer to as the **image** of a set s under a relation r. (In the relational algebra, the same kind of operation can be achieved by a combination of SELECT and PROJECT.) In terms of the table representation of binary relations, we can think of the image of a set s under a relation r as a result of a look-up operation from the left-hand column to the right-hand column of r. If r is contains and s is

```
{"moscow mule", "mickey mouse"}
```

then the image set is the set of ingredients from the right-hand column which have "mickey mouse" or "moscow mule" in the left-hand column (see Fig. 7.3).

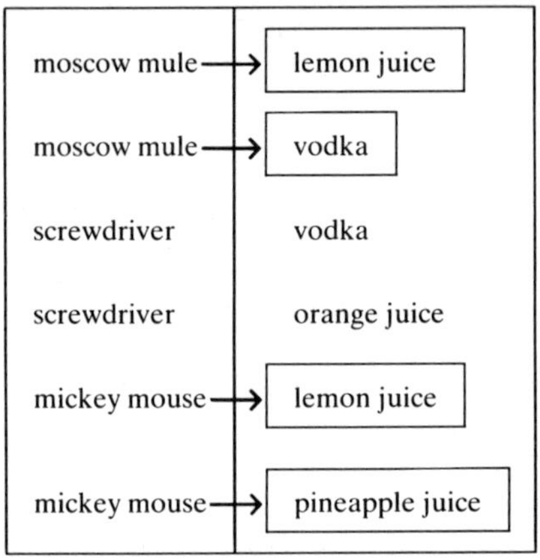

Figure 7.3 An example of the use of im.

The image relation in *me too* is called im. The operation im can be applied to contains:

```
contains im {"moscow mule", "mickey mouse"}
```

in order to discover the set of ingredients needed to make a Moscow Mule and a Mickey Mouse:

```
{"lemon juice", "vodka", "pineapple juice"}
```

Similarly, the price of a cocktail could be found from pricelist by using im. Only one price is associated with a particular cocktail, so the result returned will be a singleton set. In this case we can select the only element of that set using the:

```
the(pricelist im {"moscow mule"})
```

which returns the price we are interested in:

```
2.75
```

im takes a relation, and a set of objects of the same type as the domain of the relation, and returns a set of objects of the range type:

```
_ im _ : rel(T1,T2) x set(T1) -> set(T2)
```

The operation is defined:

```
r im s == { y | (x,y) <- r ; x member s} ;
```

or, alternatively:

```
r im s == rng(r dr s) ;
```

Another useful operation is inverse, which takes each pair in a relation and reverses the order of its two elements. In the table representation, this corresponds to swapping the first and second columns of the relation. The definition of inverse is

```
inverse : rel(T1,T2) -> rel(T2,T1)
inverse(r) == {(y,x) | (x,y) <- r} ;
```

So, for example, inverse(pricelist) has the value

```
{(2.75, "moscow mule"),
 (2.25, "screwdriver"),
 (1.75, "mickey mouse") }
```

How useful is inverse? The im operation gives us a way of looking forward through a relation, but there is no operation for a right-to-left look-up. Applying the image operation to the inverse of a relation, however, makes this possible. Suppose, for instance, that we have run out of lemon juice and pineapple juice, and want to discover which cocktails need either of these ingredients:

```
inverse(contains) im {"lemon juice","pineapple juice"}
```

gives the necessary information

```
{"moscow mule", "mickey mouse"}
```

and we can now tell customers that these cocktails are 'off'.

We have now covered all the operations on binary relations which are predefined in *me too*. To recap, they are the relation constructor, the predicate is_relation, the selectors dom, rng, dr, ds and im, and the inverse operation. Together with the set operations, the operations on binary relations provide the machinery for building, editing and querying a database of relations.

In the next section we move on to look at a more powerful object type based on sets of pairs.

7.2 Maps

He had bought a large map representing the sea,
Without the least vestige of land:
And the crew were much pleased when they found it to be
A map they could all understand . . .

Other maps are such shapes, with their islands and capes!
But we've got our brave Captain to thank
(So the crew would protest) that he's bought us the best –
A perfect and absolute blank!

Lewis Carroll

A **map**, sometimes called a *finite function*, is another yet more powerful construct for data representation. As its name suggests, it is a *mapping* between two sets of entities. In fact, a map is a special case of a binary relation; it records an association between domain elements and range elements. One extra constraint applies to maps, namely that there are no duplicated elements in the domain of a map. Elements may appear more than once in the range, however.

If we resurrect the relations from the cocktail bar example, we see that the relation contains does not satisfy this constraint, since at least one cocktail appears more than once in the domain. In contrast, there are no repeated elements in the domain of pricelist, so pricelist is, in fact, a map (see Fig. 7.4).

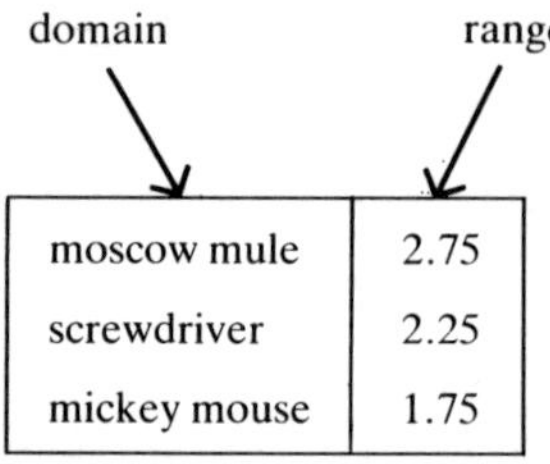

Figure 7.4 The map pricelist.

Formally, we say that a relation r is also a map if

```
card(r) = card(dom(r))
```

and, indeed, this holds true for pricelist.

We say that, in pricelist, the domain element "screwdriver" *maps onto* the range element 2.25, and so on.

The stricture that all elements of the domain are unique in the domain may appear arbitrary at first sight, but it has great mathematical significance. Any element from the domain of a map has one and only one mapping associated with it; in other words, it uniquely determines an element in the range of the map. For a map m and a domain element x, the element from the range which x maps onto is denoted by

```
m[x]
```

The reader may now be suffering from a sense of *déjà vu*. This is, of course, almost exactly the wording we used in an earlier chapter when functions were under discussion. One way of looking at maps is as a *data-oriented* representation for functions. Instead of specifying a rule for computing a range value (the result) from a domain value (the arguments), a map records explicitly in a data object the mappings between the domain and range of the function. Of course, this is possible only for finite domains, hence the alternative name: finite functions.

Consider, for example, the function not, which takes a boolean value and logically inverts it. The type Boolean is a finite domain, consisting of a set of two values, true and false. We could represent not as a function, or as a map. The function is specified thus:

```
not : Boolean -> Boolean
not(b) == if b then false else true ;
```

Alternatively, the mappings from all possible input values to the corresponding output values could be stored in a data object – a finite function or map (see Fig. 7.5).

true	false
false	true

Figure 7.5 A map representation of the function not.

We shall refer to this map as notm to distinguish it from the function not. The type of the data object notm is

map(Boolean, Boolean)

The general form of the type specification for a map is

map(T_1, T_2)

where T_1 is the type of elements of the domain, and T_2 is the type of the range elements.

Later we shall see that maps are frequently used in a way which is reminiscent of the use of functions, in particular, of function application. From a mathematical point of view, then, maps can be likened to functions.

From a computational viewpoint, maps can be regarded as data structures which resemble arrays. The domain elements of a map are the indices whereby range elements may be addressed. The map pricelist, for instance, can be viewed as an array of prices which are indexed by names of cocktails. Maps are, in fact, less limited than arrays. The indices need not be contiguous integers; in fact, they may not be integers at all. The domain of a map, like the domain of any binary relation, may be of any type, including complex types. This is true for the range as well; frequently the range type of a map will itself be a map. This means that we can construct nested maps, where the degree of nesting corresponds to the dimensionality of an array. So, for example, a two-dimensional array can be represented by a doubly nested map. Examples of nested maps will be encountered later.

In the next section we describe maps and the operations on them in greater detail, and present the *me too* notation for maps.

7.2.1 Maps in *me too*

Since maps are a special case of binary relations, they can also be represented by sets of pairs. However, it is useful to distinguish maps from other sets of pairs, and a special notation is adopted for this reason. Each mapping shows the domain element, followed by an arrow pointing to the associated range element. Here we define pricelist as a map:

```
? pricelist == {"moscow mule" -> 2.75,
                "screwdriver" -> 2.25,
                "mickey mouse" -> 1.75 } ;
= PRICELIST ;
```

and inspect the resulting value:

```
? pricelist ;
= {moscow mule -> 2.75,
   screwdriver -> 2.25,
   mickey mouse -> 1.75} ;
```

Actually, following the original definition of pricelist as a set of pairs (as a relation), this is the value which would have been returned by the *me too* shell. The shell detects cases where a relation conforms to the constraint that there are no duplicated elements in the domain, that is, where the relation is a *map*. In these circumstances, the value of the relation is printed out in map notation.

The general form for the map constructor is

$$\{e_1 \text{ -> } e_2, e_3 \text{ -> } e_4, \ldots, e_k \text{ -> } e_{k+1}\}$$

This is an instance of set enumeration, where the elements of the set are single mappings. The type specification has the form

$$\text{map}(T_1, T_2)$$

So, pricelist is of type

```
map(Cocktail, Price)
```

There is a predicate is_map which tests whether a data object is a map:

```
is_map(pricelist)
```

returns true, while

```
is_map(contains)
```

returns false. The information in the contains relation could in fact be represented in map form. We will create a new data object using map representation, and call it contains2, to distinguish it from the relation contains. Instead of having a separate entry for each ingredient, we can gather all the ingredients for each cocktail into a set. The domain elements are of type Cocktail, and the range elements are of type set(Ingredient). The type of contains2, then, is

```
map(Cocktail,set(Ingredient))
```

The map constructor may be used to build contains2:

```
contains2 ==
  {"moscow mule" -> {"lemon juice","vodka"},
   "screwdriver" -> {"vodka","orange juice"},
   "mickey mouse" -> {"lemon juice","pineapple juice"}} ;
```

This gives us a general method for converting binary relations into maps.

Since maps are sets of pairs, the standard set operations may be applied to them. And since maps are a special case of binary relations, the operations on binary relations may also be used. In addition, there is some further notation which is specific to maps.

We have seen how to construct a map by enumeration. Since maps are sets, we may also use set comprehension to construct maps from sets. In Chapter 6 we defined a set rainbow:

```
rainbow ==
  {"red","orange","yellow","green","blue","indigo","violet"};
```

and constructed a set of pairs showing the color names and the length of each name:

```
colorlengths ==
  {(color, stringlength(color)) | color <- rainbow} ;
```

colorlengths turns out to be a map, since it is a set of pairs wherein the first element of each pair is unique. This is an example of the general form

```
{(x,e) | x <- s}
```

which may be used to construct maps. There is an alternative notation, equivalent to the form above, but which emphasizes the fact that the resulting value is a map:

```
{x : s -> e}
```

which means *the set of mappings from* x *to* e *where* x *drawn from the set* s. The values of x constitute the domain, and the values of e the range of the map. The map colorlengths could equally well be constructed by the following expression:

```
{color : rainbow -> stringlength(color)}
```

which has the same value as before:

```
{"red" -> 3, "orange" -> 6, "yellow" -> 6, "green" -> 5,
 "blue" -> 4, "indigo" -> 6, "violet" -> 6}
```

Once a map has been constructed, we can look up values in the range by indexing the map by an element from the domain. This is similar to the image operation on binary relations, except that a single domain element, rather than a set of domain elements, is supplied as an argument. This operation is known as **map application** (or *finite function application*), and takes the form

```
m[x]
```

where m is a map, and x is some expression which has the value of an element from the domain of m. The domain of m is scanned for the occurrence of the value of x, and the element from the range of m which x maps onto is returned. The use of the square brackets [] is intended to be reminiscent of array subscripting. Alternatively, we can think of map application as being similar to function application, where a function is applied to an argument from the domain of that function.

The map pricelist can be applied to the name of a cocktail:

```
pricelist["moscow mule"]
```

This expression evaluates to 2.75.

The map contains2 maps cocktail names onto *sets of ingredients*. We expect an application of contains2 to return a set of ingredients:

```
contains2["screwdriver"]
```

has the value

```
{"vodka", "orange juice"}
```

The map colorlengths maps names to natural numbers, so, for example,

```
colorlengths["yellow"]
```

returns a natural number, in this case, 6.

The functionality of map application is

```
_[_] : map(T1,T2) x T1 -> T2
```

and a simple definition of the operation is

```
m[x] == the(rng (m dr {x})) ;
```

This definition ignores the case where a map m is applied to a value x which is not present in the domain of m, as in

```
pricelist["brandy bang"]
```

This cocktail is not recorded in pricelist, so the value of this expression is undefined. The *me too* shell returns the value false in these circumstances. So, the definition of the operation is not quite as simple as we have suggested; it is, in fact,

```
m[x] == if    x member dom(m)
        then the(rng(m dr {x}))
        else false ;
```

However, this is not always satisfactory, since the type of the value returned should be the same as the range type of the map. A variant of the map application operation permits the use of a default value: a value to be returned when the map is applied to a value which is not present in the domain. In the case of pricelist, we might specify a negative number as the default, as in

```
pricelist["brandy bang",-999.9]
```

which will return the value −999.9, since there is no occurrence of "brandy bang" in the domain of pricelist.

```
pricelist["screwdriver",-999.9]
```

will still return 2.25. As the domain type of contains2 is set(Ingredient), the most suitable default here is the empty set:

```
contains2["brandy bang",{}]
```

returns the empty set. For colorlengths, we might choose zero as the default value, so that

```
colorlengths["puce",0]
```

evaluates to zero. The functionality of map application with default is

```
_[_,_] : map(T1,T2) x T1 x T2 -> T2
```

so that, given a default of the correct type,

```
m[x,d]
```

is defined, and is type-wise correct, whether or not x is in the domain of m. The definition of map application with default is

```
m[x,d] == if    x member dom(m)
          then the(rng(m dr {x}))
          else d ;
```

Both versions of map application are available in the *me too* language. Supplying a default is recommended in general, but the default may safely be omitted in circumstances where x is guaranteed to be in the domain of m.

The final operation on maps is the **overwrite** operation, overwr. This corresponds to the overwrite operator of VDM, which is written as a dagger (†). overwr permits one map m1 to be overwritten by another m2 in the following way: each mapping in m1 is included in the result, unless its domain element occurs in the domain of m2. If so, it is replaced by the mapping from m2. All the mappings from m2 are included in the result.

For example, if pricelist has the same value as before:

```
{"moscow mule" -> 2.75,
 "screwdriver" -> 2.25,
 "mickey mouse" -> 1.75} ;
```

we can alter one of the prices, and add a new cocktail to the price list by

```
pricelist == pricelist overwr
                {"screwdriver" -> 2.45,
                 "brandy bang" -> 2.75} ;
```

The value of pricelist will now be

```
{"moscow mule" -> 2.75,
 "screwdriver" -> 2.45,
 "mickey mouse" -> 1.75,
 "brandy bang" -> 2.75}
```

The mapping from "screwdriver" in pricelist has been overwritten by the new mapping to the new price of $2.45. This is because, where a domain element appears in both maps, the mapping from the second map takes precedence. The two other mappings from pricelist are left intact. Finally, a new mapping has been added for "brandy bang". It is easy to verify from this example that

```
(dom(m1) union dom(m2)) = dom(m1 overwr m2)
```

The functionality of overwr is

```
_ overwr _ : map(T1,T2) x map(T1,T2) -> map(T1,T2)
```

and its definition is

```
m1 overwr m2 == m2 union (m1 ds dom(m2)) ;
```

We have now covered all of the map notation available in *me too*.

7.3 Summary

In this chapter we introduced two further *me too* data types based on sets. Binary relations and maps are both based on sets of pairs, with maps a special case of binary relations. Maps obey the constraint that domain elements are unique. Binary relations can be used to model data structures such as tables, whilst maps can be used to model powerful and versatile array mechanisms.

The following chapter completes the discussion of the *me too* notation, covering sequences and records.

7.4 Exercises

(i) The relation r is defined

```
r == {("a",1),("a",2),("b",5)} ;
```

(a) What is the type of r?
What are the values of
(b) dom(r)
(c) rng(r)
(d) r ds {"a"}
(e) r dr {"a"}

(ii) The map m is defined

```
m == {"a" -> {1,2},"b" -> {5}} ;
```

(a) What is the type of m?
What are the values of
(b) m["a"]
(c) m["c"]
(d) m["d",{}]
(e) m overwr {"a" -> {3},"c" -> {10}}
(f) { n : {1,4,9} -> n * 2}

(iii) A class register shows students and the subjects they study:

```
Register = map(Student,set(Subject))
```

A timetable shows which subjects are taught during which lessons:

```
Timetable = map(Subject,set(Lesson))
```

(a) Define an operation lessons, which takes a student, a register and a timetable and returns the set of lessons attended by that student.
(b) Define an operation attends, which returns the set of students who attend a particular lesson.
(c) Define an operation no_clashes, which, for a given register and timetable, returns true if there are no timetable clashes. (A clash occurs when two subjects taken by the same student have lessons in parallel – i.e. they occupy the same lesson slot in the timetable).

Chapter 8

me too notation – sequences and records

In this chapter we deal with the rest of the *me too* language, namely the notation for sequences and records.

8.1 Sequences

> *Salviati: . . . If I asked you, Simplicio, what the next number of the first sequence is, what would you say?*
> *Simplicio: I could not tell you. I think it is a random sequence and that there is no law in it.*
>
> Douglas Hofstadter

A sequence is an ordered collection of elements. Because it is ordered, each element has a position in the sequence. As with sets, the elements of a sequence are all of the same type; unlike sets, however, elements may appear more than once in a sequence.

8.1.1 Sequences in *me too*

Sequences may be constructed by enumeration. For example, the vowels of the English alphabet could be represented as the sequence:

```
["a","e","i","o","u"]
```

where the sequence is ordered alphabetically. The general form of the sequence constructor by enumeration is

$[e_1, . . ., e_k]$

where the elements e_i are expressions whose values are of the same type. The empty sequence is represented by

```
[]
```

For two sequences to be equal, they must not only contain the same elements; those elements must also be in the same order. So

```
["a","e","i","o","u"] /= ["u","o","a","e","i"]
```

And since elements may appear more than once in a sequence,

["a","a","e","i","o","u"] /= ["a","e","i","o","u"]

The former is a sequence of length 6, the latter of length 5.

As an example, let us design an operation to calculate the cost of a telephone bill. We will suppose that the telephone system concerned is that of some unspecified country whose unit of currency is the geld (100 gelds is written as 'G100'), with a smaller unit, the centigeld (100c = G1). Long-distance calls are charged at three different rates (peak, standard and cheap) according to the time of day. A log is kept of the duration in seconds of each call made. Since two or more calls may be of the same duration, a set would not be an appropriate representation, as any duplicates would disappear. We will use a sequence:

```
Log = seq(Call)
Call = Nat
```

The operation to calculate the cost of the calls takes an object of type Log and returns a real number representing the cost in gelds and centigelds:

```
cost : Log -> Real
```

For simplicity, we will assume that all calls are made at peak rate, and are long-distance calls. Suppose that two calls have been made so far, of 60 and 245 seconds' duration. The current state of the log can be defined as

```
log1 == [60,245] ;
```

When further calls have been made, conc can be used to concatenate two sequences:

```
log1 == [60,490] conc log1 ;
```

conc joins together two sequences q_1 and q_2 of the same type, such that the resulting sequence contains all the elements of q_1, followed by all the elements of q_2. The functionality of conc is

```
_ conc _ : seq(T) x seq(T) -> seq(T)
```

log1 now has the value

```
[60,490,60,245]
```

We can find the number of elements in a sequence by using len. Thus len(q) returns the length of sequence q. So

```
len(log1)
```

has the value 4, showing that four calls have been made to date.

Sequences may be decomposed using the selectors hd, tl, last and butlast. hd (short for *head*) returns the first element of a sequence:

```
hd(log1) = 60
```

and tl (short for *tail*) returns the rest of the sequence after the head has been removed:

```
tl(log1) = [490,60,245]
```

logl is of type seq(Call), so hd(logl) returns a value of type Call. tl(logl) returns a value of type seq(Call). In general terms,

```
hd : seq(T) -> T
 tl : seq(T) -> seq(T)
```

hd and tl are complementary operations. We can reconstitute the original sequence using conc:

```
[hd(q)] conc tl(q) = q
```

for any non-empty sequence q.

last and butlast are similar to hd and tl, except that they operate from the right-hand end of the sequence. last selects the last element from the sequence. Unlike hd, however, last returns not an element, but a singleton sequence. For example

```
last(logl) = [245]
```

butlast returns the sequence with the last element removed:

```
butlast(logl) = [60,490,60]
```

last and butlast have the same functionality as tl:

```
last, butlast : seq(T) -> seq(T)
```

Concatenation may be used to rebuild a sequence which has been decomposed using last and butlast:

```
butlast(q) conc last(q) = q
```

hd and tl are similar to the operations familiar to functional programmers, logic programmers and users of Lisp. In functional programming these operations are sometimes known as *head* and *tail*; in Lisp as *car* and *cdr*. These operations are typically used to recurse down lists from left to right; butlast and last may be used in a similar way, but recursing from right to left. In *me too*, as in VDM and Z, these operations may be used to recursively process *sequences*, rather than lists. Later we shall see that we have some sequence notation which is analogous to the set comprehension construct. These constructs may be used in many cases to avoid this kind of recursion.

Another use for *head* and *tail* in functional programming is to select an item from a particular position in a list. Here again, hd and tl, or butlast and last, may be used in this way on *me too* sequences. For example

```
hd(tl(logl))
```

selects the second item in the sequence logl, since tl(logl) returns [490,60,245], and hd applied to this sequence yields 490. Later we shall see that *me too* provides a more elegant construct for selecting an element from a sequence by position.

The sequence constructors using generators are syntactically similar to the set comprehension notation, except that sequence brackets are used.

```
[ e | x <- q ]
```

constructs a new sequence from the sequence q. Note that q must be a sequence, not a set. Each element x is drawn from q *in order*, the expression e is evaluated for each value of x, and the value of e is added to the result sequence in order. For example, if a sequence ql has the value

```
[1,10,4]
```

then the constructor

```
[x * x | x <- ql]
```

builds a sequence which reflects the ordering of ql. The value of the resulting sequence is found by evaluating

```
[1 * 1, 10 * 10, 4 * 4]
```

in exactly that order, yielding the sequence

```
[1,100,16]
```

In the telephone bill example, logl is a sequence of calls, where each call is represented as a duration:

```
logl = [60,490,60,245]
```

We assume for the moment an operation units, which returns the number of charge units used during a call:

```
units : Call -> Nat
```

The sequence constructor can be used to convert the log into a sequence of units – the units used for each call:

```
[units(c) | c <- logl]
```

Suppose that, for long-distance calls made at peak rate, 18 seconds is the time allowed per unit. One unit is registered as soon as the call is connected; thereafter another unit is charged every 18 seconds. The units operation, then, is defined:

```
units(c) == 1 + (c truncate 18) ;
```

So

```
[units(c) | c <- logl]
```

will return the sequence

```
[4,28,4,14]
```

As with sets, functions can be reduced over sequences. To determine the total number of units used so far, plus is reduced over the sequences of units:

```
+ reduce (0) [units(c) | c <- logl]
```

which expands to

```
+ reduce (0) [4,28,4,14]
```

As with sets, the unit of the reduction (here zero) is injected as a starting value. The expression is equivalent to

```
(((0 + 4) + 28) + 4) + 14
```

So, in total, 50 charge units have been used.

Since order is a feature of sequences, the binary operation involved in reduction over a sequence need not be commutative or associative. Otherwise, rules which apply to reduction over sets also apply to reduction over sequences (see Section 6.2.2).

We have now almost reached the point of calculating the charges for the calls. The other piece of information needed is the charge per unit: this is 5.06c. We can now define the operation cost, which returns the charges, in gelds and centigelds, for the logged calls:

```
cost : Log -> Real
cost(log) ==
  ((+ reduce (0) [units(c) | c <- log]) * 5.06)/100 ;
```

Notice the obligatory expression bracketing. We can now determine the cost of the calls:

```
cost(log1) = 2.53
```

The four calls logged so far will cost G2.53.

In this example we have represented a log of telephone calls as a sequence, so that any duplicate values are not removed, as they would be in a set. We can make use of this property of sequences to redefine the power function from Chapter 5, avoiding a recursive definition. power was defined as

```
power : Integer x Nat -> Integer
power(n,m) == if   m = 0
              then 1
              else n * power(n,m - 1) ;
```

One piece of sequence notation not yet encountered will be needed: the integer range constructor.

$[e_1, \ldots, e_2]$

constructs the sequence of integers from e_1 to e_2 inclusive, where e_1 and e_2 are expressions which evaluate to integers. If the value of e_1 is greater than the value of e_2, then the empty sequence is returned.

A sequence of length four, each of whose elements is the number two, can be constructed by

```
[ 2 | x <- [1,...,4]]
```

which is an example of a constructor of the form [e | x <- q] where e is *not* an expression involving x. The power 2^4 can be specified by reducing multiply over the sequence, using one as the unit:

```
  * reduce (1) [ 2 | x <- [1,...,4]]
= * reduce (1) [ 2 | x <- [1,2,3,4]]
= * reduce (1) [ 2,2,2,2 ]
= (((1 * 2) * 2) * 2) * 2
= 16
```

So, power can be specified as

```
power(n,m) == * reduce (1) [ n | x <- [1,...,m]] ;
```

where the integer range constructor is used simply to control the number of multiplications of n by itself. This is an example of the use of a general technique corresponding to iteration in imperative programming languages.

Sequence constructors may have generators with filters. We may, for example, want to extract from the telephone log all the long calls, where a 'long' call has a duration greater than one minute:

```
  [ c | c <- logl; c > 60]
= [490,245]
```

In fact, all the combinations of multiple generators, with or without filters, which may be used with sets may also be used with sequences. The general form is

$$[\, e \mid g_1, \ldots, g_k \,]$$

where each generator g_i has one of the forms

```
x <- q
x <- q; b
(e1,...,ek) <- q
(e1,...,ek) <- q; b
```

Where multiple generators are used in a sequence constructor, the generators operate from right to left. For example, in

```
[(x,y) | x <- ["a","b"], y <- [1,2]]
```

the first value of x is drawn, "a", and then each value of y is drawn in sequence. Only then is the next value of x drawn. The expression evaluates to

```
[("a",1),("a",2),("b",1),("b",2)]
```

Sequences can be represented as maps, where the domain elements of the map are positional indices, and the range of the map contains the elements of the sequence. So logl, which has the value

```
[60,490,60,245]
```

can be represented by the map

```
{1 -> 60, 2 -> 490, 3 -> 60, 4 -> 245}
```

The user of *me too* can make use of this alternative map representation. For example, when rng is applied to a sequence, the *me too* shell automatically invokes a map representation for that sequence. A sequence can therefore be converted to a set by applying the rng operation to the sequence. In our example,

```
rng(logl) = {60,490,245}
```

We will make use of rng in specifying an invariant on logs:

```
inv_Log(log) == all c in rng(log) . c > 0 ;
```

The invariant states that all calls in a log must have a duration greater than zero. We can see that inv_Log(logl) = true

This is an example of a user-defined invariant. Later in this chapter we examine a special kind of invariant in *me too* – a **record invariant**.

We have seen the effect of applying rng to a sequence; dom may also be applied to a sequence. In this case a set of position indices is returned:

dom(logl) = {1,2,3,4}

Now we can see how an element may be extracted from a sequence by position. Map application is used, so that, for example

logl[2] = 490

If no default is specified, and an attempt is made to apply a sequence to an index which is not in the domain of its map representation, then, as usual, the *me too* shell returns the value false:

logl[5] = false

To avoid this type discrepancy, we might in this case specify a default of zero, so that

logl[5,0] = 0

The map representation can also be invoked in order to replace values at given positions in a sequence.

logl overwr {4 -> 300, 3 -> 102}

replaces the fourth element of the sequence logl with the value 300, and the third with the value 102. The resulting sequence has the value

[60,490,102,300]

A special restriction is placed on the use of overwrite with sequences. In

q overwr m

all indices in the domain of q must also be in the domain of m. In other words, only those positions already present may be overwritten with new values. This restriction precludes the possibility of accidentally attempting to build a sequence whose position indices are non-contiguous. For instance,

logl overwr {10 -> 360}

is an attempt to build a sequence corresponding to the map

{1 -> 60, 2 -> 490, 3 -> 60, 4 -> 245, 10 -> 360}

This does not correspond to a valid sequence, since positions 5 through 9 are undefined. The *me too* shell prevents such invalid sequences being built by returning the original sequence unchanged in these circumstances. The value of the expression above, then, would be that of logl.

A sequence can be explicitly converted to map representation using the asm (*as map*) operation:

asm(logl) = {1 -> 60, 2 -> 490, 3 -> 60, 4 -> 245}

The inverse of this operation is called asq (*as sequence*); it takes a map and converts it into the surface representation for a sequence.

```
asq(asm(log1))
```

returns the original value of log1:

```
[60,490,60,245]
```

In general, asq should only be applied to maps which correspond to valid sequences: that is, the domain of the map consists of a set of contiguous integers including one.

We will now extend the design of the telephone bill calculator. Up to now we have assumed that all calls are long-distance and made at peak rate. We will continue to deal only with long-distance calls, but will handle three charge rates – peak, standard and cheap.

The log must now include information concerning the charge rate, as well as the duration of the call. A log is still a sequence of calls,

```
Log = seq(Call)
```

but the representation for Call is changed:

```
Call = pair(Rate,Nat)
```

Now a new type, Rate, is needed:

```
Rate = {"peak","standard","cheap"}
```

Types are sets. Integer, for example, denotes the set of integer numbers. Rate, in the type specification above, is given an enumerated set as its representation. This means that objects of type Rate have one of the values specified in the set: "peak", or "standard", or "cheap". Since the representation of a log has changed, we must respecify the invariant on logs:

```
inv_Log(log) ==
  all c in rng(log) .
    (first(c) member {"peak","standard","cheap"})
      and
    (second(c) > 0) ;
```

Let us suppose that there are three people – Rik, Mike and Vyv – sharing a house, and they each keep a separate log to avoid arguments over the telephone bill. The current state of these logs is shown in the following definitions:

```
rik  == [("peak",1470),("cheap",350)] ;
mike == [("standard", 460) ] ;
vyv  == [("peak", 1610)] ;
```

The durations of all peak calls made could be found by

```
[ d | log <- [rik,mike,vyv], (r,d) <- log; r = "peak"]
```

and the sequence returned will be:

```
[1470,1610]
```

This is an example of the use of multiple generators with filters.

The three logs can be combined using conc:

```
log2 == (rik conc mike) conc vyv ;
```

which has the value

```
[("peak",1470),("cheap",350),("standard",460),("peak",1610)]
```

The same result could be obtained by using distributed concatenation. dconc takes a sequence of sequences, and returns the sequence which results from concatenating the inner sequences together in order. For example,

```
log2 == dconc([rik,mike,vyv]) ;
```

has the same effect as the previous definition of log2.

The new representation for calls means that the units operation has to be altered. A call is now a pair of values; we must select the first element of the pair (the rate) and the second (the duration). The time allowed per unit varies with the charge rate; as before, the time unit for peak calls is 18 seconds. But for standard rate calls, the time unit is 24 seconds, and for cheap rate calls, 45 seconds. Given this information, units is redefined as

```
units(c) ==
let rate == first(c),
    dur == second(c)
in let timeunit == if    rate = "peak" then 18
                   else if    rate = "standard" then 24
                          else 45
   in 1 + (dur truncate timeunit) ;
```

The cost operation does not need to be changed. So, the cost of the calls in the current quarter can be found by

```
cost(log2)
```

which returns the value 10.12.

The cost of all calls at a particular charge rate could be found:

```
cost([(r,d) | (r,d) <- log2; r = "standard"])
```

gives the cost of all the standard calls – G1.01. Or, each individual's charges can be computed separately:

```
[cost(log) | log <- [rik,mike,vyv]]
```

which returns the sequence of charges attributable to Rik, Mike and Vyv respectively:

```
[4.554, 1.012, 4.554]
```

So, Rik, Mike and Vyv must pay G4.55, G1.01 and G4.55 towards the bill respectively.

All the operations on sequences have now been covered. In the next section we introduce the final object type in *me too*.

8.2 Records

The record is a familiar concept in programming, and needs no more than a brief introduction here. Records are data structures which hold values in named fields: a value is accessed by its field name. Each field has a type associated with it, and only values of that type are valid values for that field. Different fields in a record, however, may be of different types. *me too* records correspond to the data types known as *composite objects* in VDM.

8.2.1 Records in *me too*

me too objects may be represented as records. In the type specification a record type is named and the name and type of each of its fields is given. In addition to the (non-machine-readable) type specification, a record declaration is included as part of the machine-readable portion of the specification. On encountering the record declaration, the *me too* shell automatically generates a number of operations specific to that record type – record constructors, selectors and so on – which may then be applied to appropriate data objects. In order to illustrate the use of records in *me too*, we return to the telephone bill example.

The last version of the telephone bill calculator handled calls made at peak, standard or cheap rate. The time allowed per unit for the different charge rates was built into the units operation by means of a let expression:

```
let timeunit == if    rate = "peak" then 18
                else if    rate = "standard" then 24
                      else 45
in ...
```

However, the time allowed per unit may change from time to time, so it would be more convenient to use a data structure to hold these values. We will therefore introduce a new type, Chargetable, represented as a record. The type specification is

```
Chargetable = record(peak:Nat, standard:Nat, cheap:Nat)
```

A data object of type Chargetable is therefore a record with three fields. The fields are named peak, standard and cheap, and each holds a value of type Nat. These values will represent the number of seconds allowed per charge unit at a given charge rate. As usual, the type specification is included in the specification as commentary; in addition a record declaration must be input to the shell. The record declaration in this case takes the form

```
Chargetable :: peak standard cheap ;
```

where the names of the fields are shown, but not their types. The declaration of the record type Chargetable results in the automatic definition of a number of operations. These are

```
mk_Chargetable
is_Chargetable
inv_Chargetable
peak
standard
```

```
cheap
upd_peak
upd_standard
upd_cheap
```

mk_Chargetable is a constructor which accepts three values and builds a record of type Chargetable. We can now define a data object:

```
ct == mk_Chargetable(18,24,45) ;
```

If we inspect the value of ct, we see that the shell displays the value of a record in the form of its constructor:

```
? ct ;
= MK_CHARGETABLE(18,24,45) ;
```

The predicate is_Chargetable tests whether a data object is a record of type Chargetable, so that

```
is_Chargetable(ct)
```

would return the value true. The mk_ and upd_ operations automatically apply the is_ predicate. There is also a general predicate, is_record, which returns true when applied to a record of any type.

The record declaration also causes field selector operations to be automatically defined. The selector functions have the same names as the fields. In this case, the functions peak, standard and cheap are generated, so that, for example,

```
peak(ct) = 18
```

Whenever a record type is declared, an invariant on that type is automatically generated. In our example, an operation named inv_Chargetable is created, which enables the user to specify an invariant on the type Chargetable. The body of a record invariant initially has the value true, and must be redefined by the user in order to have any effect. Unlike the invariants we have already seen, a record invariant is *automatically* applied whenever an attempt is made to construct or update a record using the *me too* shell. So, mk_Chargetable and the associated upd_ operations first apply the predicate is_Chargetable, and, if the result is true, they then apply the invariant inv_Chargetable to the record being constructed.

In our case, we would like to ensure that the time units are ordered by charge rate, so that less time is allowed at peak rate than at standard rate, and less at standard rate than at cheap rate. We will therefore redefine inv_Chargetable:

```
inv_Chargetable(x) ==
   (peak(x) < standard(x)) and (standard(x) < cheap(x)) ;
```

Once this invariant has been redefined, any record constructed by mk_Chargetable or by one of the upd_ operations will be subject to the constraint that the number of seconds per charge unit at peak rate must be less than at standard rate, and at standard rate less than at cheap rate. So, for example, an attempt to evaluate an expression such as

```
mk_Chargetable(3,2,1)
```

would result in the invariant failing. Any expression which attempts to construct or update a record which violates the invariant on that record type will evaluate to false. If inv_Chargetable were not redefined by the user, the body of the invariant function would default to true, that is, it would have no effect.

For each of the fields, an update operation is available. For example, if the telephone company changes the time allowed per unit, the record must be updated. If the time per unit for peak calls is reduced to 15 seconds, upd_peak can be used to update the charge table:

```
ct2 == upd_peak(ct,15) ;
```

If, however, the attempt were made to change the value of this field to 25:

```
upd_peak(ct,25)
```

the invariant would be violated, and the result false would be returned.

If more than one field is to be updated, then upd_ operations can be nested:

```
upd_standard(upd_peak(ct,15),20)
```

which returns the new record with the value of the peak field changed to 15, and of the standard field changed to 20:

```
mk_Chargetable(15,20,45)
```

In any update of the form upd_<fieldname>(rec,val), the update operation checks that rec is a record, and that it contains a field named fieldname. It also checks that the result of the attempted update conforms to the invariant for that record type. If any of these tests fails, the result false is returned.

Armed with the record notation, and the new object type Chargetable, we can now respecify the units operation:

```
units : Call x Chargetable -> Nat
units(c,ct) ==
let rate == first(c),
    dur == second(c)
in let timeunit == if    rate = "peak"
                   then peak(ct)
                   else if   rate = "standard"
                        then standard(ct)
                        else cheap(ct)
   in 1 + (dur truncate timeunit) ;
```

Now the units operation will not need to be changed if the time per unit is altered for the different charge rates. The units operation is used by cost; the only remaining change, then, is to supply the charge table as an extra argument to cost, and to include the extra parameter in the call to units:

```
cost : Log x Chargetable -> Real
cost(log,ct) ==
  ((+ reduce (0) [units(c,ct) | c <- log]) * 5.06)/100 ;
```

The representation of Log has not changed, so the invariant on logs remains as before.

If log2 has the same value as before:

```
[("peak",1470),("cheap",350),("standard",460),("peak",1610)]
```

then

```
cost(log2,ct) = 10.12
```

8.3 Summary

In this chapter we have presented the *me too* notation for sequences and records. An example was developed wherein a sequence representation is preferable to a set representation because items may be duplicated. In general, sequences are appropriate where repetition of elements and/or ordering of elements is significant. The example was further developed by incorporating a record type, which improved the design by generalizing the operations.

We have now covered all of the *me too* notation, and move on in Part III to consider some larger examples and case studies illustrating the use of the *me too* method and notation.

8.4 Exercises

(i) Give the values of the following sequence expressions:
  (a) ["seek","simplicity"]
      conc (["and","trust","it"] overwr {2 -> "distrust"})
  (b) [(n, n * 2) | n <- [1,...,4]]
  (c) [(x,y) | x <- [1,2,3], y <- ["a","b"]]

(ii) A quote from Shakespeare's Macbeth is represented as a data object of type seq(String):

```
macbeth == ["fair","is","foul","and","foul","is","fair"] ;
```

  What are the values of the following expressions?
  (a) dom(macbeth)
  (b) asm(macbeth)
  (c) macbeth[7]
  (d) macbeth[8,"error"]
  Using the object macbeth, give *me too* specifications of the following:
  (e) the number of words in macbeth;
  (f) the number of *distinct* words in macbeth;
  (g) the number of times the word "foul" appears;
  (h) the set of positions where the word "foul" appears.

(iii) The sequence q is defined as follows:

```
q == dconc([[1],[4,3],[2,9]]) ;
```

  What are the values of the following expressions?
  (a) q

(b) hd(tl(q))
(c) last(butlast(q))

(iv) Vehicle details are represented by records of type Vehicle:

Vehicle = record(reg:String, year:Nat, manuf:String, model:String)

(a) Write the record declaration for the type Vehicle.
(b) Define a data object car1, of type Vehicle, whose registration is ME 2, year 1953, manufacturer Chevrolet and model Corvette.
(c) What expression will extract the model of this car?
(d) Change the year of registration of car1 to 1989.

PART III
EXAMPLES AND CASE STUDIES

The purpose of these chapters is to show the application of *me too* in a variety of areas and to consolidate learning of the *me too* notation. Chapters 9 and 10 specify larger examples than was possible when teaching the notation in Part II. Chapter 11 is included to demonstrate the application of the method in constructing a design. Finally, the remaining three chapters present case studies. These report a variety of designs undertaken by and for project teams from various divisions within International Computers Ltd (ICL), the Information Systems subsidiary of STC PLC.

Chapter 9

Example 1 – a design for a simple frames system

> *Our memories are card indexes consulted, then put back in disorder by authorities whom we do not control.*
>
> Cyril Connolly

In this section we present a *me too* specification of a simple frames system which illustrates map notation and the use of invariants.

9.1 Frames systems and inheritance

Frames systems were proposed (Minsky, 1975) as a cognitive model to explain some of the characteristics of human memory, learning and reasoning. In particular, they are meant to model our ability to process incoming information rapidly by reference to an organized body of knowledge. The artificial intelligence community has found many applications for frames systems, including natural language processing and expert systems. Irrespective of the merits or otherwise of frames systems as a cognitive model, frames have proved to be a useful concept in knowledge representation, and have made their appearance in a number of commercial applications. Frames systems prefigure many of the concepts associated with object-oriented programming, such as *classes*, *inheritance* and *procedural attachment*.

A frames system consists of a network of frames. Figure 9.1 shows a single frame of the simplest kind.

A frame collects together information concerning a named entity, in this case,

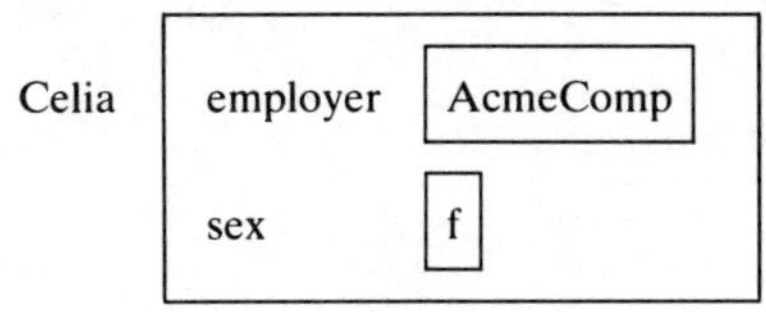

Figure 9.1 The frame Celia.

an employee named Celia. The frame has named *slots*, which in our example contain simple atomic (i.e. non-decomposable) values. The slot name and the value contained in the slot can be thought of as an *attribute–value* pair. The frame in Fig. 9.1 records the facts that Celia is employed by a company called AcmeComp, and that she is female.

Frames begin to be useful when they are linked together into a frames system.

In Fig. 9.2 the links between frames form a *kind* hierarchy (other sorts of link are also possible). The links can be thought of as slot values which act as pointers to other frames. Inheritance of slots and their values is effected by means of the kind hierarchy. Celia, by virtue of being a kind of project leader, inherits the slot *works on*, and its value *projects*. And since a project leader is a kind of manager, she also inherits the *salary* and *purpose* slots, along with their values. The manager and project leader frames are generic frames: they record stereotypic information, or

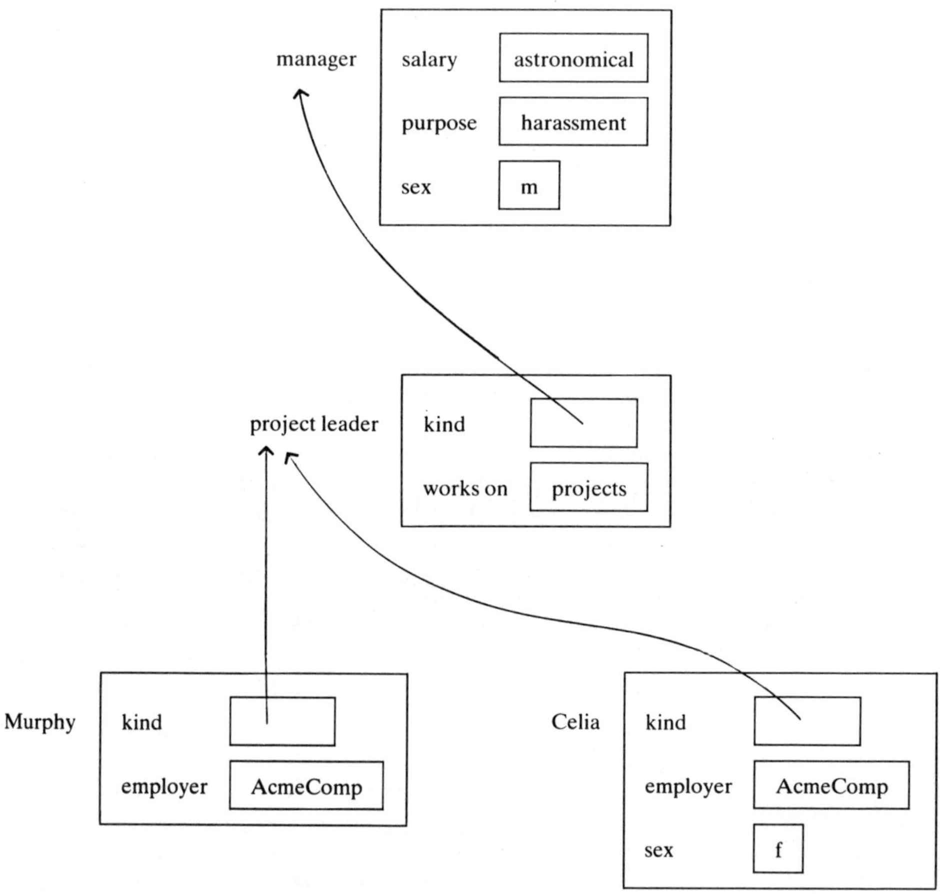

Figure 9.2 A frames system.

default expectations, concerning classes of entities. These defaults can, however, be overridden in specific instances. The Celia frame is an instance of a project leader frame, which is itself a specialization of a manager frame. However, the Celia frame does not inherit the attribute–value pair *sex–m*, because *sex–f* is stored explicitly in the frame. Slots in a frame take precedence over potentially inheritable slots from higher in the kind hierarchy.

The frames system calculator presented below, based on earlier unpublished versions by Peter Henderson and Cydney Minkowitz, allows us to construct frames systems like the one we have seen, and to retrieve values from slots in frames, using inheritance where appropriate. Slots can only contain atomic values. Multiple inheritance is not allowed, and the kind network is strictly hierarchical. For a specification of a more complex frames system, incorporating procedural attachment and embedded frames, see Henderson and Jones (1988).

9.2 The Model step

The abstract objects we are concerned with are frames and frames systems. A frames system is a database of frames; we will call the abstract object Db. We also need names of frames, attributes (slot names) and values (the contents of slots) as objects. The abstract objects, then, are

```
Name, Attr, Val, Frame, Db
```

The first operation needed is a constructor for the empty frames database:

```
emptydb : -> Db
```

Next is an operation for putting information into the frames system. putvalue inserts an attribute–value pair into a frame in the database:

```
putvalue : Name x Attr x Val x Db -> Db
```

Together, these two constructors will allow us to build frames systems such as that shown in Fig. 9.2.

Now we need an operation which will retrieve slot values:

```
getvalue : Name x Attr x Db -> Val
```

This operation must use inheritance where necessary, so we propose a subsidiary operation, inherit, to take care of this. getvalue(n,a,db) looks up the value of a in the frame named n, and, if there is no attribute a, calls inherit.

```
inherit : Name x Attr x Db -> Val
```

inherit recurses up through the kind hierarchy, looking for a value for attribute a. We expect getvalue to behave in the following way: if we ask for Celia's employer, the value returned will be "AcmeComp", found by simply looking up the value of the employer slot in the frame named "Celia". If we ask what Celia works on, the response will be "projects", by inheritance from the superordinate frame in the kind hierarchy. Celia's salary will be given as "astronomical", by inheritance through more than one level in the kind hierarchy; and Celia's sex will be given as "f" for female, since the value stored explicitly in the frame takes precedence over inheritable values. Finally, we must also consider the case where a value is neither stored nor inheritable: if we ask, say, for Celia's age, getvalue should return an error value.

The model for the frames system is now complete.

9.3 The Specify step

In the Specify step, representations are chosen for the objects. Objects of type Name, Attr and Val can be represented as strings:

```
Name, Attr, Val = String
```

A frame is an association between attributes and values; an appropriate representation would be a map:

```
Frame = map(Attr,Val)
```

Finally, the database of frames can also be a map, mapping frame names to frames:

```
Db = map(Name,Frame)
```

A kind slot in a frame will be labeled with the attribute "kind", and the frame the kind slot points to will be named by a Val, which is also of type String. Only one frame can be named by a single atomic value, so the requirement is met that a frame can have no more than one parent frame in the kind network. This is one of the necessary properties if a network is to be strictly hierarchical. We will further constrain the form a frames database can take by specifying an invariant, inv_Db:

```
inv_Db : Db -> Boolean
```

In particular, inv_Db must ensure that the kind network contains no pointers to non-existent frames, and that it is non-cyclic. If inv_Db and inherit are specified correctly, the inherit operation, and hence also getvalue, will be guaranteed to terminate.

A frames database is either empty or non-empty. If it is non-empty, it may contain a kind network, which must be hierarchical. In fact, we decide to allow disjoint hierarchies in a frames database. Each such hierarchy must have a root. The first part of the invariant on frames databases states that, in a non-empty database, there is at least one root frame:

```
(1) (db = {})
    or
    (exists f in rng(db) . not("kind" member dom(f)))
```

Secondly, we specify that all kind slots point to an existing frame:

```
(2) all f in rng(db) .
        ("kind" member dom(f)) => (f["kind"] member dom (db))
```

Finally we specify that no kind network contains cycles, by asserting that no frame is superordinate to itself in a kind network:

```
(3) not(exists n in dom(db) . n member supers(n,db))
```

where the functionality of supers is

```
supers : Name x Db -> set(Name)
```

and supers(n,db) returns the set of names of the frames which are superordinate in the kind hierarchy to the frame named n in db. The definition of supers is

```
supers (n,db) ==
  let parent == db[n,{}]["kind","undefined"]
  in if   parent = "undefined" then {}
     else {parent} union supers(parent, db ds {n}) ;
```

Before we combine the separate parts of the invariant, we note that (1) is redundant, since it is implied by the conjunction of (2) and (3). The complete invariant, then, is

```
inv_Db(db) ==
  (all f in rng(db) .
    ("kind" member dom(f)) =>
                     (f["kind"] member dom(db)))
   and
  (not(exists n in dom(db) . n member supers(n,db)));
```

In effect, an invariant on a data type subsets the data type given in the type specification. In this case, we are stating that the set of valid frames databases is that subset of the type map(String,map(String,String)) whose members satisfy the constraints specified in inv_Db.

As far as the activity of specification is concerned, the invariant acts as an assertion concerning the intended properties of the data type. Later we examine the separate issue of how the invariant may be used as part of an *executable* specification.

Now we turn to the constructor operations. An object of type Db is a map. So, the constructor for the empty database must construct the empty map. Since a map is a set of pairs, the empty map is simply the empty set:

```
emptydb() == {} ;
```

putvalue(n,a,v,db) constructs a new database from db, inserting a new value v in the slot a in the frame named n. If the frame n already exists in db, and there is a slot labeled a, its value will be overwritten. If the frame exists, but there is no slot labeled a, the frame n will be augmented by the addition of the new attribute–value pair mapping a to v. If there is no frame named n in db, a new frame with only one slot will be inserted into the database. Since a database is a doubly nested map, it should come as no surprise to see that there are two map overwrites in the definition:

```
putvalue(n,a,v,db) ==
  db overwr { n -> db[n,{}] overwr { a -> v}} ;
```

In this definition, db[n,{}] retrieves the frame n from the database. If there is no frame of that name, the map application defaults to the empty set, which is the correct value for the empty frame. The frame is then overwritten by the map containing only the new mapping from a to v. If there is a frame named n in db, the resulting frame retains any previous attribute–value pairs with the exception that, if a appeared already in this frame, its previous mapping is overwritten and it now maps to v. If there was no previous mapping from a, the new mapping is added to the frame.

The outer overwrite adds the newly constructed frame into the database. If a frame of the same name existed previously, it is replaced by the new one. If not, the database is augmented by the addition of the new frame.

If we now look ahead to the Validate step, where we will create instances of frames databases, we must consider how we will make use of the invariant when executing the specification. As it stands, the definition of putvalue permits the construction of databases which violate the constraints we have specified. We have a choice of validation strategies: firstly, we may test data objects explicitly by applying inv_Db to each instance of a frames database created. Alternatively, the invariant can be enforced by incorporating it into the putvalue operation. In the present case, we choose the latter option; we therefore redefine putvalue:

```
putvalue(n,a,v,db) ==
  let new == db overwr { n -> db[n,{}] overwr { a -> v}}
  in  if inv_Db(new) then new else db ;
```

We have chosen to prevent invalid databases ever being constructed, even at an intermediate stage. This choice constrains the order in which information can be put into the database when it is being built. For example, the value cannot be put into the kind slot in the Celia frame until the project manager frame has been put into the database. The advantage gained is that a database can never get into a state which violates the invariant.

Now we move on to the retrieval operation. getvalue looks up the value of an attribute in a frame; if that attribute is not present, the inherit operation is called:

```
getvalue(n,a,db) ==
  if    n member dom(db)
  then db[n][a,inherit(n,a,db)]
  else "undefined" ;
```

The if clause checks whether there is a frame of the specified name in the database. If not, the error value "undefined" is returned. Otherwise, there are two possibilities: either the attribute appears in the frame, or not. db[n] returns the frame, which is then applied to the attribute name to return the value in the slot. If the attribute is not present in the frame, the default is invoked – a call to the inherit operation.

The inheritance operation must look up through the kind hierarchy as far as necessary to find an inheritable value. The search may not be successful, in which case the error value is returned:

```
inherit(n,a,db) ==
  if    "kind" member dom(db[n])
  then getvalue(db[n]["kind"],a,db)
  else "undefined" ;
```

The if clause checks whether the frame is linked to a superordinate frame via a kind slot. If not, there is no possibility of inheritance, so the error value is returned.

Otherwise, the double map application in the then clause retrieves the name of the frame immediately above in the hierarchy, and getvalue is used to look up the value of the attribute in this higher frame. If necessary, getvalue calls inherit again, and the process continues until either a value is inherited or the top of the hierarchy is reached.

The if clause also acts as a terminating condition; the recursive call to getvalue in the then clause results in a recursion up the kind hierarchy. If no value is found by inheritance, at some point a root frame, which has no kind slot, will be reached. Again, the error value is returned.

This completes the specification of the frames system calculator. The complete specification appears in Appendix 2.

9.4 Executing the specification

The definitions of the operations can either be loaded from a file, or typed into the *me too* shell, as in the following interaction:

```
? emptydb() == {} ;
= EMPTYDB ;

? inv_Db(db) ==
    (all f in rng(db) .
      ("kind" member dom(f)) => (f["kind"] member dom(db)))
     and
    (not(exists n in dom(db) . n member supers(n,db)));

= INV_DB ;

? putvalue(n,a,v,db) ==
  let new == db overwr { n -> db[n,{}] overwr { a -> v}}
  in if inv_Db(new) then new else db ;
= PUTVALUE ;
.
.
.
```

Once all the operations have been defined, the database of frames is constructed:

```
? db == emptydb() ;
= DB ;
? db == putvalue("manager","salary","astronomical",db) ;
= DB ;
? db == putvalue("manager","purpose","harassment",db) ;
= DB ;
? db == putvalue("manager","sex","m",db) ;
= DB ;
? db == putvalue("project leader","kind","manager",db) ;
= DB ;
? db == putvalue("project leader","works on","projects",db) ;
= DB ;
```

We now inspect the value of db:

```
? db;
= {manager -> {salary -> astronomical,
                purpose -> harassment,
                sex -> m},
   project leader -> {kind -> manager,
                      works on -> projects}} ;
```

and check that we have a frames database containing two frames. We continue inputting information into the database until the frames system shown in Fig. 9.2 has been built. We now try to build a series of invalid databases, to test that the invariant is operating as we expect:

```
? dbl == putvalue("Murphy","kind","programmer",db) ;
= DBl ;
? db = dbl ;
= TRUE ;
```

Here we attempt to construct a new version of the database wherein a kind slot points to a non-existent frame. The invariant should fail, leaving the database unchanged. This can be verified by inspecting db and dbl, or, as we have done here, by testing their equality. (Recall that the equality operation is defined for all types in *me too*.) The fact that the old and new states of the database are equal shows that, as intended, the attempt to insert the new value has failed.

Next we might attempt to create a cycle in the kind network:

```
? db2 == putvalue("manager","kind","Celia",db) ;
= DB2 ;
? db = db2 ;
= TRUE ;
```

This change would have made the Celia frame superordinate to itself; the application of the invariant has therefore prevented the change being made.

Now the retrieval operation is tested on a variety of data. Here we show some of the tests which would be applied:

```
? getvalue("Celia","employer",db) ;
= AcmeComp ;
? getvalue("Celia","works on",db) ;
= projects ;
? getvalue("Celia","salary",db) ;
= astronomical ;
? getvalue("Celia","sex",db) ;
= f ;
? getvalue("Celia","age",db) ;
= undefined ;
```

After testing this operation on a variety of frames databases, we will eventually satisfy ourselves that the behavior of getvalue matches our intentions as stated at the beginning of the chapter. All the operations will be tested on more complex databases, until we are satisfied that a set of appropriate test cases has been covered.

In general, errors or omissions may be discovered during validation, and one or more cycles of correction and retesting will take place. Moreover, the experience of interacting with the prototype frequently results in further cycles around the Model–Specify–Validate loop. At the same time, we should review the evolving design critically. Having produced a first design for a frames system, we would now proceed to inspect the specification carefully. For example, if we started by looking only at the Model part of the specification, we would realize that the object Frame does not appear in any of the functionalities of the operations. Since we are designing a frames system, this fact should cause us some concern. A logical next step in the process would be to return to the Model step and redesign the whole system, starting with operations which manipulate single frames. We would then compare and appraise the two designs.

In later iterations we might explore alternative designs incorporating, for example, multiple inheritance, procedural attachment or embedded frames.

9.5 Summary

We have presented a design of a simple frames system, and indicated some avenues which might be explored in subsequent iterations in the design process. The design illustrates the use of map notation. Although a simple design, it incorporates inheritance of slots and default values, thus demonstrating the power and succinctness of the combination of map notation and functions. The use of invariants both as assertions in the specification, and as constraints on the execution of the prototype, has also been illustrated.

Chapter 10

Example 2 – a simple concordance package

Words, words, words.
William Shakespeare

To demonstrate the use of sequences, we present a design for a simple text processing package. The specification of this system also provides a simple illustration of how modular systems may be specified in *me too*. The complete specification can be found in Appendix 2.

10.1 Text processing

Text processing is here used in the sense of textual analysis, rather than of document preparation. A number of text processing packages are available on mainframes and microcomputers; their main purpose is as a research tool, and they are used by scholars from a wide range of disciplines.

Provided a text or body of texts is converted into machine-readable form, indexes and concordances can be produced quickly and cheaply by the use of a text processing package, whereas in the past scholars spent years of their lives compiling these research aids. Cruden, for example, is said to have worked nineteen hours a day for three years preparing his concordance of the King James Version of the Bible (Hollingdale and Tootill, 1970).

In literary studies a text processing package may be used as an aid in the stylistic analysis of the works of a particular author. Moreover, various stylistic features and statistical measures derived from such analyses – such as word frequencies, collocation patterns, type/token ratios and average sentence length – have been used to resolve questions of disputed authorship. Similar techniques have been applied in *forensic linguistics*: in some cases the results of textual analyses have been presented as expert testimony in court cases.

The design presented below provides a very simple version of some of the facilities like indexing and concordancing found in packages such as the Oxford Concordance Program (Hockey and Marriott, 1980). These facilities would typically be used in the literary and linguistic study of texts.

10.2 The Model step – version 1

Suppose our brief is to design a package providing five text processing functions realized as five user operations: wordcount, type_token_ratio, freqtab, index and concord. We have been supplied with the following requirements specification for the five text processing operations.

TEXT PROCESSING OPERATIONS

wordcount returns the total number of words (tokens) in a text.

type_token_ratio produces a statistic known as a type/token ratio, which has been used in stylistic analysis and authorship attribution studies. Given a long enough sample of text, it can be shown that a given author tends to have a more or less constant type/token ratio. The ratio is between the number of *distinct* words (types) in the text, and the *total* number of words in the text (the number of tokens). A ratio of one would mean that no word is repeated anywhere in the text. Ratios tending towards zero indicate increasing levels of repetition. For example, the following text (a short quote from Samuel Butler the younger)

I do not mind lying, but I hate inaccuracy

has a word count of 9, and a type/token ratio of 8/9 (or $0.888888\dot{8}$) since the word 'I' appears twice in the text. There are nine words in total (tokens), but only eight distinct words (types) in the text.

freqtab produces a table showing the frequency of each word type in the text. Frequency tables may be ordered alphabetically or by frequency. In this case word types will be ordered alphabetically, and raw frequencies will be shown for each word type in the text.

index produces an alphabetical index of all word types, showing the position in the text of each instance (token) of each type. Position will be by word position in the text, rather than page number, line number, stanza number etc.

concord *concords* the text, that is, it produces a concordance. A concordance entry shows a word token from the text – the *head word* – with some surrounding context, and also the position of that token in the text. The size of the context (number of words before and after the head word) will be supplied by the user as a parameter. Concordance entries are to be listed alphabetically. A concordance might be used to look up references by an author to particular words or phrases. A similar application is found in the KWIC (key word in context) indexes found in many libraries.

Having studied the requirements, we decide that the abstract objects of interest in this application are texts, types and tokens. In addition, the data object returned by the freqtab operation is a frequency table, by index an index and by concord a concordance. It will be useful too to have an abstract object to represent the entries in a concordance. Finally, we will be concerned with positions of tokens in the text. The abstract objects, then, are

```
Text
Type
Token
FreqTable
Index
Concordance
Entry
Position
```

The functionalities of the five top level operations are as follows:

```
wordcount        : Text -> Nat
type_token_ratio : Text -> Real
freqtab          : Text -> FreqTable
index            : Text -> Index
concord          : Text x Nat -> Concordance
```

These abstract objects and operations represent a first attempt at the Model step.

10.3 The Specify step – version 1

Firstly we choose representations for the objects. A text is a sequence of tokens. Types and tokens can be represented as strings:

```
Text         = seq(Token)
Type, Token  = String
```

A frequency table shows word types (ordered alphabetically) and, for each type, the frequency of tokens of that type:

```
FreqTable = seq(pair(Type,Nat))
```

We use a sequence, since the entries in the table are ordered. For the same reason, sequences are used to represent objects of types Index and Concordance. An index lists, for each word type, all the positions in the text where a token of that type is found:

```
Index = seq(pair(Type,seq(Position)))
```

A concordance has an entry for each token in the text:

```
Concordance = seq(Entry)
Entry       = pair(Text,Position)
```

The first element of an entry is of type Text, since we show the token with surrounding context. Finally,

```
Position = Nat
```

where a position of n means that that token is the nth token in the text.

Now we move on to define the five user operations on texts. These will be visible operations. In order to define them, it will be helpful to have some subsidiary (hidden) operations. These are explained as they arise.

wordcount is simple to define – the length of the sequence gives us the word count:

```
wordcount(t) == len(t) ;
```

The type/token ratio can be found by dividing the number of word types by the wordcount. The former can be found by removing duplicate words from the text:

```
type_token_ratio(t) ==
  wordcount(removedups(t)) / wordcount(t) ;
```

Here we have invented a new subsidiary operation, removedups, as the need for it arose. removedups compares all the tokens in a text for equality, and deletes all but one instance of each repeated token:

```
removedups : Text -> Text
```

However, in *me too* we have a generic predicate, =, for testing equality of data objects of any type. removedups can therefore easily be generalized to operate on sequences of any type:

```
removedups : seq(T) -> seq(T)
```

Later we will find that several of the subsidiary operations on texts which we want to specify can be specified as generic sequence operations. If we generalize these operations, we will in effect be extending the set of predefined sequence operations in *me too*. We will decide to do this, and will therefore create a separate module containing the extended set of operations on sequences. The text processing module will import operations from the sequence extensions module. removedups will be one of these imported operations. Whilst specifying the text processing module we simply note the functionalities of the sequence operations, deferring the specification of the sequence extensions module until later.

The remaining three user operations all require an alphabetic sort on texts. We will define a hidden operation, alphasort:

```
alphasort : Text -> Text
alphasort(t) ==
  if    t = [] then []
  else let x == minstring reduce ("zzz") t
        in [x] conc alphasort(delete(t,hd(positions(x,t)))) ;
```

and modify the model to include the functionality of alphasort. (This is one of many sorting algorithms which could be used.) We have introduced three further operations in the definition of alphasort. First, minstring returns the (alphabetically) lower of two strings. Its functionality is

```
minstring : String x String -> String
```

Since minstring is a basic operation on strings, we decide to specify this operation in a separate module which provides an extended set of string operations, along the same lines as the extensions to the sequence operations.

delete and positions are generic sequence operations. delete removes an element from a given position in a sequence:

```
delete : seq(T) x Position -> seq(T)
```

The positions operation returns a sequence of numbers representing the positions in a sequence where a certain element is found:

```
positions : T x seq(T) -> seq(Position)
```

Position is an object associated with sequences in general, and is not particular to texts. This object then will appear in the sequence extensions module, and will be imported to the text processing module.

In order to define freqtab, we first define another hidden operation, freq, which returns the number of instances of a particular word in a text:

```
freq : Type x Text -> Nat
freq(typ,t) == wordcount([tok | tok <- t; tok = typ]) ;
```

The functionality of freq is added to the model, and freqtab is defined in terms of freq:

```
freqtab(t) ==
  [(typ,freq(typ,t)) | typ <- alphasort(removedups(t))] ;
```

To build an index or a concordance, we need to find all the positions of the tokens of a given word type in a text. The positions operation can be used again here. The definition of index is

```
index(t) ==
  [(typ,positions(typ,t)) | typ <- alphasort(removedups(t))];
```

concord takes each word type in a text, in alphabetical order, and each instance of that word, ordered by position in the text, and builds a sequence of entries. Each entry shows a token, with some surrounding context, and its position in the text. The size of the context (number of preceding and following tokens) is supplied as a parameter:

```
concord(t,n) ==
  [(context(p,n,t),p) | typ <- alphasort(removedups(t)),
                        p   <- positions(typ,t)] ;
```

Each entry is a pair: the first element of the pair is a text – the token with its preceding and following context. The second element of the pair gives the position of that token in the text. The hidden operation context builds up a text wherein the token of interest is preceded by n words of preceding context and followed by n words of following context. In case the context overflows the beginning or end of the text, a blank string is supplied as a default for the missing tokens. The definition of context is

```
context : Position x Nat x Text -> Text
context(p,n,t) ==
  [t[pos," "] | pos <- [p - n,...,p + n]] ;
```

The user operations have now been defined. In the process, we have made decisions which have given rise to modifications to the original model. We have introduced several hidden operations and have decided to package some of them in two additional modules. We now return to the Model step to incorporate these changes.

10.4 The Model step – version 2

The model has been augmented by the addition of the functionalities of the subsidiary operations on texts. Other subsidiary operations could have been defined for texts, but were recognized as having more generality. This led to the decision to specify a modular system, with two new modules – string and sequence extensions – supporting the text processing module. There is one other change to the original model: the object Position belongs to the sequence module, and so disappears from the text processing module.

The specification document for the text processing module begins by recording the imported objects and operations, showing the modules from which they are derived. The specification document continues with the model part of the specification as usual.

SPECIFICATION OF TEXT_PROC

IMPORTS

Objects

Position	**from** Sequence_Extensions

Operations

removedups, positions, delete	**from** Sequence_Extensions
minstring	**from** String_Extensions

MODEL

Objects

Text
FreqTable
Index
Concordance
Entry
Type
Token

Visible operations

wordcount	: Text -> Nat
type_token_ratio	: Text -> Real
freqtab	: Text -> FreqTable
index	: Text -> Index
concord	: Text x Nat -> Concordance

Hidden operations

context	: Position x Nat x Text -> Text
freq	: Type x Text -> Nat
alphasort	: Text -> Text

The model for the sequence module, in which T is a type variable, is:

SPECIFICATION OF SEQUENCE_EXTENSIONS

MODEL

Objects

```
Position
```

Operations

```
removedups : seq(T) -> seq(T)
positions  : T x seq(T) -> seq(Position)
delete     : seq(T) x Position -> seq(T)
```

In our text processing example it turned out that only one string operation was needed. However, we will still have a separate module. The model is:

SPECIFICATION OF STRING_EXTENSIONS

MODEL

Operations

```
minstring : String x String -> String
```

We will have to complete the specification of the two supporting modules by going through the Specify step.

10.5 The Specify step – version 2

The TEXT_PROC module

The specification of objects and operations in this module remains unchanged.

The SEQUENCE_EXTENSIONS module

There is one abstract object, Position, which we will represent as a natural number:

```
Position = Nat
```

Next the operations are defined. removedups takes a sequence, and if any elements of the sequence are repeated, removes all but one of the duplicated elements:

```
removedups(q) ==
  if   q = [] then []
  else if   hd(q) member rng(tl(q))
       then removedups(tl(q))
       else [hd(q)] conc removedups(tl(q)) ;
```

Given an element x, and a sequence q, positions(x,q) returns a sequence showing all the positions in q (in ascending order) where x is found:

```
positions(x,q) ==
  [ p | p <- [1,...,len(q)]; q[p] = x] ;
```

delete(q,i) removes the ith element from the sequence q. To convert the sequence into map notation, asm is used, and a new map is constructed which omits the ith element of the sequence, and adjusts the indices of the following elements of the sequence accordingly. The map representation is converted back to the usual sequence representation by means of asq.

```
delete(q,i) ==
  asq({(if j < i then j else j - 1, x) | (j,x) <- asm(q);
                                          j /= i}) ;
```

All the sequence operations have now been defined, and we turn to the string module.

The STRING_EXTENSIONS module

No new objects are introduced in this module. The Specify step therefore involves defining the single new operation on strings. minstring(a,b) returns whichever of a or b is lower in the sorting order. Since the < operation in *me too* is defined for strings as well as numbers, it can be used in the definition:

```
minstring(a,b) == if a < b then a else b ;
```

We have now completed the Model and Specify steps for the three modules, and may proceed to validate the design by executing the specification.

10.6 Executing the specification

As usual, the definitions of the operations could be typed directly into the *me too* shell, or loaded from file. Here we assume that each module is stored in a separate file. The three modules are loaded into the shell, and some data objects are created. For data we use two short texts: the quote from Samuel Butler given above, and another from Saki. We start by testing texts which do not contain punctuation; at some future stage we would incorporate it.

```
? butler == ["I","do","not","mind","lying","but","I","hate",
              "inaccuracy"] ;
= BUTLER ;
? saki == ["a","little","inaccuracy","sometimes","saves","tons",
            "of","explanation"] ;
= SAKI ;
? text == butler conc saki ;
= TEXT ;
? text ;
= [I,do,not,mind,lying,but,I,hate,inaccuracy,a,little,inaccuracy,
   sometimes,saves,tons,of,explanation] ;
```

We will apply a bottom-up testing regime, starting with the sequence operations. The following interaction shows part of this testing process.

```
? removedups([]) ;
= [] ;
? removedups(butler) ;
= [do,not,mind,lying,but,I,hate,inaccuracy] ;
? removedups(saki) = saki ;
= TRUE ;
? removedups(["a","b","a","a","c","a","d","d"]) ;
= [b,c,a,d] ;
   .
   .
   .
? positions("not",[]) ;
= [] ;
? positions(" ",saki) ;
= [] ;
? positions("accuracy",butler) ;
= [] ;
? positions("inaccuracy",butler) ;
= [9] ;
? positions("inaccuracy",text) ;
= [9,12] ;
   .
   .
   .
? delete([],2) ;
= [] ;
? delete(butler,100) ;
= [I,do,not,mind,lying,but,I,hate,inaccuracy] ;
? delete(butler,0) ;
= [do,not,mind,lying,but,I,hate,inaccuracy] ;
```

At this point we have discovered an error. An attempt to delete the element at position zero of a sequence has resulted in the *first* element being removed. (The previous test attempted to remove the hundredth element of a sequence of length nine, and this left the sequence unchanged.) When specifying the operation we omitted to consider one of the possible exception cases. We must examine the definition of delete:

```
delete(q,i) ==
  asq({(if j < i then j else j - 1, x) | (j,x) <- asm(q);
                                          j /= i});
```

We can see that if i is greater than the length of the sequence, the original sequence will be rebuilt unchanged. Each position index j will be smaller than i, so the then clause will be evaluated in every case, pairing each index with its original partner. This is why the attempt to delete the hundredth element returned the original sequence. However, an attempt to delete the element at position zero erroneously deletes the first element. This is because the else clause is invoked for all positions of the sequence. All indices are decremented by one, leaving the first element at position zero. asq then rebuilds the sequence from the new position one, and the original first element is lost.

We must first decide how to handle the two kinds of exception, and then re-specify the operation. After due consideration we decide that any attempt to delete at a position greater than the length of the sequence or less than one should return the original sequence intact. delete is redefined to correct the error uncovered by the second test, and to specify the exception explicitly for both cases. Testing whether i is in the domain of the sequence covers both cases:

```
delete(q,i) ==
  if    i member dom(q)
  then asq({(if j < i then j else j - 1, x) | (j,x) <- asm(q);
                                                    j /= i})
  else q ;
```

The specification is modified, and testing continues:

```
? delete(butler,100) ;
= [I,do,not,mind,lying,but,I,hate,inaccuracy] ;
? delete(butler,0) ;
= [I,do,not,mind,lying,but,I,hate,inaccuracy] ;
? delete(butler,9) ;
= [I,do,not,mind,lying,but,I,hate] ;
? delete(butler,1) ;
= [do,not,mind,lying,but,I,hate,inaccuracy] ;
? delete(butler,3) ;
= [I,do,mind,lying,but,I,hate,inaccuracy] ;
  .
  .
```

Next the minstring operation would be tested, before we move on to the text processing module.

Firstly we test the hidden operations on texts, starting with context. We will pay particular attention to contexts which overflow the beginning and ending of the text.

```
? context(3,1,butler) ;
= [do,not,mind] ;
? context(1,3,butler) ;
= [  ,  ,  ,I,do,not,mind] ;
```

The first test covers the simple case, where the token of interest is in the middle of the text. In the second test, we request the first word in the text, with three words of context before and after. Recall that a blank string is supplied as a default when the context overflows the beginning or end of the text. The operation behaves as intended so far. Now we ask for two words of context around the ninth (the last) word in the text, and follow up by applying context to positions greater than the length of the text. An empty text is also supplied to the operation.

```
? context(9,2,butler) ;
= [I,hate,inaccuracy,  ,  ] ;
? context(10,2,butler) ;
= [hate,inaccuracy,  ,  ,  ] ;
```

```
? context(10,1,[]) ;
= [  ,  ,  ];
    .
    .
```

We could have predicted these results by examining the specification of context. By the way we deal with the beginning and ending of a text, we have made context very tolerant. In effect, we are regarding a text as a (perhaps empty) sequence of non-blank strings, with an infinite sequence of blank strings concatenated to the beginning and another to the end. Given any position, valid (such as 9) or invalid (such as 10) in the above examples, context will return a context of some kind. In the specification as it stands context is used only in concord, and here the position parameter is guaranteed to reference a valid position in the text. If we were to re-use context elsewhere, however, this could cause problems. We respecify context so that the position supplied as a parameter must be greater than zero and less than or equal to the length of the text, otherwise a null text is returned:

```
context(p,n,t) ==
  if   p member dom(t)
  then [t[pos," "] | pos <- [p - n,...,p + n]]
  else [] ;
```

Now a null context is returned when an invalid position is supplied:

```
? context(9,2,butler) ;
= [I,hate,inaccuracy,  ,  ];
? context(10,2,butler) ;
= [];
? context(10,1,[]) ;
= [];
```

The freq and alphasort operations are tested, and then we move on to the five user operations in the text processing system. (Layout and bold type are used below in order to clarify the material.)

```
? wordcount(butler) ;
= 9 ;
? wordcount(saki) ;
= 8 ;
? wordcount(text) ;
= 17 ;
? type_token_ratio(butler) ;
= 0.8888888 ;
? type_token_ratio(saki) ;
= 1 ;
? type_token_ratio(text) ;
= 0.8823529 ;

? freqtab(butler) ;
= [ ( I,          2 ) ,
    ( but,        1 ) ,
    ( do,         1 ) ,
    ( hate,       1 ) ,
    ( inaccuracy, 1 ) ,
```

```
      ( lying,        1 ) ,
      ( mind,         1 ) ,
      ( not,          1 )  ] ;

? index(text) ;
= [ ( I,              [1,7]  ) ,
    ( a,              [10]   ) ,
    ( but,            [6]    ) ,
    ( do,             [2]    ) ,
    ( explanation,    [17]   ) ,
    ( hate,           [8]    ) ,
    ( inaccuracy,     [9,12] ) ,
    ( little,         [11]   ) ,
    ( lying,          [5]    ) ,
    ( mind,           [4]    ) ,
    ( not,            [3]    ) ,
    ( of,             [16]   ) ,
    ( saves,          [14]   ) ,
    ( sometimes,      [13]   ) ,
    ( tons,           [15]   )  ] ;

? concord(butler, 1) ;
= [ ( [        , I,           do           ] , 1  ) ,
    ( [ but ,    I,           hate         ] , 7  ) ,
    ( [ lying ,  but ,        I            ] , 6  ) ,
    ( [ I ,      do ,         not          ] , 2  ) ,
    ( [ I ,      hate ,       inaccuracy   ] , 8  ) ,
    ( [ hate ,   inaccuracy ,              ] , 9  ) ,
    ( [ mind ,   lying ,      but          ] , 5  ) ,
    ( [ not ,    mind ,       lying        ] , 4  ) ,
    ( [ do ,     not ,        mind         ] , 3  )  ] ;
```

Finally, with apologies to Saki, we can alter the sentiments expressed in our text by a little textual editing:

```
? text overwr {12 -> "mathematics", 13 -> "always"} ;
= [I, do, not, mind, lying, but, I, hate, inaccuracy,
   a, little, mathematics, always, saves, tons, of, explanation];
```

We will leave the design of the text processing package at this point, noting that testing would now continue on longer texts and on texts incorporating punctuation. The specification would also be reviewed, possibly leading to further iterations through the design process. In particular, with a modularized specification we should be concerned that the abstract objects and operations are allocated to the correct modules. This is not always as simple as it seems. For example, the objects Type and Token could be regarded as generic sequence objects, and freq and even context might be redefined as generic operations on sequences. These questions could be addressed in the next iteration through the design loop.

10.7 Summary

The text processing example is an obvious application in which to use sequence notation, since texts are ordered and usually involve repetition of words.

During the Specify step, a number of subsidiary operations were created when the need arose. This involved returning to the Model step to incorporate the functionalities of the new operations. Also during the Specify step it was recognized that some of the subsidiary operations could be generalized; consequently a modular system was eventually specified. The string and sequence modules could of course be extended and reused in different systems. The decision to modularize also required iteration back to the Model step.

In the Validate step some simple errors were discovered in the specification. The Specify step was revisited in order to correct the definitions of the operations involved.

Finally, an indication was given of some possible directions subsequent iterations through the design process might take.

Chapter 11

Example 3 – applying the *me too* method

We take examples to prove other things, and if we wanted to prove the examples we should take the other things as examples of the examples. For, since we always think the difficulty lies in what we are trying to prove, we find examples clearer and an aid to demonstration.

Blaise Pascal

This example is intended to illustrate both the *me too* method and notation by means of an extended example. In particular, we wish to show how the method is used on a larger scale, developing three versions of an example system. By way of consolidation of the earlier tutorial material, much of the *me too* notation is employed in the example.

The three specifications developed in this chapter are collected together and given in full in Appendix 2.

11.1 Requirements for an automated teller machine

Imagine that we are part of a development team, with the task of designing an automated teller machine (ATM) for a bank. The requirements supplied by the bank are shown in Fig. 11.1.

It is the task of our design group to model a system which meets these requirements. In this chapter, we design only the functionality to be offered by the ATM; that is, we design the facilities of the system rather than, say, the ergonomic considerations of the machine itself or the layout of any screen incorporated in it.

11.2 The first design

The first decision to be made is whether or not the initial design will attempt to incorporate all of the given requirements. For a large or novel system, it may be appropriate to start by considering only a subset of the requirements, creating a

1. Facilities

(a) customers should be able to withdraw cash, in multiples of $5, up to the balance of their account or to a set limit (whichever is the lower)
(b) customers should be able to examine the balance of their account
(c) customers should be able to order a new check book
(d) customers should be able to order a statement

2. Security

(a) customers should gainn access to an account by means of a card supplied to the ATM
(b) a card is associated with one account
(c) a card has associated with it a personal identification number (PIN), known only to the authorized user of the account, which must be supplied independently to the ATM whenever the card is presented
(d) attempted fraud should result in the card being rendered unusable (perhaps being confiscated by the ATM)

Figure 11.1 ATM statement of requirements.

subsystem which will later be extended to the full functionality required. This example is not particularly large or novel but, for tutorial purposes, we shall begin by considering only one aspect of the problem.

We have chosen to start with the manipulation of a customer's account, since this banking activity underlies the added convenience offered by ATM facilities. Thus, in this first design, all ATM-related concepts such as 'card' or 'PIN' are ignored. The purpose of this iteration is to specify a model which provides bank staff with mechanisms for handling bank accounts at the bank counter. We do not intend these facilities to be used directly by customers. The specification created in this iteration is to be the basis for designing the ATM facilities.

11.2.1 The Model step – design 1

The *me too* method prescribes that our first activity is to determine the objects and operations of interest in the system. This may well be undertaken using analysis techniques, such as SADT (Gane and Sarson, 1979) or SSADM (Downs *et al.*, 1988); however, it is not within the scope of this book to introduce such techniques, so we adopt an informal approach in this example.

While discussing the facilities of the bank, our design team finds that it is repeatedly using terms such as 'customer', 'account', 'account number', 'amounts of money', 'deposit', 'withdrawal' and so on. Consequently, we begin to document the Model step by recording these terms associated with banking facilities:

Objects

Customer	
Account	
AccNo	account number
Amount	

Operations

OpenAccount
Deposit
Withdraw
CloseAccount

As we proceed, we anticipate that more terms may be added while others are found not to be useful in the system model we are building. Where analysis techniques are used in the Model step, they are likely to uncover such changes at an early stage; here we use the need for such changes to highlight how the method can accommodate change as the design proceeds.

The next step in clarifying our thinking about the system is to write a short description of each operation. There may be an informal summary of each operation but the main task is to write functionalities for the operations, where the functionality for each operation specifies the type of its input parameters and the type of result returned.

To start with OpenAccount: what is involved when an account is opened? The intention is that the bank adds a new customer account to the collection of accounts it already has. OpenAccount therefore starts from the existing collection, sets up a new account and adds it to the collection. An immediate problem in writing the functionality is that so far we have not given ourselves any terminology for referring to this 'collection of accounts'. So we extend the model by adding a new object called BankDb, which represents the database of account information held by the bank.

Before writing the functionality of OpenAccount, we have to decide what information is required to set up a new account. Remember that in a functional specification language like *me too*, there is no global state or global variables – any object to be manipulated by an operation has to be supplied as a parameter to that operation. Thus, since OpenAccount has to act on an existing bank database, it must be given a bank database as a parameter. We also need to supply the name of the customer requesting the new account. We decide that a new account is set up with a zero balance; later money can be deposited. The functionality of OpenAccount is therefore

```
OpenAccount : BankDb x Customer -> BankDb
```

What about depositing money in an account? Normally when accessing an account, it is identified not by the customer's name but by an account number, so the functionality of Deposit is

```
Deposit : BankDb x AccNo x Amount -> BankDb
```

indicating that the result of depositing a sum of money in a nominated account is a new version of the bank database. The intention is, of course, that the new bank database contains a new version of the appropriate account with the balance increased by the amount deposited. In the Model step, this is stated as an informal description of the operation – it will be made precise when the operation is defined during the Specify step.

The functionalities of the remaining two operations are

Withdraw : BankDb x AccNo x Amount -> BankDb

CloseAccount : BankDb x AccNo -> BankDb

All of these operations have to be supplied with an existing bank database, but at the beginning there is no such object. It is possible to defer considering this by saying that, whatever representation is used for a BankDb, the first call of OpenAccount will be supplied with an empty object of that type. However, it is normal practice to acknowledge explicitly the need for an empty bank database by providing an operation in the model whose task is to construct one, such as

NewBankDb : -> BankDb

This functionality states that the operation takes no parameters and creates a bank database. In the informal description for this operation, we record the fact that this new bank database will be empty of accounts. Once the representations for objects have been determined in the Specify step, we can state this formally.

Finally when reviewing the model, it becomes clear that, short of inspecting the entire database, there is no means of examining the balance of any account. We therefore add another operation:

Balance : BankDb x AccNo -> Amount

At the end of the first attempt at the Model step, our model of this subsystem is as follows:

MODEL

Objects

BankDb	the bank database
Customer	customer identification
Account	
AccNo	account number
Amount	a sum of money

Operations

NewBankDb : -> BankDb
OpenAccount : BankDb x Customer -> BankDb
CloseAccount : BankDb x AccNo -> BankDb
Deposit : BankDb x AccNo x Amount -> BankDb
Withdraw : BankDb x AccNo x Amount -> BankDb
Balance : BankDb x AccNo -> Amount

where

NewBankDb() creates a new bank database

OpenAccount(db,c) opens the account for customer c by adding an empty account to the database db

CloseAccount(db,n) closes account n by removing it from the database db

Deposit(db,n,m) credits the account m to account n in database db

Withdraw(db,n,m) debits account n by amount m in database db

Balance(db,n) shows the balance of account n in database db

This illustrates both the amount of detail expected at the Model step and a way of presenting it. In documenting the model, we note that the Account object has not been used directly by any of the operations. Rather than risk dispensing with it prematurely, we decide to carry on to the next step of the method, specifying the objects and the operations in order to clarify what the design group means by them.

11.2.2 The Specify step – design 1

In a model-based method such as *me too*, the first aspect of the specification to be considered is the choice of mathematical representation for the objects in the model. Until this is done, there is no basis for specifying the operations or any invariants, since these will be defined in terms of the mathematical operations available for the representation chosen. That is, it is necessary to decide if an object is to be represented by, say, a set or a sequence, before we can specify any operations or invariants which refer to that object.

The intention behind the Account object is that it should record the name of the customer together with the balance of the account. A simple way of achieving this is to use a tuple (in this case, a pair):

```
Account = tuple(Customer,Amount)
```

Accounts are held in the bank database. As decided in the Model step, the object AccNo will be used to access accounts, which suggests that a suitable representation for the database is a map from AccNo to Account:

```
BankDb = map(AccNo,Account)
```

The remaining objects in the model have the following representations:

```
AccNo    = Nat
Amount   = Integer
Customer = String
```

where the amount is in whole dollars. These decisions give the starting point for going on to specify the operations and any invariants.

As a first step, we consider what constitutes a valid bank database as a precursor to stating an invariant for the BankDb object. We wish to ensure that account numbers in the database are unique non-negative numbers. In fact, it is not necessary to specify an invariant to state this, because our choice of representation already does so. The uniqueness of account numbers in the database is asserted by choosing to represent the database as a map with AccNo as its domain. It is clear that negative account numbers are not permitted by our decision to represent them by the natural (i.e. non-negative) numbers. We turn next to specifying the operations.

In writing the specification for an operation, we ask first what its preconditions are; that is, what conditions must hold before the operation can be called. If desired, these conditions can then be incorporated into the specification of the operation.

Creating an empty bank database is trivial, since it consists of an empty map:

```
NewBankDb() == {} ;
```

This makes precise our informally stated assumption in the Model step that a new bank database is empty of any account information.

When we come to write the specification for OpenAccount, we find that the newly created account needs a new account number. In an implicit style, we could state this by specifying the relationship between the old and new versions of the bank database as follows:

```
∀ old_bdb, new_bdb : BankDb ,
  c : Customer ,
  acc : AccNo .

  (new_bdb = OpenAccount(old_bdb,c)) =>
    (new_bdb = old_bdb overwr {acc -> (c,0)})
    and not(acc member dom(old_bdb))
```

which says that a new account is created and is identified by an account number which is not already in use. There is no need in this style to indicate how that account number is generated. However, in the explicit style required for executability, we do have to generate a new account number. The most straightforward way to achieve this is to ask the caller of the operation (a member of the bank staff) to supply an account number as a parameter. The functionality of OpenAccount is therefore amended to become

```
OpenAccount : BankDb x Customer x AccNo -> BankDb
```

Because the account number is supplied as a parameter, it is now necessary to state explicitly that the new account number must not already exist. One way of writing this is to specify a boolean operation for the precondition, as in

```
pre_OpenAccount : BankDb x Customer x AccNo -> Boolean
pre_OpenAccount(bdb,c,acc) == not(acc member dom(bdb)) ;
```

This operation encapsulating the precondition can be either paired with a post-condition operation such as

```
post_OpenAccount(bdb,c,acc) == bdb overwr {acc -> (c,0)} ;
```

or invoked in the OpenAccount operation:

```
OpenAccount(bdb,c,acc) ==
  if    pre_OpenAccount(bdb,c,acc)
  then bdb overwr {acc -> (c,0)}
  else bdb ;
```

Alternatively, since specifying preconditions separately leads to a proliferation of operations, we can write the operation as

```
OpenAccount(bdb,c,acc) ==
  if    not(acc member dom(bdb))
  then bdb overwr {acc -> (c,0)}
  else bdb ;
```

taking the precondition directly into the operation. All these versions of the specification ensure that an existing account will be left unscathed by the operation.

The specification of this operation illustrates an approach to exception handling which is common in functional programming. Recall that function applications are expressions, so they return a single value and can have no side-effects. Thus imperative mechanisms such as printing an error message to the screen or to an error log (which would be side-effects of the function) are not available in the functional style of *me too*. The functionality of this operation currently states that it returns an object of type BankDb. In defining exception handling for the operation, we have to decide whether to return a suitable BankDb object, or to extend the range of types the operation can return, for example, to return an error message.

It can be advantageous to choose the former method, if it is possible, where it is likely that the returned object will be supplied as a parameter to another operation; that is, where composition of operations may be required. For example, using composition we can construct a perfectly acceptable BankDb object as follows:

```
Deposit(OpenAccount(NewBankDb(),"Smith",5123),5123,1000)
```

However, if OpenAccount could return an object other than a BankDb, then this ability to compose operations means that all other operations taking a BankDb parameter would have to make sure that that is what is supplied. Consequently, the approach taken in OpenAccount is to return a suitable object of type BankDb. In this case, the value chosen is the bank database that was originally supplied.

CloseAccount is used if an account is to be removed entirely. Unlike OpenAccount, the precondition for this operation requires that the account *must* exist in the bank database.

```
pre_CloseAccount : BankDb x AccNo -> Boolean
pre_CloseAccount(bdb,acc) == acc member dom(bdb) ;
```

If the condition is not met, then as for OpenAccount the operation leaves the bank database unchanged:

```
CloseAccount(bdb,acc) ==
  if   pre_CloseAccount(bdb,acc)
  then bdb ds {acc}
  else bdb ;
```

or, alternatively,

```
CloseAccount(bdb,acc) ==
  if   acc member dom(bdb)
  then bdb ds {acc}
  else bdb ;
```

For the rest of this design exercise, we do not state preconditions separately but incorporate them into the main operation under consideration.

If a customer has an account, they may deposit amounts of money:

```
Deposit(bdb,acc,amt) ==
  if   acc member dom(bdb)
  then let acct == bdb[acc]
       in bdb overwr {acc -> (first(acct),second(acct) + amt)}
  else bdb ;
```

This operation extracts the relevant account from the database. The balance in the account is increased by the value of amt in the expression

```
(first(acct),second(acct) + amt)
```

which reconstructs the tuple representing the account. This new account value overwrites the old account in the bank database.

The Withdraw operation is similar except that, when we consider its preconditions, we realize that the statement of requirements is unclear about the possibility of overdrafts. ATM users cannot withdraw more than the balance of their accounts, but it transpires that the bank staff can authorize overdrafts for personal callers. The operation, therefore, need not check that the amount withdrawn is covered by the balance:

```
Withdraw(bdb,acc,amt) ==
  if    acc member dom(bdb)
  then let acct == bdb[acc]
       in  bdb overwr {acc -> (first(acct),second(acct) - amt)}
  else bdb ;
```

This is so similar to the Deposit operation that it can be re-written as

```
Withdraw(bdb,acc,amt) == Deposit(bdb,acc,-amt) ;
```

This 'deposits' the negative amount in the account, thus effectively withdrawing it.

Finally, there is the operation to check the balance of an account. What value should this return when the account number refers to a non-existent account? The functionality of Balance states that it returns a value of type Amount, so one option is to return some suitable error value of this type. However, it is difficult to see what a suitable value might be, since any value could be a valid balance. We decide that we have to return an error message instead of an amount, which means extending the functionality of the operation to allow this:

```
Balance : BankDb x AccNo -> Amount union String
```

Here the functionality of Balance shows that the operation can now return either an object of type Amount or an object of type String. The type of the result is now a **union type** indicated by the union operator. As noted in the earlier description of exception handling, we must now ensure that any operations whose definitions include a call to Balance cope with the error case. The operation is specified by

```
Balance(bdb,acc) == second(bdb[acc,(" ","no such account")]) ;
```

The precondition does not have to be tested explicitly in this operation since the desired effect is achieved by supplying a default to the map application. The operation returns the balance that it finds in the account or an error message if the account is not present in the database.

This completes the specification of the model for this first attempt at the ATM design. The next step is to test the specification by executing it in the *me too* shell.

11.2.3 The Validate step – design 1

The specification is entered, exactly as it has been given above, either into a file or directly into the shell. Once this has been done, we can experiment with the objects and operations we have defined. In testing a *me too* specification, we can be guided in our choice of test cases by the specifications of the operations. For example, if the operation contains an error case, we test that an occurrence of that error is detected and correctly handled. Test cases must also be generated from the requirements of the system.

To begin with, we test NewBankDb by creating an instance of the bank database object as follows:

```
? db == NewBankDb();
= DB ;
? db;
= {};
```

(The prompts and responses from the shell are also shown.) This interaction shows the empty database as expected. The next step is to check OpenAccount. We use the operation to open some valid accounts:

```
? db == OpenAccount(db,"Ferguson",1) ;
= DB ;
? db == OpenAccount(db,"Campbell",2) ;
= DB ;
? db == OpenAccount(db,"Fraser",5) ;
= DB ;
? db == OpenAccount(db,"Beattie",8) ;
= DB;
? db;
= {1 -> (Ferguson,0), 2 -> (Campbell,0),
   5 -> (Fraser,0), 8 -> (Beattie,0) };
```

and again the database has the expected value. OpenAccount should not allow a new account to be opened with an existing account number:

```
? db == OpenAccount(db,"McGregor",2) ;
= DB ;
? db;
= {1 -> (Ferguson,0), 2 -> (Campbell,0),
   5 -> (Fraser,0), 8 -> (Beattie,0) };
```

and indeed it does not open another account for account number 2, nor does it overwrite the account already present.

We continue in a similar fashion to test Deposit and Withdraw, but for the sake of space, we list the calls rather than show details of the interaction with the shell and assume that the value of the database is checked after each call. The cases chosen show deposits to both new and existing accounts, as well as a non-existent account. Several valid withdrawals are made, one of which creates an overdraft. There is also an attempt to withdraw cash from a non-existent account. The comments shown here and in the testing throughout this chapter indicate the intended results.

```
db == Deposit(db,1,50) ;     % valid call
db == Deposit(db,5,125) ;    % valid call – first for a/c
db == Deposit(db,5,65) ;     % valid call – second for a/c
db == Deposit(db,4,5) ;      % error – no such account
db == Deposit(db,2,5) ;      % valid
```

```
db == Withdraw(db,5,21) ;   % valid
db == Withdraw(db,1,25) ;   % valid - first for a/c
db == Withdraw(db,1,25) ;   % valid - second for a/c
db == Withdraw(db,2,30) ;   % valid - overdraft
db == Withdraw(db,4,20) ;   % error - no such account
```

After this, the value of the database db is:

```
{1 -> ("Ferguson",0), 2 -> ("Campbell",-25),
 5 -> ("Fraser",169), 8 -> ("Beattie",0) }
```

We carry on to experiment with the Balance operation, covering the possible cases for the state of an account:

```
? Balance(db,2);               % valid - overdraft
= -25 ;
? Balance(db,1);               % valid - zero balance
= 0 ;
? Balance(db,4);               % valid - account not present
= no such account ;
? Balance(db,5) ;              % valid - before withdrawal
= 169 ;
? db == Withdraw(db,5,70) ;
= DB ;
? Balance(db,5);               % valid - after withdrawal
= 99 ;
? db ;
= { 5 -> (Fraser,99), 2 -> (Campbell,-25),
    1 -> (Ferguson,0), 8 -> (Beattie,0) };
```

Finally, we test CloseAccount, again considering the various states of an account:

```
? db == CloseAccount(db,8) ;   % valid - zero balance
= DB ;
? db == CloseAccount(db,5) ;   % error - positive balance
= DB ;
? db == CloseAccount(db,2) ;   % error - negative balance
= DB ;
? db == CloseAccount(db,7) ;   % error - no such account
= DB ;
? db;
= { 1 -> (Ferguson,0) };
```

Unfortunately we find that the accounts belonging to Campbell (account 2) and Fraser (account 5) have been closed as well as that for Beattie (account 8). This means that Campbell has retained $25 of the bank's money while Fraser has lost the $99 remaining in the account. This reveals an oversight in the precondition for CloseAccount, which should have additionally specified that the balance of an account which is to be closed must be zero. That is, the precondition should have been

```
pre_CloseAccount : BankDb x AccNo -> Boolean
pre_CloseAccount(bdb,acc) ==
  (acc member dom(bdb)) and (second(bdb[acc,(" ",0)]) = 0) ;
```

The operation is respecified to include the equivalent of this precondition:

```
CloseAccount(bdb,acc) ==
  if   (acc member dom(bdb))
       and (second(bdb[acc],(" ",0)) = 0)
  then bdb ds {acc}
  else bdb ;
```

We reconstruct the database and rerun the tests for CloseAccount:

```
? db == CloseAccount(db,8) ;  % valid – zero balance
= DB ;
? db == CloseAccount(db,5) ;  % error – positive balance
= DB ;
? db == CloseAccount(db,2) ;  % error – negative balance
= DB ;
? db == CloseAccount(db,7) ;  % error – no such account
= DB ;
? db;
= { 5 -> (Fraser,99), 2 -> (Campbell,-25),
    1 -> (Ferguson,0) };
```

and find, as required, that the account belonging to Beattie has been closed but not those of Campbell and Fraser.

The prototype now displays the required behavior, as demonstrated by the test cases above, indicating that the specification possesses the required properties. It is now time to consider the next iteration of the design. Before doing so, though, we note that the customer name is never used in account manipulation. This prompts us to ask what purpose this object serves *in the model we are building*. It will undoubtedly be part of the account information in the eventual system, as perhaps will be the customer's address, the date on which regular statements are to be sent, and other such information. However, none of this is directly relevant to our model. This kind of consideration is part of the design process – deciding which aspects of the system are to be included in the model. Thus in a real bank, customers' details will be associated with their accounts, but it is not necessary to record that association in our model. Removing the Customer object, then, is proposed as a change to the model as we proceed to the next design. The specification developed in this section is given in full in Appendix 2.

11.3 The second design

At this stage, we decide not to make any radical changes in our approach, but to incorporate the functionality needed by an ATM, building on top of the model (and its specification) that we have already created. However, we do decide to introduce a new module to emphasize the distinction between bank and ATM facilities. The BANK module specified in the previous iteration retains its rôle as providing manager and teller operations for the banking facilities; the new ATM_USER module provides ATM-specific facilities.

The statement of requirements shown in Fig. 11.1 is the basis of this iteration. The specification is to be evaluated against these requirements in the Validate step.

11.3.1 The Model step – design 2

The first task is to determine any new objects that will be required to provide the facilities of the ATM. Recall the requirements of the ATM: users of an ATM are to be allowed to withdraw cash, inspect the balance of their account, and order check books and statements. To gain access to the ATM, they have to present a card (which carries some kind of number identifying the account to which the card relates) and supply a personal identification number (PIN).

This suggests some new objects in the BANK module. One obvious candidate is the PIN, the secret number associated with each card. Another object is the AtmCard. The requirements say that each card has a PIN and is associated with one account. In addition, we identify each card by a card number, the object CardNo, which is distinct from both the account number and the PIN. This allows (but does not require) the bank to issue more than one card for an account, for example, to joint account holders. It is decided that PINs and card numbers will be unique within the bank.

No other objects are immediately apparent, so the next part of the Model step is to consider the operations. There are several cases to consider. First, which of the existing bank operations need to be altered or removed as a result of the changes and additions proposed? Second, are there any new bank operations to be added to the model? Third, what new operations are needed in the ATM_USER module to support the ATM user?

The BANK module

We begin with changes to existing operations. Recall that a decision resulting from the previous iteration was to dispense with the Customer object. This affects the OpenAccount operation which now has the functionality

```
OpenAccount : BankDb x AccNo -> BankDb
```

At this stage, none of the other operations already in the BANK module require any changes to their functionalities.

Next we deal with new banking facilities for bank staff, of which there are two groups, relating to orders for check books and statements, and to card issue and retention. As we consider what happens when a check book or statement is ordered, we realize that the model must include some way of recording these orders and noting when they have been fulfilled. Consequently, the bank database has to be extended to hold this additional information – some record of those accounts for which a new check book has been ordered and of those accounts for which an up-to-date statement has been ordered. The representation of this new information in the database will be made explicit in the Specify step.

The new operations for the bank staff register that the outstanding orders have been fulfilled:

```
CBooksOrdered : BankDb -> BankDb

StatementsOrdered : BankDb -> BankDb
```

CBooksOrdered handles orders for check books, and StatementsOrdered handles orders for statements.

The next group of bank operations handle the issue and retention of cards. A card is issued by associating it with an account:

IssueCard : BankDb x AtmCard -> BankDb

Along with this functionality, we state our intention that the operation will take the account number concerned from the card itself rather than as a separate parameter. This has the benefit that the card cannot accidentally be associated with the wrong account or with more than one account.

We decide to model confiscation of cards by maintaining a list of illegal cards, with the intention that the ATM operations will not permit transactions involving such cards:

RetainCard : BankDb x AtmCard -> BankDb

ReleaseCard : BankDb x AtmCard -> BankDb

where RetainCard adds the card to a list of illegal cards and ReleaseCard removes the card from that list.

There are no other staff operations needed, but we note that the operations in the BANK module repeatedly test for the presence of an account in the bank database which leads us to provide an operation encapsulating this test. The new operation is not visible outside the module; its functionality is

AcctKnown : BankDb x AccNo -> Boolean

The ATM_USER module will, we anticipate, need to make enquiries about the validity of cards, specifically whether or not they are present in the database and whether or not they have been marked as illegal. The BANK module therefore provides two new visible operations for these checks:

CardKnown : BankDb x AtmCard -> Boolean

CardLegal : BankDb x AtmCard -> Boolean

The ATM_USER module

We turn now to the specification of the ATM facilities in the ATM_USER module. The first step is to ask what the possible events at an ATM are in order to determine what operations are needed to allow that sequence of events to take place. We shall identify the significant events in a customer's transaction at an ATM and then ensure that there are operations to carry out each event. Thus,

- the bank customer supplies a card which has to be known to the bank and must be a legal card [event 1];
- a PIN is entered which must match the card [event 2];
- if the PIN does not match the card, the card should be rendered unusable [event 3];
- otherwise, the customer can order a check book [event 4a], order a statement [event 4b], ask for the balance of their account [event 4c] or withdraw some cash [event 4d];
- if cash is requested, the amount must not exceed the balance of the account or the bank's limit and must be a multiple of 5 [event 5].

We propose the following operations for these events:

Event	Operation
event 1	CardKnown and CardLegal (in the BANK module)
event 2	PINOK
event 3	RetainCard (in the BANK module)
event 4a	atm_OrderCBook
event 4b	atm_OrderStatement
event 4c	atm_Balance
event 4d	atm_Withdraw
event 5	AmountOK

The new operations are as follows:

```
atm_OrderCBook : BankDb x AtmCard x PIN -> BankDb

atm_OrderStatement : BankDb x AtmCard x PIN -> BankDb

atm_Balance : BankDb x AtmCard x PIN -> Amount union String

atm_Withdraw : BankDb x AtmCard x PIN x Amount -> BankDb
```

These four operations are visible in the module; they provide the main customer facilities required at the ATM. atm_OrderCBook adds the account number on the card to the bank's list of ordered check books, while atm_OrderStatement adds the account number to the bank's list of ordered statements. atm_Balance and atm_Withdraw make available balance enquiry and cash withdrawal, much as in the underlying banking facilities.

The subsidiary (hidden) operations are

```
PINOK : AtmCard x PIN -> Boolean

AmountOK : BankDb x AtmCard x Amount -> Boolean
```

With these new objects and operations, we proceed to the specification step.

11.3.2 The Specify step – design 2

We tackle this in two stages corresponding to the two modules identified in the Model step.

The BANK module

The bank database has become more complicated, in that it now has to hold general information about the state of the bank as well as account information. That is, the bank now has to maintain the account information, the bank's limit on the amount a customer may withdraw from an ATM, a list of illegal cards, the outstanding requests for check books and the outstanding requests for statements. What changes does this require in the representation of the bank database?

First, we consider how to represent the constituent parts of the bank database.

The account information can be represented by a map, as before. In consultation with the bank, we decide that customers will not be able to register more than one request for a check book or for a statement at a time. Because duplicate requests are not permitted and order is immaterial, the two collections of outstanding requests can be represented by sets, in this case, by sets of account numbers.

Now we can consider the new representation of the bank database. In the previous iteration, the database was the collection of accounts; now it contains that original collection together with two new collections and other information. These parts of the database are not all of the same type, so suitable representations for the database would be as a record or a tuple. Because records have named fields and the associated selection and update operations are supplied automatically, we find it convenient to represent the bank database as a record.

```
BankDb = record (accts:map(AccNo,Account),
                 limit:Amount,
                 illegal:set(AtmCard),
                 statements:set(AccNo),
                 cbooks:set(AccNo))
```

Note that, although customer names are no longer recorded, account information must now note the cards for each account. The remaining representations are as follows:

```
Account  = tuple(set(AtmCard),Amount)
AtmCard = record(acc:AccNo, cid:CardNo, pin:PIN)
Amount   = Integer
CardNo, AccNo, PIN = Nat
```

Representing bank databases and cards as records means that they have to be declared in the machine-readable part of the specification. This results in the automatic provision of operations for manipulating records of type BankDb and of type AtmCard. The declarations are:

```
BankDb :: accts limit illegal statements cbooks ;

AtmCard :: acc cid pin ;
```

Recall that this will allow field selection using these field names, as in accts(bdb), that instances of the records can be created by the operations mk_BankDb and mk_AtmCard, that instances of the records will be checked against their invariants and that fields in a record instance can be changed using the upd_ operations.

With these representations, we can redefine the record invariant on the bank database to enforce our intention that PINs and card numbers must be unique within the bank:

```
inv_BankDb : BankDb -> Boolean
inv_BankDb(bdb) ==
  let all_cards == { c | a <- rng(accts(bdb)),
                         c <- first(a) }
  in let cids == { cid(c) | c <- all_cards },
         pins == { pin(c) | c <- all_cards }
     in (card)cids) = card(all_cards))
        and
        (card(pins) = card(all_cards)) ;
```

This invariant ensures that there are no duplicate card numbers or PINs by collecting them together in two separate sets and checking that there is one card number and one PIN for each known card. It does not prohibit overlap between card numbers and PINs, however. If we wish to extend the restriction, the invariant becomes

```
inv_BankDb(bdb) ==
  let all_cards == { c | a <- rng(accts(bdb)),
                         c <- first(a) }
  in let cids == { cid(c) | c <- all_cards },
         pins == { pin(c) | c <- all_cards }
     in (card(cids) = card(all_cards))
        and
        ((card(pins) = card(all_cards))
        and
        ((cids inter pins) = {})) ;
```

All of the existing operations are retained in this iteration of the design, but most of them are affected by the changes in representation given above. We start by respecifying OpenAccount:

```
OpenAccount(bdb,acc) ==
  if   AcctKnown(bdb,acc)
  then bdb
  else upd_accts(bdb, accts(bdb) overwr {acc -> ({},0}) ;
```

As before, this checks that the account does not already exist before adding it, except that now it uses the operation AcctKnown introduced in this iteration of the design. The expression accts(bdb) extracts the account information from the database, and a new version of the database is created by the upd_accts operation which overwrites the accts field to include the new account number and its empty account.

The functionalities of the other operations from the first design are unchanged but the specifications have to be modified in line with the new representations as follows:

```
NewBankDb() == mk_BankDb({}, 0, {}, {}, {}) ; % zero limit

CloseAccount(bdb,acc) ==
  if   AcctKnown(bdb,acc) and (second(bdb[acc,("",0)]) = 0)
  then upd_accts(bdb,accts(bdb) ds {acc})
  else bdb ;

Deposit(bdb,acc,amt) ==
  if   AcctKnown(bdb,acc)
  then let acct == accts(bdb)[acc]
       in upd_accts(bdb,accts(bdb) overwr
                                  {acc -> (first(acct),second(acct) + amt)})
  else bdb;

Balance(bdb,acc) ==
  if   AcctKnown(bdb,acc)
  then second(accts(bdb)[acc])
  else "no such account" ;
```

In order to be consistent with the other operations, Balance now makes use of the new hidden operation, AcctKnown, to guarantee that the account is present in the database. The Withdraw operation is unchanged from the previous iteration and so is omitted here.

The next pair of operations removes the outstanding orders for statements and check books:

```
CBooksOrdered(bdb) == upd_cbooks(bdb,{}) ;

StatementsOrdered(bdb) == upd_statements(bdb,{}) ;
```

As far as the bank database is concerned, clearing the backlog of orders simply involves removing the orders from the database – the mechanics of printing statements, registering check books and supplying these items to customers are not of interest here and so are not included in our model.

The operations for card handling are as follows. IssueCard checks that the account identified on the card is known before adding the card to the set of cards available for that account:

```
IssueCard(bdb,c) ==
  if   AcctKnown(bdb,acc(c))
  then let acct == accts(bdb)[acc(c)]
       in let new == upd_accts(bdb,accts(bdb) overwr
                              {acc(c) -> (first(acct) union {c},
                                          second(acct))})
          in if inv_BankDb(new) then new else bdb
  else bdb ;
```

RetainCard adds the given card to the set of illegal cards while ReleaseCard removes it from that set:

```
RetainCard(bdb,c) == upd_illegal(bdb,illegal(bdb) union {c}) ;

ReleaseCard(bdb,c) == upd_illegal(bdb,illegal(bdb) diff {c}) ;
```

Finally in the BANK module, we specify the operations which make the various checks required:

```
AcctKnown(bdb,acc) == acc member dom(accts(bdb)) ;

CardKnown(bdb,c) ==
  AcctKnown(bdb,acc(c)) and
  (c member first(accts(bdb)[acc(c),({},0)])) ;

CardLegal(bdb,c) == not(c member illegal(bdb)) ;
```

The ATM_USER module

Now we turn to the specification of the new ATM_USER module. This imports the BankDb and AtmCard objects from the BANK module (along with their associated record manipulation operations). It also imports the checking operations CardKnown and CardLegal, together with Balance and Withdraw to support their ATM counterparts.

First we specify the visible operations.

```
atm_OrderCBook(bdb,c,p) ==
  if   (CardKnown(bdb,c) and PINOK(c,p)) and CardLegal(bdb,c)
  then upd_cbooks(bdb,cbooks(bdb) union {acc(c)})
  else bdb ;
```

The group of checks in this operation are standard checks that are going to reappear in every ATM user operation. Consequently, we package them together in a new hidden operation TransactionOK which we add to the model:

```
TransactionOK : BankDb x AtmCard x PIN -> Boolean
```

With this operation available, the specifications of the ordering operations are

```
atm_OrderCBook(bdb,c,p) ==
  if   TransactionOK(bdb,c,p)
  then upd_cbooks(bdb,cbooks(bdb) union {acc(c)})
  else bdb ;

atm_OrderStatement(bdb,c,p) ==
  if   TransactionOK(bdb,c,p)
  then upd_statements(bdb,statements(bdb) union {acc(c)})
  else bdb ;
```

Ordering a check book or statement adds the account number from the card to the appropriate collection in the bank database. Because these collections are sets, adding a new account number is achieved using the union operator. Since union amalgamates two sets, the account number is first made into a singleton set by the expression {acc(c)}. Note that using a set to represent these collections means that multiple requests by a customer will be lost, since only one check book and one statement may be on order for an account at any given time.

A balance enquiry simply makes use of the BANK operation Balance:

```
atm_Balance(bdb,c,p) ==
  if   TransactionOK(bdb,c,p)
  then Balance(bdb,acc(c))
  else "transaction refused" ;
```

Similarly, the withdrawal operation makes use of the BANK Withdraw operation, but some additional checks on the amount requested have to be made:

```
atm_Withdraw(bdb,c,p,amt) ==
  if   TransactionOK(bdb,c,p) and AmountOK(bdb,c,amt)
  then Withdraw(bdb,acc(c),amt)
  else bdb ;
```

Finally we have to specify the hidden operations which perform the checks required:

```
PINOK(c,p) == pin(c) = p ;

TransactionOK(bdb,c,p) ==
  (CardKnown(bdb,c) and PINOK(c,p)) and CardLegal(bdb,c) ;
```

```
AmountOK(bdb,c,amt) ==
  ((amt < limit(bdb)) and ((amt mod 5) = 0))
  and (amt <= second(accts(bdb)[acc(c),({},0)])) ;
```

The two modules have now been specified and it is time to test them.

11.3.3 The Validate step – design 2

Testing the BANK module
We rerun all the test cases for OpenAccount from the first iteration which yields, as expected, the bank database

```
MK_BANKDB({1 -> ({},0), 2 -> ({},0), 5 -> ({},0), 8 -> ({},0)},
          0, {}, {}, {} )
```

The different presentation is due to the change in representation of the bank database. Of the five fields, the bank limit is set to zero, there are no illegal cards and the two collections of orders are empty at present. Running the remaining transactions from the first iteration returns equivalent results (i.e. the balances are as before and no other information has been changed in the database):

```
MK_BANKDB({1 -> ({},0), 5 -> ({},99), 2 -> ({},-25)},
          0, {}, {}, {} )
```

Having tested the modified operations, we move on to the new operations. The operations CBooksOrdered and StatementsOrdered deal with customers' orders. However, we cannot test them effectively without the ordering operations in the ATM_USER specification; we therefore defer these test cases until that specification is tested.

Next we test the operations for creating and manipulating cards. We need to create some cards to begin with:

```
c11 == mk_AtmCard(1, 12, 123) ;
c12 == mk_AtmCard(1, 23, 234) ;
c13 == mk_AtmCard(1, 34, 345) ;
c24 == mk_AtmCard(2, 45, 456) ;
c55 == mk_AtmCard(5, 56, 567) ;
c57 == mk_AtmCard(5, 78, 789) ;
c86 == mk_AtmCard(8, 67, 678) ;
```

With these cards available, we can test IssueCard. After each call below, we check that the database is correct.

```
db == IssueCard(db,c11) ;  % valid – first card
db == IssueCard(db,c12) ;  % valid – second card
db == IssueCard(db,c13) ;  % valid – third card
db == IssueCard(db,c24) ;  % valid
db == IssueCard(db,c55) ;  % valid
db == IssueCard(db,c24) ;  % no effect – card already issued
db == IssueCard(db,c86) ;  % error – no such account
```

Also we test that we can mark a card as being illegal (and therefore make it unusable) and then make it legal again; the database is checked after each call:

```
db == RetainCard(db,c11) ;
db == RetainCard(db,c13) ;
db == ReleaseCard(db,c11) ;  % illegal card
db == ReleaseCard(db,c55) ;  % legal card - no effect
```

At the end of this group of tests, the database has the value

```
MK_BANKDB({5 -> ({MK_ATMCARD(5,56,567)},99),
           1 -> ({MK_ATMCARD(1,12,123),
                  MK_ATMCARD(1,34,345),
                  MK_ATMCARD(1,23,234)},0),
           2 -> ({MK_ATMCARD(2,45,456)},-25)},
           0, {MK_ATMCARD(1,34,345)},{}, {})
```

The only operations remaining in the BANK specification are those testing error conditions:

```
? AcctKnown(db,1) ;     % a/c in bank
= TRUE ;
? AcctKnown(db,5) ;     % a/c in bank
= TRUE ;
? AcctKnown(db,8) ;     % a/c closed
= FALSE ;
? AcctKnown(db,12) ;    % a/c never existed
= FALSE ;

? CardLegal(db,c11) ;   % was illegal but okay now
= TRUE ;
? CardLegal(db,c55) ;   % never illegal
= TRUE ;
? CardLegal(db,c13) ;   % card illegal
= FALSE ;
? CardLegal(db,c86) ;   % unissued card
= TRUE ;
```

This last case shows that the definition of legality of a card does not depend on the card being known to the bank. However, there is already an operation to check this:

```
? CardKnown(db,c11) ;         % yes
= TRUE ;
? CardKnown(db,c13) ;         % yes (but illegal)
= TRUE ;
? CardKnown(db,c86) ;         % no such account
= FALSE ;
? CardKnown(db,c57) ;         % card never issued
= FALSE ;
```

The testing strategy above has verified that the BANK specification is behaving as required, so we move on to test the operations in the ATM_USER specification.

Testing the ATM_USER module

We start by testing the hidden operations which check for error conditions:

```
? PINOK(c12,234) ;                  % valid
= TRUE ;
? PINOK(c13,345) ;                  % valid
= TRUE ;
? PINOK(c55,234) ;                  % error
= FALSE ;

? AmountOK(db,c55,20) ;             % error – bank limit zero
= FALSE ;
? db == upd_limit(db,50) ;          % reset limit
= DB ;
? AmountOK(db,c55,20) ;             % now call is valid
= TRUE ;
? AmountOK(db,c55,60) ;             % error – over bank limit
= FALSE ;
? AmountOK(db,c55,12) ;             % error – not multiple of 5
= FALSE ;
? AmountOK(db,c24,10) ;             % error – overdraft exists
= FALSE ;
? AmountOK(db,c11,5) ;              % error – over balance
= FALSE ;

? TransactionOK(db,c11,123) ;       % valid
= TRUE ;
? TransactionOK(db,c11,234) ;       % error – wrong PIN
= FALSE ;
? TransactionOK(db,c13,345) ;       % error – illegal card
= FALSE ;
? db == ReleaseCard(db,c13) ;       % card legal again
= DB ;
? TransactionOK(db,c13,345) ;       % call valid now
= TRUE ;
? TransactionOK(db,c86,678) ;       % error – no such a/c
= FALSE ;
? TransactionOK(db,c57,789) ;       % error – unissued card
= FALSE ;
```

The above tests demonstrate that these subsidiary operations are behaving as required. We now test the four user operations, starting with those for ordering check books and statements, and checking the value of the database after each call:

```
db == atm_OrderCBook(db,c12,234) ;  % valid
db == atm_OrderCBook(db,c11,123) ;  % not added again
db == atm_OrderCBook(db,c55,567) ;  % valid
db == atm_OrderCBook(db,c86,678) ;  % error (no such a/c)
```

Note that the earlier tests of the operation TransactionOK mean that we do not have to test every failure condition individually – it is enough to check that the ATM user operations handle a failure as intended. Now we order some statements, again covering the necessary cases: a valid order, a subsequent order and a failure case:

```
db == atm_OrderStatement(db,c24,456) ;  % valid
db == atm_OrderStatement(db,c24,456) ;  % ignored
db == atm_OrderStatement(db,c57,789) ;  % error (no card c57)
```

At this stage, the database has the value

```
MK_BANKDB({5 -> ({MK_ATMCARD(5,56,567)},99),
           1 -> ({MK_ATMCARD(1,34,345),
                  MK_ATMCARD(1,12,123),
                  MK_ATMCARD(1,23,234)},0),
           2 -> ({MK_ATMCARD(2,45,456)},-25)},
          50,{},{2},{1,5})
```

To test atm_Balance, we make several valid calls:

```
? atm_Balance(db,c11,123) ;  % valid
= 0 ;
? atm_Balance(db,c13,345) ;  % same a/c, other card
= 0 ;
? atm_Balance(db,c24,456) ;  % valid
= -25 ;
? atm_Balance(db,c55,567) ;  % valid
= 99 ;
```

and an invalid call:

```
? atm_Balance(RetainCard(db,c11),c11,123) ;
= transaction refused ;
```

We make the following calls to test atm_Withdraw, again checking the database after each call. We have already tested AmountOK and TransactionOK, the constituent parts of the condition in the operation, so we include only one failure case for each of them:

```
db == atm_Withdraw(db,c55,567,20) ;  % valid
db == atm_Withdraw(db,c24,456,10) ;  % error - overdraft
db == Deposit(db,2,60) ;             % clear overdraft
db == atm_Withdraw(db,c24,456,10) ;  % valid
db == atm_Withdraw(db,c86,678,10) ;  % error - no a/c
```

As we test atm_Withdraw, it occurs to us that there is another situation when an ATM can refuse to dispense cash, namely when it has no more cash available. We note this omission from the requirements.

All that remains is to test order handling in the operations CBooksOrdered and StatementsOrdered in the BANK specification. Each operation is tested with orders present in the database and with no orders present, checking the database after each call:

```
db == CBooksOrdered(db) ;       % clears list
db == StatementsOrdered(db) ;   % clears list
db == CBooksOrdered(db) ;       % no further change
db == StatementsOrdered(db) ;   % no further change
```

The database now has the value

```
MK_BANKDB({5 -> ({MK_ATMCARD(5,56,567)},79),
           1 -> ({MK_ATMCARD(1,12,123),
                  MK_ATMCARD(1,23,234),
                  MK_ATMCARD(1,34,345)},0),
           2 -> ({MK_ATMCARD(2,45,456)},25)},
          50, {}, {}, {} )
```

This completes our testing of the two specifications created in this second iteration of the design.

We have completed our design according to the statement of requirements, having provided all the facilities and security measures requested. In the process, we have discovered a failure condition not mentioned in the requirements. The bank confirms that this is an omission from the requirements, so we embark on a third iteration to rectify this.

11.4 The third design

This iteration is to address the restriction, not explicitly stated in the requirements, that the amount of cash available for withdrawal is limited by the amount of money the ATM is currently holding. When the ATM exhausts its supply, it has to refuse customers' attempts to withdraw cash, irrespective of any other conditions stipulated for withdrawal. At the same time, there should be some mechanism to allow an ATM to be restocked. As we consider these issues, we see that another question not covered by the original requirements is 'Can an individual bank install more than one ATM?'. If it can, what effect does that have on our model?

11.4.1 The Model step – design 3

The unresolved issues above are going to necessitate some substantial changes to the ATM model constructed in the previous two iterations. Recording the amount of money held in an ATM implies that some object will be needed to represent an ATM, whereas up to now the ATM has not been explicit in the model (and has probably been seen as 'just' the user interface to the operations provided by the bank).

If ATMs are to be distinct objects in a bank, then it will be necessary to distinguish between data specific to an ATM and data belonging to the bank. For example, the account information clearly belongs to the bank. Alternatives such as restricting a customer to use of a specific ATM, or holding and managing duplicated information among the ATMs, do not seem to be reasonable options. On the other hand, the amount of money currently held in an ATM is clearly ATM-specific. If the orders for check books and statements were made specific to an ATM, either this would result in allowing customers to order more than one statement or check book by using different ATMs or the system would have to merge the collections of requests centrally to eliminate duplicate requests. We decide to avoid these complications by retaining this information in the bank database, which coincides with our intuition that this is not ATM-specific information.

With these thoughts in mind, the list of objects becomes

BankDb	the bank database

Atm	ATM-specific information
AtmId	ATM identifier

with other objects as before.

What new operations are going to be required? There is to be a check on an ATM's cash supplies:

```
EnoughCash : Atm x Amount -> Boolean
```

which determines whether or not the ATM has sufficient cash for a given transaction. In addition, we provide the bank staff with two operations which allow cash to be added to or removed from an ATM:

```
AddCash : Bank x AtmId x Amount -> Bank

RemoveCash : Bank x AtmId x Amount -> Bank
```

AddCash increases the amount held by the ATM and RemoveCash decreases the amount held by the ATM. All these operations are in the BANK module.

Although we suspect that more changes may be needed, it is not obvious what they are at the moment, so we move on to the Specify step.

11.4.2 The Specify step – design 3

The BANK module

The model of the bank has to change to accommodate the new Atm object. As our design team debates how to incorporate the new object in the representations of the model, it is agreed that adding ATM descriptions to the bank database would be straightforward enough, but would not reflect the fact that the database and ATMs are distinct entities belonging to a particular bank. Accordingly, we try introducing a new object: a Bank, which owns a collection of one or more ATMs and a bank database.

```
Bank = tuple(BankDb,map(AtmId,Atm))
BankDb = record(accts : map(AccNo,Account),
                limit : Amount,
                illegal : set(AtmCard),
                statements : set(AccNo),
                cbooks : set(AccNo))
Atm = Amount
AtmId = String
```

with all other objects as in the previous iteration. For now, there does not seem to be any ATM-specific information other than the amount of cash available to be dispensed so we represent an ATM by the amount of money it contains. Because we require access to individual ATMs, they need some form of identification within the bank, so they are held in a map indexed by an identifier.

The redefinition of the record invariant inv_BankDb introduced in the previous iteration of the design remains unchanged: it continues to guarantee the uniqueness of card numbers and PINs known to the bank.

As we go on to consider the operations in the model, it becomes clear that the introduction of the Bank object affects many of the operations in the model – some will now apply to a bank, some may apply to ATMs and others to the bank database. Thus, this clarification of what is meant by the objects in the model requires that we abandon the specification of this module and return to the Model step.

The ATM_USER module
Changes are also needed in the ATM_USER module, arising from the potential multiplicity of ATMs. In the bank, each ATM has an identifying name. When a customer engages in a transaction, we need to know what ATM is in use. In reality, of course, the ATM is selected when a customer walks up to it and inserts their card. In our specification, we model this by making each atm_ operation identify the ATM to be used. At the moment, only the atm_Withdraw operation has any effect on an ATM (reducing the amount of cash it is holding), but for consistency and to allow for possible future enhancements, it is decided to make all ATM transactions identify themselves.

11.4.3 The Model step revisited – design 3

Our first step is to reconsider the modularization of the design. Because we have added new objects, the Bank and the Atm, we need to incorporate operations to make a new bank, add ATMs and a bank database, and so on. We decide to split the BANK module into two parts: the BASIC_BANK specification creates and manipulates the basic objects in the model while BANK_STAFF provides the banking staff operations. ATM_USER remains as before.

The BASIC_BANK module
This specification 'owns' all the objects in the design as listed earlier; the other modules import them as necessary. It has an operation to create the bank object:

```
NewBank : -> Bank
```

and dispenses with NewBankDb which is no longer needed. Informed by our earlier attempt at this third design, we do not anticipate needing operations to make ATMs (because each ATM simply consists of an amount) or bank databases or cards (because they are to be represented as records). We do expect, though, to need to update the value of an ATM or a bank database so we provide these facilities in the operations:

```
ReplaceAtm : Bank x AtmId x Atm -> Bank
ReplaceBankDb : Bank x BankDb -> Bank
```

The enquiry operations are presently supplied with the bank database. We could have them all operate on the bank instead, but most of them are subsidiary operations, called from within the main bank transaction operations, and the result would be repeated extraction of the bank database from the bank. For now at least, we decide to leave them as they stand. There is also the new operation EnoughCash:

```
EnoughCash : Atm x Amount -> Boolean
```

and, in line with the other enquiry operations, we provide a new operation which checks that a named ATM is known to the bank:

```
AtmKnown : Bank x AtmId -> Boolean
```

The BANK_STAFF module

All the remaining operations of the BANK module in the second design are now in this module. Those which previously accepted a BankDb parameter are changed to take a Bank parameter. That is,

```
OpenAccount : Bank x AccNo -> Bank
Deposit : Bank x AccNo x Amount -> Bank
Withdraw : Bank x AccNo x Amount -> Bank
Balance : Bank x AccNo -> Amount union String
CloseAccount : Bank x AccNo -> Bank
CBooksOrdered : Bank -> Bank
StatementsOrdered : Bank -> Bank
IssueCard : Bank x AtmCard -> Bank
RetainCard : Bank x AtmCard -> Bank
ReleaseCard : Bank x AtmCard -> Bank
```

In addition, there are the two new operations for managing cash stocks in an ATM:

```
AddCash : Bank x AtmId x Amount -> Bank
RemoveCash : Bank x AtmId x Amount -> Bank
```

The ATM_USER module

The only changes in this module are that the atm_ operations are supplied with a Bank instead of a BankDb and additionally need to be given an AtmId naming the ATM in use. The atm_ operations now have functionality

```
atm_Withdraw : Bank x AtmId x AtmCard x PIN x Amount -> Bank
atm_Balance : Bank x AtmId x AtmCard x PIN -> Bank union String
atm_OrderCBook : Bank x AtmId x AtmCard x PIN -> Bank
atm_OrderStatement : Bank x AtmId x AtmCard x PIN -> Bank
```

As in the BANK_STAFF module, we decide that the subsidiary operations in this module will still operate on a BankDb and so are unchanged in this iteration.

The entire module has now been revised to include the new Bank and Atm objects and we can return to the Specify step.

11.4.4 The Specify step revisited – design 3

The BASIC_BANK module

The representations of the objects in the model are unchanged from our previous attempt at this iteration so that we require the following record declarations:

```
BankDb :: accts limit illegal statements cbooks ;
AtmCard :: acc cid pin ;
```

Note that if we had chosen to represent the Bank object by a record rather than by a tuple, we would not need the operation ReplaceBankDb since its function would be performed by an upd_ operation. Because of our decision to use a tuple to represent a bank, we also introduce operations to access the constituent parts of a bank: the selector operations bdb and atms:

```
bdb : Bank -> BankDb
bdb(b) == first(b) ;

atms : Bank -> map(AtmId,Atm)
atms(b) == second(b) ;
```

adding their functionalities to the model.

We start with operations for making and updating banks and their components:

```
NewBank() == (mk_BankDb({}, 0, {}, {}, {}),{}) ;

ReplaceAtm(bank,aid,atm) ==
  (bdb(bank),atms(bank) overwr {aid -> atm}) ;

ReplaceBankDb(bank,db) == (db,atms(bank)) ;
```

The existing enquiry operations remain as in the previous iteration, with the addition of:

```
EnoughCash(atm,amt) == atm >= amt

AtmKnown(bank,aid) == aid member dom(atms(bank)) ;
```

The BANK_STAFF module

Now that these operations are supplied with a Bank object, they have to extract the database from the bank before manipulating or using it and then, if the value of the database is changed, construct a new Bank object containing the new BankDb object. Remember that the database itself is specified as in the previous iteration of the design, so its manipulation and use is unchanged. The original operations are rewritten as follows:

```
OpenAccount(bank,acc) ==
  let db == bdb(bank)
  in if    AcctKnown(db,acc) then bank
     else ReplaceBankDb(bank,
                           upd_accts(db,accts(db) overwr {acc -> ({},0)})) ;

CloseAccount(bank,acc) ==
  let db == bdb(bank)
  in if    AcctKnown(db,acc) and (second(db[acc,(" ",0)]) = 0)
     then ReplaceBankDb(bank,upd_accts(db,accts(db) ds {acc}))
     else bank ;

Deposit(bank,acc,amt) ==
  let db == bdb(bank)
  in if    AcctKnown(db,acc)
     then let acct == accts(db)[acc]
          in  ReplaceBankDb(bank,
                               upd_accts(db,accts(db) overwr
                                   {acc -> (first(acct),second(acct) + amt})))
     else bank ;
```

```
Withdraw(bank,acc,amt) == Deposit(bank,acc,-amt) ;

Balance(bank,acc) ==
  if   AcctKnown(bdb(bank),acc)
  then second(accts(bdb(bank))[acc])
  else "no such account" ;
```

Handling orders simply constructs a new bank with a suitable value for the bank database – there is no need to refer to the existing value:

```
CBooksOrdered(bank) ==
  ReplaceBankDb(bank,upd_cbooks(bdb(bank),{})) ;

StatementsOrdered(bank) ==
  ReplaceBankDb(bank,upd_statements(bdb(bank),{})) ;
```

Next we have the operations for card handling:

```
IssueCard(bank,c) ==
  let db == bdb(bank)
  in if    AcctKnown(db,acc(c))
     then let acct == accts(db)[acc(c)]
          in let new == upd_accts(db,accts(db) overwr
                              {acc(c) ->
                               (first(acct) union {c},second(acct))})
             in if   inv_BankDb(new)
                then ReplaceBankDb(bank,new) else bank
     else bank ;

RetainCard(bank,c) ==
  ReplaceBankDb(bank,
                upd_illegal(bdb(bank),illegal(bdb(bank)) union {c})) ;

ReleaseCard(bank,c) ==
  ReplaceBankDb(bank,
                upd_illegal(bdb(bank),illegal(bdb(bank)) diff {c})) ;
```

Two new operations are provided for managing cash stocks, and our first task is to consider their preconditions. In both operations, one case to consider is when the named ATM is not present in the bank. We can either allow the transaction to succeed, creating a new ATM in the process, or we could insist that the ATM has already been created using ReplaceAtm and fail the transaction. We decide it is more realistic to insist that ATMs should be set up explicitly and choose the latter option. For RemoveCash, there is another condition to consider, namely when the amount requested exceeds the ATM's supply. We cannot allow removal of the requested amount – an ATM cannot have an overdraft – but we still have two options. We can refuse the transaction or we can permit staff to remove what cash there is. We choose this second option. The operations are therefore specified as

```
AddCash(bank,aid,amt) ==
  if   AtmKnown(bank,aid)
  then ReplaceAtm(bank,aid,atms(bank)[aid] + amt)
  else bank ;
```

```
RemoveCash(bank,aid,amt) ==
  if    AtmKnown(bank,aid)
  then let atm == atms(bank)[aid]
       in if    atm < amt
          then ReplaceAtm(bank,aid,0)
          else ReplaceAtm(bank,aid,atm - amt)
  else bank ;
```

The ATM_USER module

The specification of this module is affected by three changes: the use of the Bank object in place of a BankDb, the identification of individual ATMs and accounting for money removed from an ATM. The first point to note is the addition of a new check to the precondition operation TransactionOK, since we do not wish to allow non-existent ATMs to be named in these operations:

```
TransactionOK : Bank x AtmId x AtmCard x PIN -> Boolean
TransactionOK(bank,aid,c,p) ==
  CardKnown(bdb(bank),c)
  and (PINOK(c,p)
  and (CardLegal(bdb(bank),c)
  and AtmKnown(bank,aid))) ;
```

We alter the model to reflect this change in functionality.

atm_Withdraw now needs to check that the ATM has sufficient funds to meet the request. If all the checks succeed, the requested amount is removed from the ATM's stocks:

```
atm_Withdraw(bank,aid,c,p,amt) ==
  if    TransactionOK(bank,aid,c,p)
        and AmountOK(bdb(bank),c,amt)
  then if    EnoughCash(atms(bank)[aid],amt)
       then Withdraw(RemoveCash(bank,aid,amt),acc(c),amt)
       else bank
  else bank ;
```

atm_Balance is also modified to take the ATM identifier parameter, which it hands on to TransactionOK; there are no other changes.

```
atm_Balance(bank,aid,c,p) ==
  if    TransactionOK(bank,aid,c,p)
  then Balance(bank,acc(c))
  else "transaction refused" ;
```

The operations for handling orders for check books and statements are essentially the same as in the previous iteration, but now the bank has to be decomposed (to extract the bank database) and then reconstructed:

```
atm_OrderCBook(bank,aid,c,p) ==
  let db == bdb(bank)
  in if    TransactionOK(bank,aid,c,p)
     then ReplaceBankDb(bank,
                        upd_cbooks(db,cbooks(db) union {acc(c)}))
     else bank ;
```

```
atm_OrderStatement(bank,aid,c,p) ==
  let db == bdb(bank)
  in if    TransactionOK(bank,aid,c,p)
     then ReplaceBankDb(bank,
              upd_statements(db,statements(db) union {acc(c)}))
     else bank ;
```

11.4.5 The Validate step – design 3

As in the second iteration, there are two classes of tests to be run: regression tests, which demonstrate that the design retains the functionality of the previous version, and tests of the new facilities added in this iteration.

The BASIC_BANK module

The new facilities in this module are concerned with banks and ATMs – we test these by creating a bank:

```
? b == NewBank() ;
= B ;
? b == ReplaceAtm(ReplaceAtm(b,"atm1",100),"atm2",200) ;
= B ;
? b == ReplaceBankDb(b,upd_limit(bdb(b),200)) ;
= B ;
```

which results in the bank

```
( MK_BANKDB({},200,{},{},{}),
  {"atm1" -> 100, "atm2" -> 200} )
```

with two ATMs and a bank limit of $200. This allows us to test the new operations EnoughCash and AtmKnown. Note that testing EnoughCash requires us to extract the relevant ATM explicitly from the bank:

```
? EnoughCash(atms(b)["atm1",0],50) ;    % valid
= TRUE ;
? EnoughCash(atms(b)["atm1",0],150) ;   % too much for "atm1"
= FALSE ;
? EnoughCash(atms(b)["atm2",0],150) ;   % valid for "atm2"
= TRUE ;
? EnoughCash(atms(b)["atm3",0],50) ;    % no such atm
= FALSE ;

? AtmKnown(b,"atm1") ;
= TRUE ;
? AtmKnown(b,"atm3") ;
= FALSE ;
```

We leave regression testing of the other operations until we have created an instance of a bank which possesses some accounts.

The BANK_STAFF module

Regression testing in this module consists of substituting the bank b for the bank database db in the tests created for the previous iteration. Rerunning these amended tests produces equivalent results, yielding the bank

```
( MK_BANKDB({5 -> ({MK_ATMCARD(5,56,567)},99),
             1 -> ({MK_ATMCARD(1,12,123),
                    MK_ATMCARD(1,23,234),
                    MK_ATMCARD(1,34,345)},0),
             2 -> ({MK_ATMCARD(2,45,456)},-25)},
           200,{MK_ATMCARD(1,34,345)},{},{}),
  {"atm1" -> 100,"atm2" -> 200 })
```

Note that the cash in the ATMs is unchanged, as no ATM transactions have taken place yet.

With this bank b, we can now test the remaining operations in the BASIC_BANK module. The only change required to the test script is to substitute bdb(b) for db in the calls as these operations still take a bank database as a parameter. We rerun the tests and find that they all return the same results as before.

Returning to the BANK_STAFF module, its new facilities allow bank staff to control the amount of cash held in an ATM. We make the following calls, involving ATMs which exist in the bank, checking the value of the bank after each call:

```
b == AddCash(b,"atm1",500) ;          % stock = 600
b == AddCash(b,"atm2",25) ;           % stock = 225
b == RemoveCash(b,"atm2",200) ;       % stock = 25
b == RemoveCash(b,"atm1",700) ;       % stock = 0
```

resulting in the following cash stocks in the ATMs in b:

```
{"atm1" -> 0, "atm2" -> 25 }
```

since the attempt to remove $700 from "atm1" emptied that ATM. Next, we test the case where the named ATM does not exist in the bank:

```
b == AddCash(b,"atm4",50) ;
b == RemoveCash(b,"atm3",75) ;
```

The bank is, as required, unchanged by these transactions.

The ATM_USER module

There are no major new facilities in this module so the main task is to rerun the previous tests, substituting b for db in the calls on the appropriate operations and supplying an ATM identifier in the atm_ calls. One of the original withdrawals fails because it is requested at an ATM with insufficient cash, so we extend the testing by replenishing the ATM concerned:

```
b == atm_Withdraw(b,"atm1",c55,567,20) ;   % fails, no cash
b == AddCash(b,"atm1",200) ;               % stock = 200
b == atm_Withdraw(b,"atm1",c55,567,20) ;   % valid
```

and add another to test that TransactionOK detects an invalid ATM identifier:

```
? TransactionOK(b,"atm4",c11,123)
= FALSE ;
```

At the end, the bank has value

```
( MK_BANKDB({5 -> ({MK_ATMCARD(5,56,567)},79),
             1 -> ({MK_ATMCARD(1,12,123),
                    MK_ATMCARD(1,23,234),
                    MK_ATMCARD(1,34,345)},0),
             2 -> ({MK_ATMCARD(2,45,456)},25)},
            200,{MK_ATMCARD(1,34,345)},{},{}),
  {"atm1" -> 170,"atm2" -> 25 })
```

This completes our testing of this third iteration of the design, having given us confidence that the specifications satisfy the stipulated requirements. Other facilities, restrictions and modifications could be added in further iterations; however, this design has now served its purpose of illustrating the method in use, so we make no further changes.

11.5 Summary

The procedure followed in this chapter shows a typical approach to a design undertaken with *me too*. Initially only a small part of the problem was considered and a first model was developed. Validating the specification revealed an oversight; when suitable corrections were made, this first model was considered to be an adequate basis for going on to design the functionality which would meet the remaining requirements for the ATM.

The second iteration was intended to complete the design of the ATM and indeed it met the original requirements. However, the activity of specification illuminated the fact that those requirements were incomplete and that the design would have to be extended.

In the third iteration, the complexity of the principal objects increased. When their representations were considered, it became clear that these changes affected many of the operations in the model. Accordingly, the specification was discarded and the third iteration restarted with this additional feedback. Making these changes did not prove difficult or time-consuming, and the resulting design meets the requirements supplied.

Clarifying requirements, feedback from validation, detecting omissions, incremental construction of the design – these are all consequences of applying the *me too* method. Also, the example has underlined the point that the iterative loop of the method is not restricted to that shown in Fig. 4.1 but can occur at almost any stage in the method. In the first iteration, an error in the specification was corrected before completing the validation. In the third iteration, the specification was discarded before validation and the model was reconsidered.

Furthermore, the changes within and between iterations were achieved rapidly. Had it proved necessary, the entire model could have been abandoned and the design restarted. The effort invested in each iteration of the design is sufficiently small that designers have the freedom to radically alter the entire design in the light of lessons from earlier iterations.

Chapter 12

Case study 1 – networks and protocols

This chapter shows how *me too* has been used as a means of exploring new ideas to determine their potential for future investment. It describes a relatively small and simple specification from the area of network design, originally undertaken by an industrial design team. The discussion of this specification necessarily differs from those given earlier, as the authors were not present to observe how the method was applied or what testing was undertaken. Consequently, the design is presented as supplied by the design team. We then examine how it might be modified to explore alternative solutions.

12.1 Introduction

The work reported in this case study was undertaken by a project team in ICL's Network Systems Division and shows the application of *me too* to a networking problem. Of course, *me too* is not the only specification method which can be applied to network problems. Many other means of describing network applications have been used, ranging in formality from varieties of state transition diagrams (ISO, 1985), through Petri nets (Diaz, 1982), to LOTOS (Turner, 1987) and Z (Till and Potter, 1987). However, *me too* was chosen by the team because it provided an opportunity to explore the feasibility of a new system at low cost, despite the overhead of training the team in the use of the method. Another reason for choosing *me too* was the additional benefit of producing a working prototype.

12.2 The domino problem

In setting up computer networks, it is often necessary to connect unlike components, which do not 'speak' the same protocols. At one end of the spectrum, the difficulty might be in connecting an unusual printer to a PC, but the same issues arise when configuring a large network over many sites.

The end result of this connection problem is that there is a multitude of different kinds of adaptor boxes and cables, capable of connecting unlike components. These range from simple 'gender changers', that is, plug-to-socket adaptors, to highly complex and expensive network gateways. Figure 12.1 illustrates the principle, where a single adaptor is sufficient to connect the two components. Here

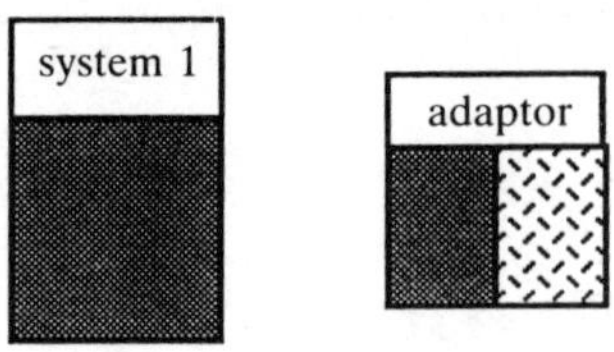

Figure 12.1 A single adaptor between systems.

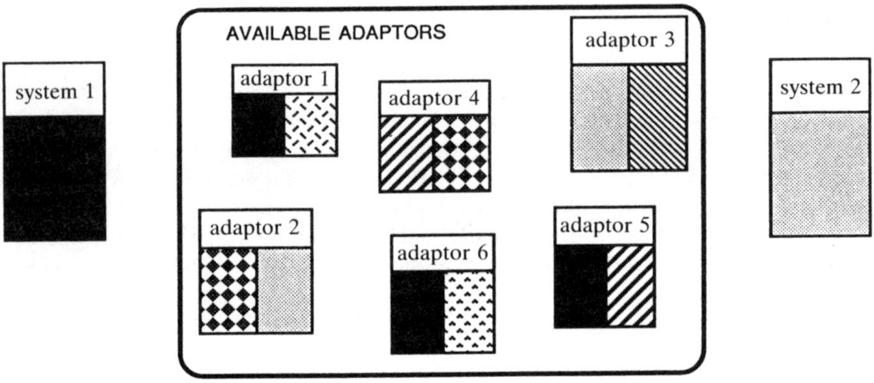

Figure 12.2 A more complicated case.

Figure 12.3 The required set of adaptors.

system 1 and system 2 are incompatible, and need an adaptor which allows communication between the different end-systems.

However, there may not be such an adaptor available. In such circumstances, it might be necessary to create a chain of adaptors between the two systems to be connected. Indeed, there are benefits in offering a standard set of adaptors which together solve a range of interconnection problems. The problem then for the network engineer is the selection of a suitable set of adaptors between end-systems. Fig. 12.2 gives an example where the engineer has to choose from an assortment of gateway components to connect the systems.

The solution for this example is given in Fig. 12.3. It shows why the problem has been called the 'domino' problem, since the task for the engineer is like selecting dominoes which match end-to-end and which create a path between the two fixed end-points.

Network Technology Unit (NTU) in ICL Network Systems wished to assess the feasibility of developing a tool to help the network engineer to identify an appropriate set of adaptors when configuring and connecting a network. The NTU design team decided to use *me too* as a prototyping mechanism in order to establish the feasibility of the tool and to demonstrate a pilot system.

12.3 The domino specification

The specification is explained, rather than developed, in this section. That is, we do not proceed through the steps of the *me too* method, but present the entire specification as delivered by the NTU designers.

First, then, what abstract objects are to be part of a tool to solve the domino problem? An obvious choice is a Domino, which will have to contain some information about the systems which it is able to connect. The network engineer is also concerned about the two end-systems which have to be connected. These are represented by EndSystem objects. Finally, for now, we require some means of holding the collection of dominoes from which the network engineer may choose, the domino database Db.

Next, we consider the representation of these initial objects. The choices here depend on what constitutes the 'pattern' of a domino, that is, the attributes of a domino which make it distinctive. In the world of networks, these properties are defined as protocols by ISO standards for Open Systems Interconnection (OSI). OSI sets out various layers of protocols, but only two aspects are relevant here: the upper application layers and the lower interconnection layers. The application layers define what kind of activity is happening (such as file transfer) while the interconnection layers define how the connections supporting the applications are achieved. In this chapter, we refer to these two aspects as the application and transport layers. A domino is constrained to operate at a single application layer; that is, only dominoes for one particular kind of application layer can be connected together. Within this, the two 'sides' of a domino are defined by the connections it can make in the transport layer.

There are standard pieces of information which define the interfaces of these layers, and the object representations below make use of these standard forms. Thus, a domino holds information about the connections it can make in the following record:

```
Domino = record (name:Name, upper:AppType,
                 tt1:TransType, tt2:TransType)
```

The upper field identifies the application layer supported by the domino, while the tt1 and tt2 fields describe the two types of connection possible in the lower transport layer. The dominoes from which the network engineer may select are held together in the database:

```
Db = set(Domino)
```

The details of the possible transport layer connections are held in the TransType object:

```
TransType = record(prot:Protocol, attr:Attribute)
```

These objects have introduced a number of subsidiary objects, which in this prototype are simply held as strings:

```
Name, AppType, Protocol = String
Attribute = { "NULL", "+", "−" }
```

For example, the application type might be "ftf" to indicate file transfer or "v" for voice. Protocols include ICL's CO3, IBM's SNA, and international standards such as X25. Attributes could have many forms, but for the purposes of this study, it was sufficient that they indicate the *gender* of the connection – positive, negative or not-applicable – in order to allow for asymmetric protocols which can be connected only in matched pairs.

EndSystem objects are similar to dominoes, in that they are defined as operating for particular application and transport layers, but obviously they only know one kind of connection in the transport layer, given here in the field bottom:

```
EndSystem = record(top:AppType, bottom:TransType)
```

Now we have to consider how the various objects will be used. The first requirements are simply to be able to create a domino database, to add dominoes to the database and to remove them:

```
mk_Db : -> Db
mk_Db() == {} ;

add_domino : Db x Domino -> Db
add_domino(db,d) == db union {d} ;

del_domino : Db x Name -> Db
del_domino(db,n) == { d | d <- db; name(d) /= n } ;
```

How are dominoes to be matched alongside each other? The first step is to inspect the necessary values of fields in the dominoes. Recall that declaring the records defined above automatically generates operations to create the records, for example, mk_Domino, and to extract the fields by name, as in upper or attr. The following additional selection operations are used to extract the specific information needed from the lower transport layer definitions:

```
prot1 : Domino -> Protocol
prot1(d) == prot(tt1(d)) ;

prot2 : Domino -> Protocol
prot2(d) == prot(tt2(d)) ;

gender1 : Domino -> Attribute
gender1(d) == attr(tt1(d)) ;

gender2 : Domino -> Attribute
gender2(d) == attr(tt2(d)) ;
```

The matching of dominoes is tackled in the next group of operations, each of which checks one aspect of the connection. The matches operation ensures that the application layers are the same and calls gender_match to check the transport layers.

```
matches : Domino x Domino -> Boolean
matches (d1,d2) ==
  (upper(d1) = upper(d2)) and gender_match(d1,d2) ;
```

gender_match handles only one aspect of the layer, ensuring that the protocol for the second part of the first domino can be matched to the protocol for the first part of the second domino, e.g. both are X25, both are CO3, etc., before calling another operation, connectable, to check the attributes of the layers.

```
gender_match : Domino x Domino -> Boolean
gender_match(d1,d2) ==
  (prot2(d1) = prot1(d2))
  and
  connectable(gender2(d1),gender1(d2)) ;
```

Finally, in this section, connectable ensures that either the protocols are symmetric or that asymmetric protocols are correctly matched.

```
connectable : Attribute x Attribute -> Boolean
connectable(a1,a2) ==
  ((a1="NULL") and (a2="NULL"))
  or
  (((a1 = "+") and (a2 = "-"))
   or
   ((a1 = "-") and (a2 = "+")) ) ;
```

These operations give us the means to see if dominoes may be placed next to each other. The network engineer, though, has to see how dominoes can be placed between end-systems. One option would be to specify versions of all these operations which take an end-system in the first or second domino position. This would give rise to a family of several similar operations. Or the operations could be more complicated, and distinguish between dominoes and end-systems supplied as parameters.

The NTU team chose a third option, though, which takes an end-system and creates, in effect, a 'one-sided' domino from it. In fact, to take care of the right- and left-handedness of the end-systems, they introduced two operations, one for each end of the chain. The conversion operations are fromES which takes a left-hand end-system at the start of the chain and turns it into a domino, and toES which takes the end-system at the end of the chain and creates a domino from it, as illustrated in Fig. 12.4.

The operations are specified as:

```
fromES : EndSystem -> Domino
fromES(e) == mk_Domino ("ES1",top(e),"dummy",bottom(e)) ;

toES: EndSystem -> Domino
toES(e) == mk_Domino("ES2",top(e),bottom(e),"dummy") ;
```

Now all the operations can deal solely with dominoes.

The first step in extracting a chain of dominoes from one end-system to the other is to specify a way of stepping from one domino to the next, that is, finding all the possible successors to a given domino:

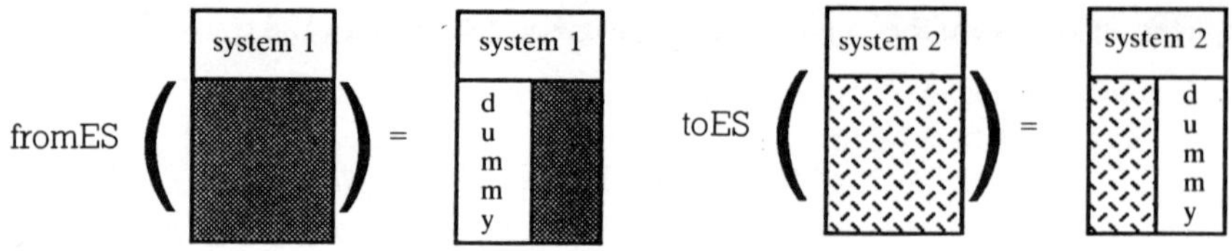

Figure 12.4 Converting end-systems to dominoes.

```
successors : Domino x Db -> set(Domino)
successors(d,db) ==
  { dl | dl <- db ; matches(d,dl) } ;
```

It starts from a given domino and extracts each domino from the database in turn (by the expression dl <- db), collecting together all the ones which can be set to the right of the given domino, indicated by matches(d,dl) returning the value true.

With these operations, we can now set about producing the kind of answers needed by the network engineer. Consider what is required: to be able to supply the two end-systems plus a collection of dominoes and be given back the names of all the dominoes (in order) which are needed to link the end-systems. This determines the functionality of the gateways operation:

```
gateways : EndSystem x EndSystem x Db -> Route
```

In this definition, a new abstract object has been introduced – the ordered collection of dominoes which have to be chained together, called a Route. Because it involves specifying an order, it is represented by a sequence; in this case, a sequence of the names of the dominoes required:

```
Route = seq(Name)
```

To find the best chain of dominoes between two end-systems, we find all the possible orderings of dominoes that will have the desired effect and pick one of them. Thus, gateways is specified as:

```
gateways : EndSystem x EndSystem x Db -> Route
gateways(e1,e2,db) ==
  find_shortest(find_routes(fromES(e1),toES(e2),db)) ;
```

find_routes is the most complicated operation in the design. It starts from the left-hand end-system (converted to look like a domino) and searches through the database for all possible successors. When it finds a successor, its name is added to the front of all routes returned from a recursive call on find_routes, starting this time from the chosen successor. This is a standard algorithm from graph theory (Harary, 1969). Thus, dl always holds the current left-hand end of the chain. In order to prevent cyclic chains, as a domino is used in a route, it is removed from the database being used for that route. Each branch of the search ends when the current left-hand side (dl) matches the domino for the end-system (which is always held in d2).

```
find_routes : Domino x Domino x Db -> set(Route)
```

```
find_routes(d1,d2,db) ==
  if    matches(d1,d2)
  then { [] }
  else { [name(next)] conc r | next <- successors(d1,db),
                               r <- find_routes(next,d2,
                                        del_domino(db,name(next))) } ;
```

Given a set of possible routes, the network engineer has to select one. There may be many bases for this decision, not least the cost of the components and whether the engineer is employed by the seller or the buyer of components. For simplicity, in this version of the design NTU decided to choose the shortest route, that is, the one involving the least number of connecting components.

```
find_shortest : set(Route) -> Route
find_shortest(rs) ==
  the ({ r | r <- rs; len(r) = len_of_shortest(rs) }) ;

len_of_shortest : set(Route) -> Integer
len_of_shortest(rs) ==
  min reduce (999) { len(r) | r <- rs } ;

min : Number x Number -> Number
min(a,b) == if a < b then a else b ;
```

len_of_shortest creates a set containing all the lengths of the routes supplied, and then extracts the minimum length from the new set. The expression

```
min reduce (999) S
```

is an application of set reduction with the function min, which determines the smallest integer is the set S. We assume that all routes in S have length less than 999. The operation find_shortest then searches the set of routes to find the shortest one.

However, there is a problem with this algorithm. If there is only one route of this length, using the the operator will extract it. If there is more than one, the cannot be applied as the result is undefined. This situation arises because we have not made our selection criteria strong enough to support the design decision that the engineer is to be returned a single answer. Either we must give the tool more information on which to base its choice, sufficient to ensure that only one route meets those criteria, or the tool must return the choice of routes and allow the network engineer to make the decision. This second alternative yields the changed operations:

```
gateways : EndSystem x EndSystem x Db -> set(Route)
gateways(e1,e2,db) ==
  find_shortest(find_routes(fromES(e1),toES(e2),db)) ;

find_shortest : set(Route) -> set(Route)
find_shortest(rs) ==
  { r | r <- rs; len(r) = len_of_shortest(rs) } ;
```

where now a set of routes is returned as the result. Using the is no longer necessary.

Having presented the NTU specification, its properties can now be examined by testing it. For the sake of space, the details of the low-level testing are omitted here. The first step is to create some end-systems and a collection of dominoes:

```
e1 == mk_EndSystem("ftf",mk_TransType("co3","-")) ;
e2 == mk_EndSystem("ftf",mk_TransType("oslan","NULL")) ;
e3 == mk_EndSystem("ftf",mk_TransType("x25","+")) ;
e4 == mk_EndSystem("voice",mk_TransType("v24","NULL")) ;
e5 == mk_EndSystem("voice",mk_TransType("oslan","NULL")) ;

db == mk_Db() ;
db == add_domino(db,
                 mk_Domino("r1","ftf",
                           mk_TransType("co3","+"),
                           mk_TransType("x25","-"))) ;
db == add_domino(db,
                 mk_Domino("r2","ftf",
                           mk_TransType("x25","+"),
                           mk_TransType("oslan","NULL"))) ;
db == add_domino(db,
                 mk_Domino("r3","ftf",
                           mk_TransType("co3","-"),
                           mk_TransType("x25","+"))) ;
db == add_domino(db,
                 mk_Domino("r4","ftf",
                           mk_TransType("x25","+"),
                           mk_TransType("co3","+"))) ;
db == add_domino(db,
                 mk_Domino("r5","ftf",
                           mk_TransType("v24","NULL"),
                           mk_TransType("oslan","NULL"))) ;
db == add_domino(db,
                 mk_Domino("r6","ftf",
                           mk_TransType("pstn","NULL"),
                           mk_TransType("v24","NULL"))) ;
db == add_domino(db,
                 mk_Domino("r7","ftf",
                           mk_TransType("x25","-"),
                           mk_TransType("v24","NULL"))) ;
```

Now it should be possible to construct routes between the systems by means of the dominoes:

```
? gateways(e1,e2,db) ;        % omits [r1,r4,r3,r7,r5]
= {[r1,r2]} ;
? gateways(e1,e3,db) ;        % only route
= {[r1]} ;
? gateways(e3,e2,db) ;        % only route
= {[r7,r5]} ;
? gateways(e3,e1,db) ;        % fails for given orientation
= {} ;
? gateways(e4,e5,db) ;        % no "voice"-level dominoes
= {} ;
```

and indeed gateways acts as expected.

At this stage, having created a specification which achieved their purpose, the NTU team ended their investigations. Had time been available, it would have been perfectly reasonable for them to revisit some of the decisions made and explore some alternative arrangements. In the course of design, for example, they might have noted that the name of a domino is used only to label it, and that holding it in the domino itself complicates the specification of some of the operations. We consider some other possibilities for revising the specification in the next section.

12.4 Revising the specification

More radical changes than the one suggested above are indicated by two deficiencies in the specification. The first is that the conversion of end-systems to dominoes is ungainly, requiring dummy names and not one but two conversion operations. The second deficiency was discovered during execution of the prototype and is illustrated in Fig. 12.5. The domino at the top would connect the end-systems in the middle but not those at the bottom. Yet the only difference is that the order of the end-systems has changed. This point was illustrated by the test case gateways(e3,e1,db) which fails to produce a route despite the fact that gateways(e1,e3,db) succeeds. This suggests that some mechanism for considering both orientations of a domino is needed.

We try addressing both these problems by making a single change to the model. Consider removing the concept of right- and left-sidedness from a domino and simply noting the two possible connections for the transport layer. The two transport layer fields are replaced by the lower field:

```
Domino = record(name:Name, upper:AppType,
                lower:set(TransType))
TransType = record(prot:Protocol, attr:Attribute)
```

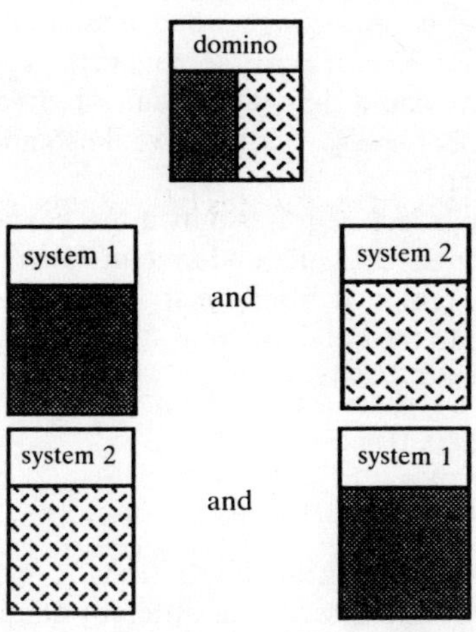

Figure 12.5 Reversing the order of end-systems.

This has the added advantage that it can be generalized to end-systems as well – the lower field for an end-system will be a singleton set containing the TransType for its transport layer connection. What changes are needed in the rest of the specification? In the gateways operation, the calls to fromES and toES are removed:

```
gateways : EndSystem x EndSystem x Db -> set(Route)
gateways(e1,e2,db) ==
  find_shortest(find_routes(e1,e2,db)) ;
```

No other changes are needed until the detailed checks at the transport layer are considered in gender_match and connectable. Indeed, since connectable deals with just a pair of attributes, it seems that only gender_match will have to be altered.

As we consider what changes are necessary, we recall how these matching operations are used by the successors operation. There is a given domino (the current end of the chain reaching out from the first end-system) and successors attempts to find another domino from those remaining to place alongside it as the next link in the chain. Thus the domino from which we are attempting to move *must* have a fixed orientation in the transport layer. That is, once a domino has been selected, it has to be clear which 'side' has been matched and which has become the new end of the chain. It is still possible to represent the side of a domino or end-system by a set, as above, but since sets have no concept of order it seems appropriate to explore an alternative representation.

The approach taken here is to give the domino an arbitrary order to begin with which can later be reversed ('flipped') if necessary. In addition, we still wish to avoid special operations pertaining to end-systems, as in our previous attempt. Accordingly, we make the following definitions:

```
Domino,EndSystem = record(name:Name, upper:AppType,
                          lower:Connection)
Connection = tuple(TransType,TransType) union TransType
TransType = record(prot:Protocol, attr:Attribute)
```

where the difference between end-systems and dominoes lies, as before, in the lower field. A domino has a pair of possible connections (in some order) and an end-system has just one. We could change the name of this abstract object to reflect its dual rôle, to Component or Node say, but to save time and editing, we leave it as a Domino in this development.

It turns out that this approach requires only a few changes to the specification. As before, gateways no longer uses the end-system conversion operations. These conversion operations are removed from the specification.

When adding a domino to the database now, it is necessary to check that it is not already present in its 'flipped' form:

```
add_domino : Db x Domino -> Db
add_domino(db,d) ==
  If flip(d) member db then db else db union {d} ;
```

Note that this, as in the NTU definition of add_domino, regards dominoes with the same 'pattern' but different names as being different dominoes.

The change in representation means that we have to be able to distinguish between dominoes and end-systems. The test for an end-system examines the lower field to see if it contains a single TransType record:

```
is_EndSystem : Domino -> Boolean
is_EndSystem(d) == is_TransType(lower(d)) ;
```

where is_TransType is an operation provided as a result of declaring the TransType record.

The tt1 and tt2 operations were previously provided as field selectors for the Domino record. They are respecified as follows:

```
tt1 : Domino -> TransType
tt1(d) ==
  if is_EndSystem(d) then lower(d) else first(lower(d)) ;

tt2 : Domino -> TransType
tt2(d) ==
  if is_EndSystem(d) then lower(d) else second(lower(d)) ;
```

As a result of providing these low-level operations capable of handling both types of component in the chain, no other changes are needed to the matching operations.

The only other issue is the consideration of both views of a domino when searching for a domino to be placed at the current end of the chain. The selection of dominoes is done by successors so this is where dominoes may need to be flipped:

```
successors : Domino x Db -> set(Domino)
successors(d,db) ==
  {d1 | d1 <- db; matches(d,d1) }
  union
  {flip(d1) | d1 <- db; matches(d,flip(d1)) } ;

flip : Domino -> Domino
flip(d) ==
  if    is_EndSystem(d)
  then d
  else upd_lower(d,(tt2(d),tt1(d))) ;
```

This completes the revised version of the Domino specification. We test it again, using the previous data, suitably altered to use the new representations. That is, both dominoes and end-systems are created by mk_Domino. For example, the e1 end-system is defined by

```
e1 == mk_Domino("e1","ftf",mk_TransType("co3","-")) ;
```

and the r2 domino is defined by

```
mk_Domino("r2","ftf",
            (mk_TransType("x25","+"),
             mk_TransType("oslan","NULL")) ) ;
```

The testing shows that gateways continues to handle the previous cases correctly. In addition, flipped dominoes are not added to the collection of dominoes and gateways yields the correct results irrespective of the order in which the end-systems are supplied.

12.5 Summary

The NTU design team produced a prototype which was acceptable to them, yielding answers to the questions they had posed about the potential value and cost of such a tool. The design was achieved relatively quickly – in a matter of days – given that this was their first use of *me too*. Using the *me too* notation forced the designers to clarify the exact nature of the objects being modeled and the functions needed, without the vagueness or ambiguity usually associated with such an early stage of development. Given a prototype, the team was able to demonstrate the kind of tool which could be provided to solve the domino problem.

Often the most difficult part of system development is establishing the requirements for a new product. One approach is to explore and evaluate ideas, expressed informally at first, perhaps, by producing prototypes of the system. The specification of the domino tool is an example of how *me too* can be used in this way, transforming vague initial ideas into a demonstration of the product. In this, the work by NTU confirmed similar experiences reported by Bonet and Kung (1984) and Gomaa (1983).

Chapter 13

Case study 2 – a database application

What were all the world's alarms
To mighty Paris . . . ?
W.B. Yeats

A legitimate issue in respect of any design method concerns whether or not it can be applied to existing systems as well as to entirely new systems. In particular, can the method be used to design enhancements to existing systems? This chapter describes specifications which were created to explore proposed changes to a database system which had already developed through two versions. The exercise is also of note because it was undertaken not by a technical or design team but within a quality assurance group.

13.1 Introduction

International Computers Limited markets and supports a wide range of hardware and software products. In order to support them, a reliable and accessible record of faults, alerts, problems, solutions, repairs, avoidance actions and so on has to be kept. 'PARIS' is ICL's Problem And Resolution Information System, a database containing support and maintenance information covering their entire software and hardware product range (Denny, 1987). It has been developed by ICL's Group Information Systems (GIS), as an internal product for use within ICL. This section outlines the context in which PARIS is used and then looks at some of the demands on the system which led to the exploratory work described in this chapter.

When a customer reports a problem, there are two groups involved in the resolution process. The problem is initially reported to a customer support unit whose task is to determine whether or not a solution is already known; that is, if it is already registered in PARIS. If it is, they pass the solution on to the customer. If no solution is found, the report is sent to the product support unit (PSU) responsible for the product in question. Once they have determined a solution, the necessary entries are placed in the PARIS database for future reference and the solution is given to the customer.

Quite apart from the necessary task of recording such information, a key feature of PARIS is its search capabilities. It contains information about a great many products, each of which may exist in more than one version and be available in more than one system environment. Problems may manifest themselves by a variety of symptoms, not all of which may be apparent to or reported by an individual customer when a fault is notified. Support units have to be able to supply partial descriptions of a fault and still be able to retrieve its solution, if it is present in PARIS.

The existing PARIS system is based on a sophisticated Codasyl network database product. In providing search facilities, the design both relies on and is constrained by the design of the network of data structures in the database. That is, the network can be designed to accommodate complex searches, but once the database is designed and populated it can be difficult to add new search strategies. Even if new searches can be added, the existing network structure may not offer acceptable performance.

An alternative, more flexible approach would be to hold the information in a relatively unstructured way, and offer fast and powerful search procedures for scanning it. Such facilities are provided by ICL's Content Addressable File Store. which allows rapid searching of large volumes of data based on the contents of the data rather than on its location in the store. As a further development of PARIS, called 'devolved PARIS', it was proposed that some exploration be made of the possibility of using this alternative data storage as the basis of the search facilities. That exploration was undertaken using *me too*.

The team undertaking this design had two objectives in specifying the functionality of PARIS. The first was to demonstrate the applicability of *me too* to database problems. Secondly, they had to specify a search operation which did not rely on navigation paths through the database. Both of these were subject to the constraint that the specification had to be completed within a (relatively short) agreed timescale, to ensure that excessive resources were not spent on the exercise.

13.2 Overview of PARIS

It should be noted at the start that in considering the objects and operations for PARIS, the model was heavily constrained by the existing system. Accordingly, we begin by describing PARIS in more detail.

At the heart of PARIS lies its catalog of **support knowledge entries** (SKEs), each of which identifies a particular fault or problem and, if a solution is known, points to the solution or action required to resolve it. A SKE is found by traversing a complex network of information relating to the location, type and symptoms of the problem. In devolved PARIS, that network is simplified into a flat file structure, but first it is necessary to introduce the various SKE-finding concepts, since they have been retained in the *me too* model.

The maintenance system that preceded PARIS had several disadvantages. It held information against components, with the description of the problem and solution in free-format text. As a result, the quality of data varied a great deal, making it hard to recognize a particular known error or to detect when two entries represented the same error. Secondly, searching for an entry was inefficient, since each entry for the component had to be scanned. The more complex data and network structures in PARIS reflect the need for efficient and accurate searching of the entries, particularly with the trend towards automatic fault diagnosis and correction.

In order both to control the quality of SKE data and to define access routes for retrieving SKEs, PARIS requires that SKEs comply with certain predefined standards. PARIS holds **global SKE standards**, which define the various attributes held by all products recorded in PARIS. However, when a PSU takes on responsibility for supporting a product, it also defines the way in which support knowledge for it is to be held on PARIS. Thus, before a SKE can be created against a particular product, the PSU responsible for the product must define local SKE standards which specify what data is required and the format in which it is to be held.

What constitutes a SKE standard? PARIS recognizes the following classes of information: product-group, entry-class and symptom.

A **product-group** may be a single installable and supported product or it may be a grouping of such products. Product-groups may be organized in hierarchies. For example, a hierarchy is appropriate when representing the VME operating system since this is divided into chapters, each of which is further divided into subsystems, and so on. Product-groups are not only part of the route-finding mechanism for SKEs, however. The SKE standards defined by a PSU are related to a particular level of the hierarchy, that is, the PSU can choose the level of precision at which problems are reported. For VME, therefore, it could be at the system, chapter or subsystem level.

The purpose of an **entry-class** is to group a set of like SKEs. This grouping may be based on such things as cause of failure, problem type or manifestation of failure. For instance, entry-classes based on problem type might be:

1. installation
2. documentation
3. operating failures
4. operating deficiencies
5. enhancement requests.

Keywords can also be defined to act as alternative keys for entry-classes, in case the exact designation is not known.

A **symptom** is a measurable or codifiable manifestation of a product problem, and may be split into symptom-type and symptom-value. For example, an error code might be specified in PARIS by the symptom-type 'EC' whose associated symptom-value represents the actual code returned. Symptom-types can, like entry-classes, have keywords associated with them to aid in locating a SKE. For example, the keywords for the symptom-type EC might be Response, Result and Code. Within product-group and entry-class, the symptom can be further qualified by specifying the format of the value (e.g. numeric or text) and possibly pre-populating the database with valid values (such as the known error codes).

SKEs are retrieved using the function **SearchSKE**. This requests the user to supply the identifying data of a SKE, namely the product-group, entry-class and symptoms.

If all the identifying data cannot be supplied, PARIS will use what is given to narrow the field of search as much as possible and then prompt the user to select from a series of possibilities, such as the list of entry-classes that exist for a specified product-group. The user can either refine the identifying data or request that all possibilities for the unknown data be included in the search.

PARIS also provides a set of functions to perform enquiries on the SKE standards, for example to find an entry-class or symptom-type by keyword or to list the entry-classes that use specified symptom-types. These functions can be used to maintain product SKE standards or to help locate a SKE.

13.3 Specifying devolved PARIS

The design of PARIS given here aimed to incorporate much of the functionality for locating SKEs as described above. However, it takes only a rudimentary view of standards, omitting the concept of global standards so that all standards are stored against product-groups, nor does it handle partial searches.

13.3.1 The model and specify steps

PARIS objects

PARIS is modeled by two data stores, one for the SKEs and the second for SKE standards. The SKE data store consists of the collection of SKEs known to PARIS, each of which contains information about the attributes which can be used to locate it, namely its product-group, entry-class and symptoms. Not surprisingly, the main object is the SKE object, together with a way of grouping SKEs:

```
SKEs = set(SKE)
SKE = record(sid:SKEid, pg:ProdGp, ec:EntryCl, syms:Symptoms)
```

Because SKEs are unique, a collection of them can be represented as a set. In this representation, each SKE contains its identifier as well as its attributes. It might seem that an alternative representation would be to separate the identifier and use it as a means of accessing the SKE:

```
SKEs = map(SKEid,SKE)
```

However, it must be remembered that a SKE is retrieved not by its identifier but by its contents. Indeed, the purpose of the search is to retrieve the SKE identifiers, since these are the index into the solution/action records in the PARIS database. Consequently, the second representation given above is not appropriate. The chosen representation introduces a number of subsidiary objects:

```
Symptoms = map(SymType,set(SymValue))
SKEid = Integer
SymType, ProdGp, EntryCl = String
SymValue = String union Number
```

The second data store records the standards that are laid down for SKEs:

```
Standards = map(ProdGp,ECstandard)
```

Standards are set at the product-group level, but may vary across the different entry-classes, depending on the requirements of each class:

```
ECstandard = map(EntryCl,SKEstd)
SKEstd = map(SymType,Format)
```

Thus, each entry-class for the product-group has a standard for its SKEs, which defines how symptoms can be described in them. This leads to the subsidiary objects:

```
Format = record(mand:Boolean, multi:Boolean, type:ValType, maxv:Integer)
ValType = {"Number", "Text"}
```

For each symptom-type, this notes whether or not it is mandatory, whether or not it may have more than one value, the kind of value it may contain and its maximum value. This latter attribute is relevant only for text values, giving the maximum length of text permitted.

PARIS operations

As indicated in the overview of PARIS, the main operation in the model is SearchSKE, which is given information about a fault and returns the identifiers of any SKEs matching that description:

```
SearchSKE : SKEs x Standards x ProdGp x EntryCl x Symptoms
                                                    -> set(SKEid)
```

where the product-group, entry-class and symptoms supplied are specific to the enquiry being made. The operation is defined to be:

```
SearchSKE(skes,stds,pgroup,eclass,symp) ==
  if    valid_symptoms(stds[pgroup,{}][eclass,{}],symp)
  then { sid(ske) | ske <- skes; SKEmatches(ske,pgroup,eclass,symp) }
  else {} ;
```

This operation extracts the relevant SKE standard; that is, the format with which any enquiry must comply. Since this format also defines how the SKEs appear in the data store, an enquiry matching this format must also match the relevant SKEs. The supplied symptoms are validated against the standard by the subsidiary operation valid_symptoms. If this succeeds, the operation collects together the identifiers of all the SKEs which match the parameters given, delegating the actual comparison to the operation SKEmatches.

First, we consider the validation of the enquiry against the prescribed format:

```
valid_symptoms : SKEstd x Symptoms -> Boolean
valid_symptoms(std,symp) ==
  let mands == { st | (st,fmt) <- std; mand(fmt) },
      singles == { st | (st,fmt) <- std; not(multi(fmt)) },
      nums == { st | (st,fmt) <- std; type(fmt)="Number" },
      texts == { st | (st,fmt) <- std; type(fmt)="Text" }
  in  check_mand(mands,symp)
      and (check_all(dom(std),symp)
      and (check_num(nums,symp)
      and (check_text(texts,symp)
      and (check_single(singles,symp)
      and check_values(std,texts,symp))))) ;
```

This operation extracts from the standard all the relevant information for checking the enquiry and then supplies it to the appropriate check_ operation. Section 13.4

describes an alternative way of specifying the validation of search parameters. However, the subsidiary operations for the original GIS version are those described here.

The first operation compares the names of mandatory symptoms with the names of the symptoms supplied in the enquiry:

```
check_mand : set(SymType) x Symptoms -> Boolean
check_mand(mands,symp) ==
  (mands = {}) or ((symp dr mands) /= {}) ;
```

Until this point, it might have been thought that the 'mandatory symptom-type' flag meant that *each* symptom-type with the flag set has to be supplied as part of the enquiry. The specification of this operation makes it clear that the actual requirement is merely that *at least one* of the symptom-types with the flag set be present in the enquiry. It is possible that there are no mandatory symptom-types for a particular standard; if so, this check has no effect.

The next check ensures that only symptom-types valid for the entry-class have been supplied:

```
check_all : set(SymType) x Symptoms -> Boolean
check_all(alls,symp) == dom(symp) subset alls ;
```

Remember that all SKEs in the data store conform to the appropriate standard. Consequently, this check makes it impossible to supply symptom-types that do not appear in SKEs for the named product-group and entry-class.

In checking the types of symptom-values, it is necessary to consider all the values of each symptom-type since there may be more than one. The GIS team specified the operation as

```
check_num : set(SymType) x Symptoms -> Boolean
check_num(nums,symp) ==
  { sv | (st,svs) <- symp dr nums, sv <- svs; not(is_number(sv)) }
  = {} ;
```

The approach here is to restrict the symptoms to those which should contain numeric values and then collect any values which are not numeric. Since this is a collection of erroneous values, the check fails if the resulting set is not empty.

This can be expressed more simply using set quantification (at the time when the original specification was written, set quantifiers were not available in the *me too* notation):

```
check_num(nums,symp) ==
  all sv in dunion(rng(symp dr nums)) . is_number(sv) ;
```

which says that all the symptom-values for all numeric symptom-types must be numeric. A similar operation checks textual values:

```
check_text : set(SymType) x Symptoms -> Boolean
check_text(texts,symp) ==
  all sv in dunion(rng(symp dr texts)) . is_string(sv) ;
```

Symptom-types which do not have the 'multiple-value' flag set must only have single values supplied:

```
check_single : set(SymType) x Symptoms -> Boolean
check_single(singles,symp) ==
  all svs in rng(symp dr singles) . card(svs) = 1 ;
```

This extracts all the sets of values for symptom-types which do not have the flag set and checks that each of those sets has only one member.

The following operation checks the actual symptom-values supplied. It is only relevant to textual symptom-values as it checks the length of text supplied against the maximum permitted length:

```
check_values : SKEstd x set(SymType) x Symptoms -> Boolean
check_values(std,texts,symp) ==
  let sym_rel == { (st,sv) | (st,svs) <- symp dr texts, sv <- svs }
  in  all (st,sv) in sym_rel . stringlength(sv) <= maxv(std[st]) ;
```

For easier checking of each value, the portion of the symp map relating to text symptom-types is converted to a binary relation. This associates a symptom-type with each of its values separately. These can then be validated individually against the standard. We assume that an operation stringlength is available (see Section 6.2).

The remainder of the specification is concerned with comparing the validated symptoms with SKEs known to the system in order to extract those that are relevant. As specified earlier in SearchSKE, the operation responsible for this is SKEmatches:

```
SKEmatches : SKE x ProdGp x EntryCl x Symptoms -> Boolean
SKEmatches(ske,pgroup,eclass,symp) ==
  (pgroup = pg(ske))
  and ((eclass = ec(ske))
  and (all st in dom(symp) .
          values_match(symp[st],syms(ske)[st,{}]))) ;
```

This compares the product-group, entry-class and symptoms, calling a subsidiary operation values_match to compare the two sets of values:

```
values_match : set(SymValue) x set(SymValue) -> Boolean
values_match(inpv,skev) ==
  (inpv = skev)
  or ((inpv subset skev)
  or (skev subset inpv)) ;
```

This specifies the somewhat unusual relationship between the values in the SKE and those supplied for a particular symptom-type. The obvious case is when both sets are the same size, since all the values must then match (that is, the sets must be equal). When fewer values are supplied than are in the SKE, it is reasonable to conclude that all the values given must be present in the SKE. The less obvious case is when *more* values are given than are in the SKE; here, all the SKE values must be present among those supplied.

This completes the specification of search facilities in the design of devolved PARIS.

13.3.2 Executing the specification

This section demonstrates some of the cases entered in the *me too* shell as part of the validation of this design.

The first step is to define standards for SKEs. There are two product-groups, each of which has an entry-class called "crash" to record program failures and a second entry-class called "doct" to record deficiencies in documentation of the products. The general SKE formats required by these products are defined in an ECstandard:

```
ECstd == { "doct" ->
             {"VOL" -> mk_Format(true,false,"Text",10),
              "PGS" -> mk_Format(false,true,"Number",0)},
           "crash" ->
             {"PN" -> mk_Format(true,true,"Text",10),
              "EC" -> mk_Format(true,true,"Number",0),
              "Desc" -> mk_Format(false,false,"Text",80)} };
```

This general standard states that documentation problems must supply a single volume name and may optionally supply one or more page numbers. A program crash SKE must either name the offending procedure(s) or give the error code(s) or both, and may also give a textual description of the problem. The actual standards for the product-groups are defined as follows:

```
p2_std == ECstd overwr
             {"crash" -> (ECstd["crash"] overwr
                           {"EC" -> mk_Format(true,false,"Number",0)} )} ;

stds == { "prod-1" -> ECstd,
          "prod-2" -> p2_std } ;
```

The first of these definitions specializes one aspect of the "crash" entry-class for the "prod-2" product-group, stating that only one error code may be supplied for such failures. The overall standards are then set up in stds, retaining the general standards for "prod-1" and using the specialized version for "prod-2"; this is the set of standards that is to be supplied when checking enquiries on the SKE database.

The next step is to record all known problems in a SKE database:

```
SKEs ==
  { mk_SKE(1,"prod-1","crash",{"PN" -> {"procX"},
                               "EC" -> {213,214}}),
    mk_SKE(2,"prod-1","crash",{"PN" -> {"procX"},
                               "EC" -> {215}}),
    mk_SKE(3,"prod-1","crash",{"PN" -> {"procV"},
                               "EC" -> {214,216}}),
    mk_SKE(4,"prod-2","crash",{"PN" -> {"procV","procZ"},
                               "EC" -> {215}}) } ;
```

There are four known problems. SKE number 1 says that "procX" in "prod-1" may fail with error code 213 or 214, while SKE number 2 describes a different failure in the same procedure, this time involving error code 215. SKE number 3 notes that "procV" may fail, returning codes 214 or 216. Only one problem is recorded for "prod-2", in SKE number 4, which says that both "procV" and "procZ" can fail with error code 215. With the two data stores SKEs and stds set up in this way, we can attempt to find SKEs that match symptoms supplied in various enquiries.

First we try some invalid data:

```
% no mandatory types supplied
searchSKE(SKEs,stds,"prod-1","crash",{"Desc" -> {"fail"}}) ;

% no such product group
searchSKE(SKEs,stds,"prod-6","crash",{"EC" -> {213}}) ;

% no such entry class
searchSKE(SKEs,stds,"prod-2","install",{"EC" -> {215}}) ;

% multiple values not allowed for prod-2
searchSKE(SKEs,stds,"prod-2","crash",{"EC" -> {213,215}}) ;

% no skes for entry class
searchSKE(SKEs,stds,"prod-2","doct",{"VOL" -> {"vol.1"}}) ;

% numeric value for text symptom-type
searchSKE(SKEs,stds,"prod-2","crash",{"PN" -> {5}}) ;

% text value for numeric symptom-type
searchSKE(SKEs,stds,"prod-2","crash",{"EC" -> {"procZ"}}) ;

% text value too long
searchSKE(SKEs,stds,"prod-2","crash",
          {"PN" -> {"very-long-procedure-name"}}) ;

% unknown symptom-type
searchSKE(SKEs,stds,"prod-2","crash",{"dump" -> {"yes"}}) ;
```

These enquiries all fail as required, returning the empty set to indicate that no matching SKEs were found. Now, can we find a SKE when given valid data? Some test enquiries follow:

```
? searchSKE(SKEs,stds,"prod-1","crash",{"EC" -> {214}}) ;
= {1,3} ;
? searchSKE(SKEs,stds,"prod-1","crash",{"EC" -> {213,214,215}}) ;
= {1,2} ;
? searchSKE(SKEs,stds,"prod-2","crash",{"PN" -> {"procZ"}}) ;
= {4} ;
? searchSKE(SKEs,stds,"prod-1","crash",{"PN" -> {"procX"}}) ;
= {1,2} ;
? searchSKE(SKEs,stds,"prod-1","crash",{"EC" -> {216},
                                         "PN" -> {"procV"}}) ;
= {3} ;
```

and they return the expected answers. The first case supplies fewer values than are held in the relevant standard, while the second case supplies more values than the standard. Both match on one of the two possible symptom-types, while the third case matches with the other symptom-type. The final case matches on the basis of both symptom-types.

The testing of the prototype uncovered no faults in this version of the design. However, lest it be thought that the specification was correct at the first attempt, it should be noted that the design given in this section was the subject of considerable iteration and development by GIS. This was mainly due to their unfamiliarity with formal methods and mathematics in general, and with *me too* in particular. For example, the functional paradigm, with its declarative approach, lack of global state and disavowal of side-effects, was entirely new to the team. However, with the confidence engendered by their first use of *me too*, they are prepared to embark on further applications of the method.

13.4 Revising the specification

The specification given in the previous section satisfied the objectives of the GIS team; however, it is excessively constructive in approach and can be re-written in a more declarative style. By way of illustrating the different styles, we present a second version in this section.

In fact, we retain the search part of the specification as it stands, changing only the operations which validate the symptoms supplied in the search enquiry. We begin by rewriting valid_symptoms as follows:

```
valid_symptoms : SKEstd x Symptoms -> Boolean
valid_symptoms(std,symp) ==
  if    dom(symp) subset dom(std)
  then (has_mand_sym(std) => contains_mand_sym(std,symp))
        and
        (all (st,v) in symp . valid_format(std[st],v))
  else false ;
```

The predicate in the conditional expression replaces the check_all operation from the previous version; if it fails, no further checks are made. The second says that if the standard names any mandatory symptom-types, the symptoms must satisfy the condition in contains_mand_sym; this clause replaces the check_mand operation in the previous version. The last clause says that each symptom value given must conform to the standard for its symptom-type.

Now we specify the new subsidiary operations introduced by this definition; first, the operations concerning mandatory symptom-types:

```
has_mand_sym : SKEstd -> Boolean
has_mand_sym(std) ==
  exists fmt in rng(std) . mand(fmt) ;

contains_mand_sym : SKEstd x Symptom -> Boolean
contains_mand_sym(std,symp) ==
  exists st in dom(symp) . mand(std[st]) ;
```

Finally, we need the operation which validates individual symptom-values against the relevant standard:

```
valid_format : Format x set(SymValue) -> Boolean
valid_format(fmt,values) ==
  (not(multi(fmt)) => (card(values) = 1))
  and
  (((type(fmt) = "Text") =>
    (all v in values . is_string(v) and (stringlength(v) <= maxv(fmt))))
```

```
and
((type(fmt) = "Number") => (all v in values . is_number(v)))) ;
```

The first clause replaces the operation check_single, the second replaces check_text and check_values, and the third replaces check_num.

Together, these operations replace the previous version of valid_symptoms and all its subsidiary operations. No changes have been made to the representations of objects in the model, so we can test the new version of the specification by re-running the previous test cases. The Validate step shows that all tests return the same results as before, so we have demonstrated that the two specifications exhibit the same behavior.

13.5 Summary

This chapter has presented a specification of some aspects of a database product and demonstrates yet another use of *me too*. All the other examples and case studies described in this book were fresh developments, whereas this chapter has presented a specification based on an existing system.

The specification in this chapter is only part of the work undertaken by the GIS team. Together the various designs they produced met their objectives as listed earlier. This highlights an important issue in modeling and prototyping techniques. These activities are only a means to an end. However rewarding, challenging or satisfying they may be, when they have achieved their objectives, it is time to stop and move on from design to the next phase of development. This also underlines the importance of setting those objectives before embarking on the exercise in the first place, otherwise there is no means of determining when it should finish.

Chapter 14

Case study 3 – designing a system architecture

I do not approve of the federal system; it is too perfect.
Simón Bolívar

The case study described in this chapter shows another use of *me too*. Rather than starting with a clean sheet for design, an informally expressed high-level design already existed. The purpose of the work with *me too* was to explore the system concepts in that document in collaboration with the designer responsible for it. It was expected that this exercise would both clarify any issues arising from the informal (English) description of the architecture and identify any omissions and ambiguities. In addition, this case study demonstrates the application of *me too* to a systems problem, rather than to a single product as in previous chapters.

14.1 Introduction

A federated system is a kind of distributed system, consisting of a collection of computer systems which act together to provide larger-scale computing facilities than could be offered by a single system. However, each member system has an independent life as well as contributing to the federation. There is no single or central repository of information about the federation; instead, a member has to deduce the current situation either from locally stored information or from information passed around by other members. Indeed, it was a design objective of the work described here to ensure that there is no master or global view held in the federation, since this can cause bottlenecks and reduce reliability.

The collaboration described here had two distinct phases. First, *me too* was used to clarify the basic concepts of the federated architecture proposed in McVitie (1987a); that is, the fundamental model of a federated system and how its members relate to each other. This model is called the Fundamental Association Model (FAM) and is described in Section 14.2. The second phase elaborated this model by examining one particular aspect of it, namely some of the security issues arising from allowing many systems potential access to each other.

The overall design resulting from this collaboration is described in Alexander and McVitie (1988). The architecture documents on which the work is based are McVitie (1987a, b) but this chapter introduces the essential concepts underlying the architecture to avoid the need to refer to these documents.

14.2 The Fundamental Association Model

As far as we are concerned, a federated system consists of a number of **servers** which, as their name suggests, offer some kind of service to the overall system. Examples of such services might be electronic mail or word processing at the user level, together with supporting services which administer and maintain the federation and which allow users access to the facilities of the system.

To achieve the offering and subsequent use of some service in the system, there must be some means of connecting servers together. In the FAM, our interest is in establishing the basic concepts underlying such connections.

If two servers are to work together in some activity, they need to be able to communicate with each other. In order to communicate, they first have to be linked in some way. This link is called an **association**; such an association must exist between two servers before they can talk to each other. In any particular association, one of the servers always acts as the provider of a service while the other acts as a user of that service.

Once two servers are associated, a conversation between them can only be held within the context of a **connection** across the association. During the time for which the association exists, there may be one or more connections across it to enable the servers to converse. Thus an electronic mail server may offer a mail service to the entire system, whilst a user of a word-processing server may wish to make use of the mail facilities. An association between the two allows the possibility of sending several word-processed documents by electronic mail, with a separate connection established for mailing each document.

Every connection between two servers is asymmetric in that the server at one end starts the connection process. This server is called the **initiator** while that at the other end is called the **responder**. The responder is the server offering the service to the federated system; the initiator asks to use that service when it asks for a connection.

The FAM describes how a responder and an initiator become associated in the system. In setting up an association, as opposed to using it, the responder acts first, belying its name. That is, the responder decides to offer a service of some kind to the federated system and creates an instance of that service (a **service instance**, or SI). It sends details about the service availability to other servers in the system in a package of information called a **token**. To create an association between the responder and another server, that server (which will subsequently be the initiator of any connections across the association) must receive the token and accept it into its pool of tokens (see Fig. 14.1).

Once the association has been established, the initiator can create connections across it by returning a token to its responder with a request to set up a connection over that association. Either the initiator or the responder may decide to terminate an association. Communication between the associated servers is possible only when a connection is established across the association. Only one connection may

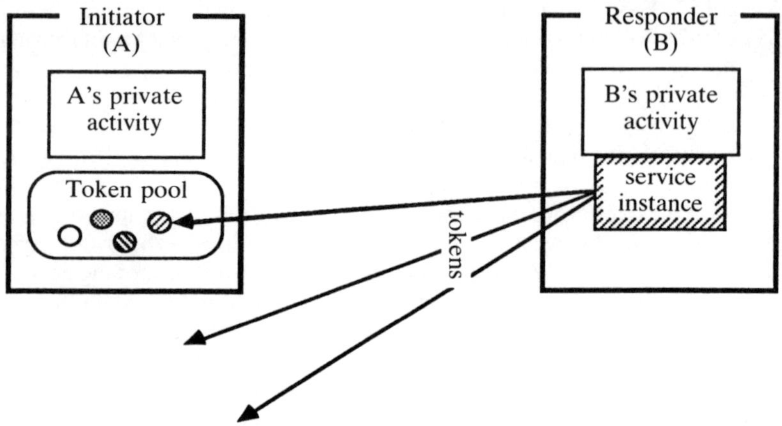

Figure 14.1 Components of an association.

exist across the association at a time, but there may be many such connections during the lifetime of the association.

The above is a basic description of the FAM, derived from that supplied in McVitie (1987a). It was specified in *me too*, resulting in some clarifications and changes to the original description, as presented in the next section.

14.3 Specifying the FAM

The above overview of the FAM is sufficient to allow a simplified version of the specification to be presented. In the process, we show how *me too* led to clarifications in the original design, by explaining some of the changes that were made.

14.3.1 FAM objects

Three basic kinds of objects are identified – namely Server, Token and ServiceInstance (known as an SI, for short). Other objects are introduced mainly to organize these three. For example, a server is held in a database of all servers. This particular organization is purely for convenience and is not intended to imply that a federated system would maintain a single record of all servers in the system. Here is an example of a specification not necessarily indicating how the system would actually be implemented – the model is for the purposes of exploration and establishing concepts rather than specifying an implementation structure for the system.

Server details are extracted from the database using a server identifier ServerId; this can be thought of as a record-key for a server. In this version of the model, a service instance just contains its token.

Thus, the federated system is represented by the collection of servers in the server database. Each server may have a pool of tokens for the associations in which it acts as initiator, having received those tokens from other servers in the system. Each server may also have a collection of service instances (SIs) for the

---

SPECIFY

Objects

```
ServerDb = map(ServerId,Server)
Server = record(tokens:Tokens, SIs:Tokens )
Tokens = map(TokenId,TokenBody)
TokenBody = record(respr:ServerId, initr:ServerId, conn:Status)
Token = record(tkid:TokenId, tkbody:TokenBody)
ServerId, TokenId = String union {"NONE"}
Status = { "REQU", "ACCPT", "ACK", "NONE" }
```

---

associations in which it acts as responder, having offered those services to others in the system. The private data and activities of a server are of no concern and so are omitted.

A complete token consists of an identifier and a body; only complete tokens are sent from one server to another. In a server, though, the identifiers are indices into the server's collection of token bodies. These collections are represented by the object Tokens, which (being a map) makes it clear that the token identifiers are unique. The body of a token records the servers at each end of the association for which it is used and whether or not there is a current connection. The only information required about a service instance is a copy of the token which is sent out to make that service known to other servers, so for now there is no SI object.

The representations of these objects were the result of various decisions about the meaning of statements in the original design and involved several iterations of the specification. For example, the earliest specification of the FAM contained the objects Association and Connection, since these terms are clearly central to the model. Consider how to represent these: an Association could note the names of the two associated servers and whether or not a connection exists across it. A Connection object is probably redundant in this case. But where would systems keep these Associations? Remember that these are *federated* systems and that they hold no global record of their state. Records of an association, then, cannot be held in a single place but must be within the members of the federation, probably in those to which it refers. This effect is achieved by the objects specified here, without explicit Association or Connection objects, since all the relevant information is held in the tokens residing in the servers.

14.3.2 FAM operations

The specification of FAM which follows was an attempt to understand the concepts in the architecture document. During its development, several questions arose regarding issues that were not clear or explicit in the document. As the specification is presented, we highlight areas where *me too* helped to clarify these issues.

The operations are described in a number of related groups. Where the definitions are not relevant to an understanding of the model, only the functionalities are given.

Database and connection status manipulation

```
EmpyDb : -> ServerDb
EmptyDb() == {} ;

AddServer : ServerDb x ServerId x Server -> ServerDb
AddServer(sdb,sid,s) == sdb overwr {sid -> s} ;
```

These operations allow the creation of an empty database and the addition of servers to it.

```
NewConnectI : Server x TokenId x Status -> Server

NewConnectR : Server x TokenId x Status -> Server
```

These operations are provided to update the connection status in a token held in a token pool or service instance. They are for convenience in later parts of the specification, rather than an essential part of the model, and so are not explained here. It is sufficient to note that NewConnectI extracts the indicated token from the token pool, changes the connection status and replaces the token in the pool with the new version, while NewConnectR performs a similar function for a token in a service instance.

Connection checking

These operations check for conditions which affect whether or not a connection can be established. The rules on connection, as specified in this version of the model, were not stringent nor were they particularly realistic. Connection is the most complex aspect of the FAM and was not covered in detail in the document supplied. Consequently, a certain amount of license was exercised in the specification. This area became the subject of further study in the second part of the collaboration.

A connection is deemed to exist (more accurately, to have at least been started) if the token contains a status of "ACK" or "ACCPT":

```
Connected : TokenBody -> Boolean
Connected(tb) ==
  (conn(tb) = "ACK") or (conn(tb) = "ACCPT");
```

ForThisInit is used by an initiator to check that the token it has been given has been accepted into its pool while ForThisResp is used by a responder to check that the token it has been given is for one of its service instances:

```
ForThisInit : Server x TokenId -> Boolean
ForThisInit(I,tid) == tid member dom(tokens(I)) ;

ForThisResp : Server x TokenId -> Boolean
ForThisResp(R,tid) == tid member dom(SIs(R)) ;
```

Handling associations

This section describes the operations needed to create and destroy associations between servers. The specification assumes that some activity in a server decides to offer a service and calls an operation like StartResp to create the service instance and token. This token is then 'sent' (as described below) to a server which is to be the initiator. Receiving and acting upon such a token is modeled by a call on StartInit.

One issue which was unclear in the original design concerned whether or not a responder knows about its partner(s) in advance. In particular, does a responder nominate a specific server or servers to which it offers its services? This arose from the original description, which reads

> *The Association is always invented by the Responder, and so server B [the Responder] thinks that it is associated with server A before server A thinks that it is associated with server B.*

In early versions of the specification given above, the decision was made that the responder would know its potential partners for a service instance (supplied in the call of StartResp) and that that information would also be noted in the token corresponding to that service instance to ensure that only suitable initiators accepted it. That proved to be the wrong decision; to make this clear, the design document was changed to make it explicit that the responder does not know the identity of any potential partners.

To create an association, the responder creates a service instance containing a token for use in communicating across the association:

```
StartResp : ServerDb x ServerId x TokenId -> ServerDb
StartResp(sdb,rid,tid) ==
  let resp == sdb[rid],
      tb == mk_TokenBody(rid,"NONE","NONE")
  in AddServer(sdb,rid,upd_SIs(resp, SIs(resp) overwr {tid -> tb})) ;
```

An association is established by StartInit when an initiator server accepts the token into its pool. A second question arose here, namely whether or not a service instance should record who is its partner at the initiator end. No mention was made of this in the original design. In the *me too* specification, it was decided not to hold this information separately in the responder, but rather to record it in the instance of the token being used for the association, both in the initiator's pool and in the service instance. Accordingly, the token sent to the initiator is modified to record its name so that the responder knows with whom it is conversing when each connection is created:

```
StartInit : ServerDb x ServerId x Token -> ServerDb
StartInit(sdb,iid,tok) ==
  let init == sdb[iid], tid == tkid(tok), tb == tkbody(tok)
  in AddServer(sdb,iid,upd_tokens(init,
                           tokens(init) overwr {tid -> upd_initr(tb,iid)})) ;
```

Either server can terminate the association, as shown in the operation EndAssoc:

```
EndAssoc : ServerDb x ServerId x TokenId -> ServerDb
EndAssoc(sdb,sid,tid) ==
  AddServer(sdb,sid,mk_Server(tokens(sdb[sid]) ds {tid},
                              SIs(sdb[sid]) ds {tid})) ;
```

This removes the token from the pool and from any service instance containing the named token. For any given server and token, only one of these actions will have any effect, depending on whether the server is responder or initiator for the association indicated by the token. Once the association has been ended (by either server), the specification does not permit any further connections to be made. If the responder ends the association, the initiator can attempt to start a connection but the request will not be accepted by the responder. The specification assumes a one–one correspondence between associations and service instances, in that ending an association deletes the service instance.

Handling connections

Connections are started by the initiator, which sets up the token ready for return to the responder. In the specification, this action is modeled by StartConnect which simply sets the connection status to "REQU", for 'requested'. In a real system, we assume that the initiator would also add data pertinent to its intended use of the service.

```
StartConnect : ServerDb x ServerId x TokenId -> ServerDb
StartConnect(sdb,iid,tid) ==
  let I == sdb[iid]
  in if    not(ForThisInit(I,tid))
           or Connected(tokens(I)[tid])
     then sdb
     else AddServer(sdb,iid,NewConnectI(I,tid,"REQU")) ;
```

Connections are accepted or rejected by the responder. The token is 'sent' to the responder (see *Token sending*) using AcceptConnect which checks that the token contains a connection request, that the token is known to one of its service instances and that there is not already a connection over that association:

```
AcceptConnect : ServerDb x ServerId x Token -> ServerDb
AcceptConnect(sdb,rid,tok) ==
  let R == sdb[rid], tid == tkid(tok),
     tb1 == upd_conn(tkbody(tok),"ACCPT")
  in if    not((conn(tkbody(tok)) = "REQU") and ForThisResp(R,tid) )
           or Connected(SIs(R)[tid])
     then sdb
     else AddServer(sdb,rid,upd_SIs(R,SIs(R) overwr
                                        {tid -> tb1}));
```

The final step in establishing a connection is to send an acknowledgement back to the initiator, by means of ConfirmConnect:

```
ConfirmConnect : ServerDb x ServerId x Token -> ServerDb
ConfirmConnect(sdb,iid,tok) ==
  let I == sdb[iid],
     tid == tkid(tok)
  in if    not((conn(tkbody(tok)) = "ACCPT") and ForThisInit(I,tid))
           or Connected(tokens(I)[tid])
     then sdb
     else AddServer(sdb,iid,NewConnectI(I,tid,"ACK")) ;
```

When it comes to ending a connection, the original design document says:

The normal order of termination of a period of connection is . . . where the Responder terminates slightly before the Initiator, although this may not be the case in some error situations.

The specification has to be rather more explicit. As stated here, it allows connections to be ended by either server but it also regards a connection to have been removed only when both servers have agreed to end it.

Connections are normally served by the responder first, using EndConnect, which clears the connection status in the service instance. The connection is completely removed when the initiator also severs it, using DelConnect. This order is not enforced, however – if either server breaks the connection, no further conversation can take place. No connections can be re-established across the association until both servers have ended the existing connection. The operations are:

```
EndConnect : ServerDb x ServerId x TokenId -> ServerDb
EndConnect(sdb,rid,tid) ==
  AddServer(sdb,rid,NewConnectR(sdb[rid],tid,"NONE")) ;

DelConnect : ServerDb x ServerId x TokenId -> ServerDb
DelConnect(sdb,iid,tid) ==
  AddServer(sdb,iid,NewConnectI(sdb[iid],tid,"NONE")) ;
```

The process of connection gave rise to many questions, particularly concerning the security of a connection. This became the focus of attention in the second part of the collaboration and is described in Section 14.4.

Token sending

The design document identifies no explicit mechanism for token passing; in the *me too* design, the action is modeled by extracting a token from a server and then supplying it in a call involving a second server. These two operations extract a token from a server:

```
RespToken : ServerDb x ServerId x TokenId -> Token
RespToken(sdb,rid,tid) ==
  mk_Token(tid,SIs(sdb[rid])[tid]) ;

InitToken : ServerDb x ServerId x TokenId -> Token
InitToken(sdb,iid,tid) ==
  mk_Token(tid,tokens(sdb[iid])[tid]) ;
```

Both operations have to construct a complete token, since extracting it from the token pool or service instance only returns the token body. With these operations, sending the token Token1 from responder B to initiator A can be modeled by the following interaction:

```
? tok1 == RespToken(db,"B","Token1");
= TOK1;
? db == StartInit(db,"A",tok1);
= DB;
```

or alternatively by

```
? db == StartInit(db,"A",RespToken(db,"B","Token1"));
= DB;
```

Similarly the responder is given a token, extracted from the initiator, when asked to accept a connection request.

For convenience in running the prototype, this token-passing mechanism has been encapsulated in three operations, representing the three occasions on which a token is passed between servers: when creating an association, when requesting a connection and when acknowledging a connection. Only the functionalities are given:

```
RespToInit1 : ServerDb x ServerId x ServerId x TokenId -> ServerDb
InitToResp : ServerDb x ServerId x ServerId x TokenId -> ServerDb
RespToInit2 : ServerDb x ServerId x ServerId x TokenId -> ServerDb
```

RespToInit1 extracts the token from the responder and supplies it to the initiator in a call of StartInit, InitToResp extracts the token from the initiator and returns it to the responder in a call of AcceptConnect, and RespToInit2 extracts the token from the responder and returns it to the initiator in a call of ConfirmConnect.

14.3.3 Executing the specification

Calls to set up various associations and connections are given below:

```
db == EmptyDb();
db == AddServer(db,"a",mk_Server({},{}));
db == AddServer(db,"b",mk_Server({},{}));
db == AddServer(db,"c",mk_Server({},{}));
db == AddServer(db,"d",mk_Server({},{}));
db == AddServer(db,"e",mk_Server({},{}));

% start a, b and c as responders
db == StartResp(db,"a","t1");
db == StartResp(db,"b","t2");
db == StartResp(db,"c","t3");

% send tokens to some potential initiators
db == RespToInit1(db,"a","b","t1");
db == RespToInit1(db,"b","e","t2");
db == RespToInit1(db,"a","d","t1");
```

At this point, the database shows that b–a, e–b, and d–a are associated, and that there are no connections. As yet, there is no association with c using token t3 because the token has not been accepted into the token pool of any server. The next step is to try ending associations:

```
db2 == EndAssoc(db,"a","t1");    % valid association
db2 == EndAssoc(db2,"e","t6");   % no such association
```

The database now shows that only e–b are associated. Alternatively, if we call

```
db2 == EndAssoc(db,"b","t2");
```

the database shows that b–a, and d–a are associated.

Now that we can create and remove associations, we test connection handling:

```
% make connections, starting them in the initiator ...
db == StartConnect(db,"b","t1");
db == StartConnect(db,"d","t3");       % no association
```

```
db == RespToInit1(db,"b","a","t2");   % another association
db == StartConnect(db,"e","t2");

% ... and sending the tokens back to the responders
db == RespToInit2(InitToResp(db,"e","b","t2"),"b","e","t2");
db == RespToInit2(InitToResp(db,"b","a","t1"),"a","b","t1");
db == RespToInit2(InitToResp(db,"d","c","t3"),"c","d","t3");
```

After executing these calls, the database shows, as required, that b–a, d–a are associated using token t1 and that a–b, e–b are associated using token t2. Of these, b–a, e–b have connections across them. There is still no association with the responder c.

We end the b–a connection:

```
db == EndConnect(db,"a","t1");
```

but because we have not completely removed it using DelConnect in the initiator b, we cannot restart a connection across this association. Thus

```
db == InitToResp(StartConnect(db,"b","t1"),"b","a","t1") ;
```

fails until after

```
db == DelConnect(db,"b","t1");
```

Further testing shows that after the responder has ended a connection, another initiator associated with it may start a different connection; that after an initiator ends the connection, it may not restart it until the responder has ended it; and that ending an association ends a connection across it.

14.4 Security aspects of connection

In a federated system, one important consideration is that of security, ensuring that only those with permission to access servers do so. In particular, when a connection is requested, some check has to be made concerning the validity of that connection. Is the initiator sure that the responder is sufficiently secure for its needs? Is there a suitable route between the servers that will preserve the security of their conversations? Is the responder prepared to be used by the connecting initiator? McVitie (1987b) addressed these and other questions in order to begin to establish a security mechanism for federated systems.

This was a considerably more complex design task than that of the FAM, but could be built upon the basic model described in the previous section. Rather than give the full *me too* specification for this extended design, which is lengthy, this section looks at some 'edited highlights', picking out the ideas which were established or made clearer as a result of the specification exercise. The full specification is given in Appendix 2.

Before presenting the specification and discussing its value, though, it must be said that the original document supplied by the systems architecture group was simply a discussion document, intended for an audience knowledgeable about security matters. Consequently, it did not set out to make detailed definitions of concepts since these were assumed to be understood. Submitting it to the scrutiny of a non-expert from the *me too* project team meant that more precise definitions had to be extracted in order to make sense of the design. The original lack of precision is not a reflection on the quality of the design (whose structure and contents stood up remarkably well to the specification process); but it does highlight the clarity of definition which can be achieved using *me too*.

Before dealing with connection itself, it is necessary to introduce the underlying concepts involved. These are essential to an understanding of the connection process and were the subject of much debate, some of which is summarized below.

14.4.1 Security concepts – original definitions

This section describes the security ideas as presented in the original design document. They may appear to be difficult to grasp or inadequately described – the reader should appreciate that this underlines the general difficulty of expressing new and complex ideas in an informal language.

The original description introduces some of the basic concepts of security when discussing whether a connecter can be 'trusted' or not, where **connecter** is a general term for associated servers:

> ***Trusted*** *implies the ability to discriminate security levels in a qualitative way...* ***Untrusted*** *implies the inability to [do so]. This is rather simplified. Any Connecter is likely to be trusted with respect to some security factors and not others.*

This has introduced the ideas of security levels and of security factors pertaining to each level. The definitions concerned with 'exact' levels also give more information about these ideas:

> *An* ***exact*** *level is one where all information handled (over the connection) is of a single security significance. An* ***inexact*** *level is one where information handled may be of several different security significances, and this level determines both the significance of any security factors which cannot be discriminated (exact factors) and the discriminatory powers of the level (trust factors).*

This begins to reveal that a level is in some way made up of factors, which may be exact or inexact. We also have a new concept: the 'security significance' relating to a level. An immediate question concerns the relationship between factors and significances – are they synonymous or not?

The design also defines the concept of a level being 'included' in another level. It was originally defined as follows:

> *If A and B are security levels, A* ***includes*** *B if A can discriminate at least all the security levels which B can discriminate, and A can discriminate or is allowed to pass the exact levels which B can pass but not discriminate.*

To the uninitiated reader, this was not easily comprehensible ... What does it mean to 'pass' levels, for example?

Finally in this section, another definition is relevant:

> *The concepts [above] ... cannot be known in an absolute manner by any single authority [but are] accumulated as the process of connection takes place ... by combining various* ***ratings****... A rating is a local view of a security level.*

Initial attempts at specifying the ideas introduced above were not particularly successful, partly because there were few clear definitions, partly due to assumptions on the part of the system architect and partly due to the specifier's unfamiliarity with the application area. The specification required several iterations with much discussion between architect and specifier before the final version was produced. The eventual description of these concepts and their *me too* specification (where appropriate) are given in the next section. It will be seen that terms like 'security significance', 'trust factors' and 'passing security levels' did not survive into the final version.

14.4.2 Security concepts – as revised

Security is described by means of **security levels**, which may be possessed by servers or by routes between servers. However, it is important to remember that the systems under consideration are federated systems; that is, they are distributed systems with no central controller or data store. Consequently, there is no single repository of wisdom about security levels in the system. In order to assess the security level of an entity in the system, we have to consider the various locally held views of it. A local view of a level is called a **rating**; that is, a rating is a concrete indication of how a server or route is seen – it has a particular value which can be set, inspected and/or manipulated.

A rating is made up of **security factors**, where each factor can have one or more values associated with it. Thus, a factor might be color with the values red, blue, and yellow, or day with the single value Monday. A factor can be represented as a set of such values. A rating is represented as a mapping from factor names to factors.

```
Rating = map(FactorName,Factor)
Factor = set(Value)
FactorName, Value = String
```

Thus, the color factor above is represented as {"red","blue","yellow"} and day is {"Monday"}. One server might have a rating of

```
{ "Color" -> {"red","blue"}, "Day" -> {"Monday"} }
```

while a second has

```
{ "Color" -> {"red"},
  "Day" -> {"Sunday","Monday","Tuesday","Wednesday",
            "Thursday","Friday","Saturday"} }
```

Intuitively, we would expect this to mean that these two servers could communicate for activities rated

```
{ "Color" -> {"red"}, "Day" -> {"Monday"} }
```

but not for activities with ratings where the color factor is {"blue"} or the day factor is {"Tuesday"}, for example.

With this foundation, saying what is meant by exact and inexact levels and factors becomes straightforward. A factor that contains a single value is called an **exact** factor; a factor with more than one value is **inexact**. A level which is described by a rating containing only exact factors is an exact level; any other level is inexact. An inexact level may contain both exact factors and inexact factors.

These definitions are expressed in the following *me too* operations which test for these properties of a factor:

```
exact : Factor -> Boolean
exact(f) == card(f) = 1 ;

inexact : Factor -> Boolean
inexact(f) == not(exact(f)) ;
```

The question of empty factors, which are deemed to be inexact by these definitions since they have a cardinality of zero, is addressed in Section 14.4.4

The definition of inclusion becomes much simpler too. If A and B are security ratings, then A **includes** B if each factor in B is present in A, and if the values of each factor in B form a subset of the values for the same factor in A. The *me too* operation capturing this property is

```
includes : Rating x Rating -> Boolean
includes(a,b) ==
  all (fn,f) in b . f subset a[fn,{}] ;
```

The final definitions remaining from the previous section concern the trustedness of connecters. A **trusted** connecter is one which is able to discriminate between security levels. This ability is indicated by the fact that its rating contains at least one inexact factor. An **untrusted** connecter is unable to discriminate security levels in any way. In other words, it is constrained to operate at a single point in the multidimensional space of possible security values. That single point is defined by the exact factors making up its rating.

An alternative way of expressing this is that an untrusted connecter *must* operate at an exact level. Note that a connecter may be trusted with respect to some security factors and not others – since some degree of trust is involved, it is referred to as a trusted connecter. The *me too* specification provides operations which check whether a rating indicates that the connecter is trusted or not:

```
trusted : Rating -> Boolean
trusted(r) == exists (fn,f) in r . inexact(f) ;

untrusted : Rating -> Boolean
untrusted(r) == not(trusted(r)) ;
```

14.4.3 Binding ratings

The previous section introduced the notion of using several local views of levels (i.e. ratings) to determine the security level of a connection:

> *[Levels are] accumulated as the process of connection takes place ... by combining various ratings.*

In this section, we examine the means of combining ratings, a process called **binding**. The original description of this process was

> *The binding has the effect of eliminating trustedness from the resulting security level. Exact security factors must either match each other or correspond to a true subset of the*

> *trusted (discriminatory) powers and then the power is subsetted. If an exact factor does not match, the connection will be failed.*

which introduced another unexplained term 'power'.

This definition lent itself to a number of interpretations, represented in early *me too* specifications by a number of alternative versions of a binding operation. For a start, the definition makes no explicit mention of how to handle inexact factors, although the use of the term 'subsetting' gives some idea of the intentions. By way of illustration, let us define the following ratings and examine some options:

```
r1 == {"Color" -> {"red","yellow"}} ;
r2 == {"Color" -> {"red"}} ;
r3 == {"Color" -> {"yellow","blue"}} ;
r4 == {"Color" -> {"red","yellow","blue"}} ;
```

For simplicity at this stage, all of these only involve one factor, common to all the ratings. The possibilities will be extended in discussion below.

What should happen if r1 and r2 are bound together? The color factor is exact in r2 and so the definition states that it should be a 'true subset' of the values for the same factor in r1. The meaning of this was unclear. After some discussion, it was taken to mean subset in the normal mathematical sense. In this case r2 meets the requirement, so we subset the result accordingly. bind(r1,r2) therefore returns the rating

```
{"Color" -> {"red"}}
```

Note that this has indeed 'eliminated the trustedness' in r1, in that it has been reduced to an exact factor. On the other hand, if r2 and r3 are bound together, the color factor in r2 is not a subset of that in r3 and so the operation fails.

Now consider binding r1 and r3. Here there are different values in the color factor, an occurrence not mentioned in the definition. Subsetting is not possible here, since r1 is not a subset of r3, nor is r3 a subset of r1. Perhaps this binding operation should fail? An alternative is to return to the idea of eliminating trustedness, so that it might be appropriate to consider the intersection of factors rather than subsetting them, since the intersection

```
{"red","yellow"} ∩ {"yellow","blue"}
```

is

```
{"yellow"}
```

which is an exact factor. This has an intuitive correspondence to the intention behind the binding process; that is, to agree on a security level for a connection. If the initiator asks to converse with a responder using "red" and "yellow", where the responder is willing to converse only at "yellow" and "blue", then it seems reasonable that they can decide on a level which includes the color "yellow", the one color value on which they agree. Failure, in this approach, is when the intersection of common factors results in an empty factor, since this indicates that there are no values on which the ratings agree.

What about r3 and r4? Here, intersection of the factors produces {"blue","yellow"}. As above, it seems reasonable that the two servers should restrict themselves to levels of mutual agreement. This example illustrates that the scheme introduced above (intersection rather than subsetting) can be applied to both exact and inexact factors, since any two exact factors will be forced to match (if they do not, the intersection of the two singleton sets is empty and the binding fails). It should be noted, though, that this approach to binding has not 'eliminated' trustedness, as stated in the original definition, but has merely reduced it. It was decided that this was a more elegant and flexible solution and was adopted by the architect.

Now that we have explored the ideas involved in the process, we can specify a bind operation with more confidence. In the absence of errors, the functionality would be

```
bind : Rating x Rating -> Rating
```

as the operation is to return the combined rating. However, this operation also has to handle the case when the binding fails. It could return an error rating of some description, for example, an empty rating. The approach taken here, however, was to return a special error flag when the binding failed. This choice was made because a failure in binding would need to be easily detectable by the connection operations requesting the binding and because it was felt that choosing an error rating might be difficult (it turned out that an empty rating would be a valid rating, for example). Consequently the functionality specifies that either a valid rating is returned or the error value "FAIL".

```
bind : Rating x Rating -> Rating union {"FAIL"}
```

and the operation is specified as:

```
bind(r1,r2) ==
  let R == {(fn, r1[fn] inter r2[fn]) | fn <- dom(r1)}
  in  if any_empty(R) then "FAIL" else R ;
```

where any_empty scans a rating to see if it contains any empty factors:

```
any_empty : Rating -> Boolean
any_empty(r) == {} member rng(r) ;
```

If these operations are used with the ratings defined earlier, they produce the expected results. Let us be more ambitious with the ratings to be bound and introduce more than one factor:

```
r5 == {"Color" -> {"pink","red"},"Code" -> {"secure"}} ;
r6 == {"Color" -> {"red","blue"}, "Code" -> {"secure","topsecret"}} ;
```

Combining r5 and r6 using the bind operation is straightforward, resulting in a new rating of

```
{"Color" -> {"red"},"Code" -> {"secure"}}
```

But what happens if we combine r2 with r5? In fact, the answer depends on the order in which the ratings are supplied as parameters. bind(r2,r5) returns

```
{"Color" -> {"red"}}
```

while bind(r5,r2) returns "FAIL", because r2 does not have a code factor. This raises two questions: should the order of the ratings matter, i.e. should one have precedence over the other, and how should omitted factors affect the result? The definition of bind above gives precedence to the first rating supplied (which can be interpreted as 'this is the security level I *must* have') over the second rating (meaning 'this is the best security I can offer'). These issues are not addressed at all in the original document.

The approach above dictates that an omitted but required factor necessarily causes the binding to fail. It could be made even stricter, by asking that all the factors from both ratings be considered:

```
bind(r1,r2) ==
  let R == {(fn, r1[fn] inter r2[fn]) | fn <- dom(r1) union dom(r2)}
  in if any_empty(R) then "FAIL" else R ;
```

This is achieved in the expression dom(r1) union dom(r2) which adds in the factors from the second rating as candidates for checking.

A more lenient alternative would allow omitted factors to be added into the result, taking a slightly different interpretation of the term 'combining'. With this in mind, the bind operation becomes

```
bind(r1,r2) ==
  let R == r1 overwr
          {(fn, r1[fn] inter r2[fn]) | fn <- dom(r1) inter dom(r2)}
  in if any_empty(R) then "FAIL" else R ;
```

which firstly takes factors in r1 and then overwrites the common factors as they are combined. It ensures that only factors common to both ratings are considered by the expression dom(r1) inter dom(r2) since this yields only factors present in both ratings.

Note, though, that this still gives the first rating precedence over the other, and factors in the second which are not present in the first will simply disappear. If we wish to avoid that, the operation is respecified as

```
bind(r1,r2) ==
  let R == r1 overwr (r2 overwr
          {(fn, r1[fn] inter r2[fn]) | fn <- dom(r1) inter dom(r2)})
  in if any_empty(R) then "FAIL" else R ;
```

which takes all the non-common factors from both ratings into the result and attempts to combine only the common factors. Binding r2 with r5 now yields

```
{"Color" -> {"red"},"Code" -> {"secure"}}
```

irrespective of the order of ratings given to bind, while bind(r2,r6) returns

```
{"Color" -> {"red"},"Code" -> {"secure","topsecret"}}
```

In fact, this last version of bind is the one which was chosen to express the meaning of the process. This was not without much debate about the rôle of ratings during the connection process and the practicalities of how much security information would be likely to be supplied. This gave rise to a more general consideration about omitted security information; this subject is covered in the next section.

14.4.4 Special cases

As mentioned above, there are some special cases of ratings and factors, each involving some omitted information, which were not considered at all in the original design. The cases are:

1. A connecter (or its environment) has no rating for some entity involved in the connection process.
2. A rating omits one or more of the possible factors.
3. A rating contains a factor with no associated values.

There are two possible approaches to dealing with omissions: prohibitive and permissive. That is, omission can mean 'I cannot or will not talk to anyone about this security rating or factor' or it can mean 'I do not care what happens about this security rating or factor'. The approach outlined above is generally permissive, with the result that an omitted rating or factor is deemed to have been defaulted.

The rationale behind this treatment of defaulted factors is based on the view that security is protected by the one who knows what is required and can therefore take the responsibility for that security. If a factor is not known to an object, its security rating cannot contribute to any discussion of that factor, and so the factor is omitted. Thus, in building the composite picture of a security level, those who know about a factor contribute that knowledge to the level from their ratings. Where a factor is omitted by a requester of a service (the initiator), the success or failure of the request will depend on the evaluation of that initiator by other servers involved in supplying the service.

Taking this view, the special cases listed above are handled as follows:

1. If a rating is omitted, this is equivalent to it being present with all factors defaulted.
2. If a factor is omitted from a rating, this is equivalent to that factor being present with all possible values; i.e. an omitted factor implies that the factor does not constrain the security aspects of the connection.
3. A present but empty factor is not allowed. Prohibition can be explicitly requested by the special factor value "NULL", which says the object thus rated will not talk to anyone who tries to mention that factor. An alternative method is for individual ratings to include a special value which they interpret as a prohibitive value.

As a result, it is now appropriate to define an invariant on ratings, which states that a valid rating must not contain any empty factors. The invariant is expressed by means of an operation called inv_Rating:

```
inv_Rating : Rating -> Boolean
inv_Rating(r) == not({} member rng(r)) ;
```

This can be used in the bind operation to check whether it has succeeded or not. It also means that inexact cannot be applied to empty factors, since the invariant states that these are not valid factors.

Note that most of the cases described above are already handled in the specification. Case (1) – missing ratings – is handled by providing an empty rating as the default when looking it up in the environment, and then relying on the handling of missing factors. Case (2) – missing factors – is covered because non-common factors in the ratings are added into the result. Further, the second approach to prohibition mentioned in Case (3) requires no change to binding, since it is implemented by judicious use of the existing mechanisms.

Handling the special prohibitive value does affect the specification, though, and is seen in the following operations. The first, prohibited, checks for the names of any prohibited factors in a rating:

```
prohibited : Rating -> set(FactorName)
prohibited(r) == { fn | (fn,f) <- r; f = "NULL" } ;
```

This is used in an expanded version of the binding operation:

```
bind : Rating x Rating -> Rating union {"FAIL"}
bind(r1,r2) ==
  let r1OK == r1 ds prohibited(r1),
      r2OK == r2 ds prohibited(r2)
  in if    ((( prohibited(r1) inter dom(r2OK)) /= {})
            or (( prohibited(r2) inter dom(r1OK)) /= {}))
      then "FAIL"
      else let R == r1 overwr (r2 overwr
                       {(fn, r1[fn] inter r2[fn]) |
                                              fn <- dom(r1OK) inter dom(r2OK)})
           in if inv_Rating(R) then R else "FAIL" ;
```

In this, the first step is to determine which factors each rating prohibits from being mentioned by the other and to remove these factors from the ratings. This yields ratings which contain only factors with actual values (r1OK and r2OK). The check on prohibited factors is enforced by

```
(((prohibited(r1) inter dom(r2OK)) /= {})
  or ((prohibited(r2) inter dom(r1OK)) /= {}))
```

which determines whether or not factors prohibited by r1 (given by prohibited(r1)) appear in the actual factors in r2 (the factors in r2OK), and vice versa. If the ratings are invalid, the intersection of these two sets contains the names of the offending factors. Note that it is acceptable for a factor to be prohibited by *both* ratings, since r1OK and r2OK only contain factors with non-"NULL" values. If the check had been

```
(((prohibited(r1) inter dom(r2)) /= {})
  or ((prohibited(2) inter dom(r1)) /= {}))
```

using r1 and r2 instead, this case would also cause the binding to fail. The binding process itself is almost identical to the operation given in the previous section, the only difference being that r1OK and r2OK are used instead of r1 and r2 in generating the factors to be intersected. Both this and the previous version adhere to the rules (1) and (2) given above for defaults.

14.4.5 The connection process

Now that we have described ratings and the mechanics of how they are combined, we can examine their use in establishing a connection between two associated servers. This is the core of the design documents, both as originally supplied and as subsequently revised during this collaboration.

One change to the original specification of the FAM involves the introduction of environments, where an **environment** is the context in which servers operate, holding data related to its own servers and others in the system. For example, it holds information about communication routes between servers as well as security ratings for servers and routes. In *me too*, this results in the following definitions:

SPECIFY (changes only)

Objects

```
FedSystem = map(Id,Environment)
Environment = record(servers:map(Id,Server),
                     FAMdata:Security,
                     routeinfo:RouteInfo)
```

Servers now located in environments; routes are between servers

```
Where = record(envId:Id, servId:Id)
RouteInfo = set(Routes)
Routes = record(from_wh:Where, to_wh:Where, how:set(RouteId))
```

Security can refer to a server or a route

```
What = Where union RouteId
Security = map(What,Rating)

Server = record(tokens:map(TokenId,TokenBody),
                SIs:map(TokenId,TokenBody))
```

TokenBody now incorporates a rating and a route id

```
TokenBody = record(respr:Where, initr:Where, conn:Status,
                   SL:Rating, route:RouteId)
```

As a result, there were a number of changes to the FAM specification, but we omit most of them as not being of particular interest here. However, a useful operation, which also shows something of the flavor of these changes, is GetServer, which extracts a named server from its environment in the system:

```
GetServer : FedSystem x Where -> Server
GetServer(sys,wh) ==
  let eid == envId(wh),
      sid == servId(wh)
  in
      servers(sys[eid,EmptyEnv()])[sid,EmptyServer()] ;
```

This looks more complicated than it really is because defaults have been supplied to the extraction of values from the maps. For clarity, if we omit the defaults, the body of the let expression is

```
servers(sys[eid])[sid]
```

which looks up the environment in the system, extracts its servers and chooses the one identified in the call.

We now turn to the connection process. The original document identifies a number of steps in the process for each of the partners in the association, which we shall now consider.

When asking for a connection, the initiator supplies an optional rating expressing its security requirements. This is one of a set of parameters pertaining to the 'Quality of Service' across the association, hence this rating is referred to as the QOS rating. After some initial checks (such as, is there an existing connection across this association? and, does the association exist?) this rating is set as the **required security level** (RSL) for the connection. The original description involved making use of local ratings held by the initiator in setting the RSL, the explicitly described rules for which were discovered to be much as for the binding process described earlier. Because of this similarity, this step was initially simplified to binding the local ratings together, but later these ratings were removed altogether.

The next step is to bind the RSL with the initiator's environment's ratings for both the initiator (called rating R1) and the responder (called rating R2). The result of this is the security level achieved at stage 2, **LA2**. Because the issues of binding and defaulted factors and ratings have been resolved, this step is also straightforward, being handled by the operation setLA2:

```
setLA2 : FedSystem x Where x Where x Rating -> Rating union {"FAIL"}
setLA2(sys,wh_i,wh_r,RSL) ==
  let R1 == EnvRating(sys,envId(wh_i),wh_i),   % Init rating
      R2 == EnvRating(sys,envId(wh_i),wh_r)    % Resp rating
  in
      bind(bind(RSL,R1),R2) ;
```

Finally, at the initiator end, the environment has to compare LA2 against all potential routes to the responder in order to select a suitable route. This step can be quite elaborate but remained materially unchanged in the revised design, so it suffices to note that the result of binding LA2 with the rating for the chosen route is called **LA3**.

The part of connection that gave rise to most discussion (and to changes, deletions and additions to the design) concerned what security information should be sent to the responder and how the responder should react to it. Recall that we are dealing with a federated system, where servers may be in different host computers, may be widely disparate in their approaches to offering and using services in the system and may have security ratings set by different agencies. How these servers view each other is central to handling security correctly.

For example, if the initiator's environment does not trust the responder at all, that is, it holds a rating for it which contains only exact factors, then it will not be prepared to discuss security with the responder. The initiator therefore takes all the responsibility for the security of the connection it is requesting and will not send LA3 as part of the connection request. All the responder's environment can do is ensure, from the ratings it holds for the responder, initiator and the chosen route, that it can protect its own security.

Originally, there were many rules for this part of the connection scattered through two different sections of the design document, and as a result the early *me too* specification was cluttered with expressions to handle the rules and special cases. The complexity of the specification acted as a signal that the design should be reconsidered more carefully. This may not always result in a simpler solution, but in this case the matter became very straightforward. Most of the rules and special cases became redundant once it had been decided that each end of the connection should be responsible for protecting its own security, and should achieve this by means of the existing binding mechanism. The description that follows is of the simplified design.

Where the servers attempt any discussion of security, they must have an appropriate overlap of concept, sharing the same security vocabulary. That is, for any factor transmitted to the responder, the initiator and responder must agree on the possible values of that factor. At a minimum, this ensures that LA3 is understood at the responder end and that the initiator understands any level returned to it.

When the initiator decides to send security information to the responder, it need not send all the factors in LA3. What is sent depends on what the initiator thinks of the responder, shown by the rating R2 mentioned above. Since inexact factors in R2 represent the initiator's view of what the responder can discuss, only factors in LA3 which correspond to those inexact factors in R2 are sent in the connection request. We can define an operation to achieve this filtering of factors:

```
filter_exact : Rating x Rating -> Rating
filter_exact(mask,r) ==
  { (fn,f) | (fn,f) <- r; inexact(mask[fn]) } ;
```

where R2 would be supplied as the mask and LA3 as the rating to be filtered. This operation extracts each (FunctionName,FunctionValue) pair from the given rating and constructs a new rating containing only those pairs which correspond to an inexact factor in the mask. Recall that when a factor is defaulted, this is treated as being present with all its potential values. We wish, therefore, to send factors in LA3 which are defaulted in R2. filter_exact is modified to include these factors explicitly:

```
filter_exact : Rating x Rating -> Rating
filter_exact(mask,r) ==
  { (fn,f) | (fn,f) <- r; not(fn member dom(mask))
                           or inexact(mask[fn]) } ;
```

When the request is received, possibly containing a rating in the token, the responder has to bind the various ratings in the normal way. This activity is defined in three operations:

```
ReceiveConnect : FedSystem x Where x Token -> FedSystem
ReceiveConnect(sys,wh_r,tok) ==
  let resp == GetServer(sys,wh_r),
      tid == tkid(tok), tb == tkbody(tok)
  in if   not((tid member dom(SIs(resp)))
              or (conn(tb) = "REQU"))
     then sys
     else AcceptConnect(sys,initr(tb), wh_r,tid,SL(tb),route(tb)) ;
```

```
AcceptConnect : FedSystem x Where x Where x TokenId x Rating
                                                x RouteId -> FedSystem
AcceptConnect(sys,wh_i,wh_r,tid,LA3,rid) ==
  let LA6 == setLA6(sys,wh_i,wh_r,tid,
                     setLA5(sys,wh_i,wh_r,rid,LA3))
  in if    LA6 = "FAIL"
     then sys
     else AckConnect(sys,wh_i,wh_r,tid,
                     if    LA3 = EmptyRating()
                     then EmptyRating() else LA6,rid) ;

AckConnect : FedSystem x Where x Where x TokenId x Rating
                                                x RouteId -> FedSystem
AckConnect(sys,wh_i,wh_r,tid,SLA,rid) ==
  NewTokenR(sys,wh_r,tid,
            mk_TokenBody(wh_r,wh_i,"ACCPT",SLA,rid)) ;
```

The first of these, ReceiveConnect, checks that the token has arrived at the right server and that it contains a connection request before extracting salient pieces of information to hand on to AcceptConnect. The operation AcceptConnect binds the responder's rating of the route with the rating passed in the token, by a call on setLA5, and binds the result with the local rating associated with the service instance, by calling setLA6. The result is the Security Level Achieved (SLA) for the connection. AckConnect sets up the token in the responder ready for sending back to the initiator to inform it of the success or otherwise of the connection request. If the initiator was prepared to talk about security with the responder, then the SLA is returned in the token.

The relative simplicity of the new description of the responder end of the connection is due in large measure to the questions raised by the process of specifying these activities in *me too*. A full but informal description of the architecture can be found in Alexander and McVitie (1988).

14.5 Summary

The examples given above of changes to the specifications are not exhaustive. In the work described in Section 14.4, several other revisions emerged from the specification exercise. For example, as mentioned in passing above, the number of ratings held in the system was markedly reduced. This was partly for practicality (it would be a considerable overhead to maintain the original number proposed) but also because it was recognized that a server is only as secure as its environment, so that holding separate views of the server and its environment was not useful.

The work described here confirms the value of *me too* as a means of clarifying ideas expressed in an existing informal specification. As this chapter has shown, *me too* made it possible to detect omissions, conflicts, oversights and ambiguities, resulting in a design document which the original designer felt expressed his intentions more clearly and precisely, even though it was still written in English and did not resort to mathematics or diagramming techniques. This result is relevant for designers or design groups who wish to use *me too* but who have to communicate their designs in non-formal documents and discussions.

Chapter 15

me too in context – conclusions

> *At first sight the idea of any rules or principles being superimposed on the creative mind seems more likely to hinder than to help, but this is really quite untrue in practice. Disciplined thinking focuses inspiration rather than blinkers it.*
>
> Gordon L. Glegg

At the beginning of the book, analysis of some of the difficulties associated with systems and software development led to the suggestion that the software engineering techniques of formal methods and rapid prototyping offered some hope for improvements in the development process. Now that *me too* has been presented by tutorial and example, it is time to re-examine its place in that process. As part of this examination, we compare *me too* with some other approaches to design, since this helps to identify the strengths, weaknesses, scope and applicability of *me too*.

15.1 Overview of *me too*

me too grew out of research into applications of functional programming. The first component of *me too* is its language, which is based on the mathematics of functions, sets and tuples. As such, it has a precise meaning, and offers a way of unambiguously documenting abstract descriptions of a system. It is based in part on notations already available in Z and VDM.

The second component of *me too* is the method advised for its use. There are three steps (Model, Specify and Validate) in an iterative cycle which encourages experimentation with the design. The details of each step provide a discipline by which *me too* specifications are developed and validated. The method encourages designers to design a system in terms of its objects and their associated operations. The specification is tested by executing it under the *me too* shell. This is obviously useful in detecting errors in the specification, but it has the added advantage of allowing the design to be demonstrated. Executing specifications has proved helpful in detecting omissions and also in stimulating suggestions for improvements or changes. These feed into further iterations of the design until it meets the requirements set for it. The resulting design can be used as a basis for subsequent implementation; it specifies the properties of the implemented system and possibly the structure of the implementation too.

The examples given in the book show some of the ways in which *me too* can be applied. For example, the case studies in Part III demonstrate that database, networks and system architectures are three areas where industrial groups have found value in constructing and expressing their designs using *me too*. These are not the only systems to which *me too* has been applied – some other application areas are listed in the next section.

15.2 Applications of *me too*

The PARIS case study in Chapter 13 showed that *me too* could be used to specify a CAFS-style database system. Other data organizations have also been specified, including a small relational database package, a functional database and a semantic network database (Jones, 1984). Moving from databases to knowledge bases, one of the earliest (and largest) specifications reproduced the functionality of a proprietary expert system shell called ExpertEase* (V. M. Jones *et al.*, 1985). ExpertEase employs deductive inference, that is, it is not supplied with rules for knowledge handling directly, but derives them from example cases supplied by the expert. Other experiments involved specifying a production-rule system (Henderson and Minkowitz, 1986) and a rule-based expert system shell, complete with Bayesian logic (Bruce, 1986).

The NTU group responsible for the Domino specification in Chapter 12 also found an entirely different use for *me too*. Part of the ISO work on communications standards involves defining protocols for routing traffic within a network. The standard for this is formulated at a relatively abstract level, leaving implementors to resolve a number of issues such as the design of the databases which hold the routing information. ICL produced a product specification document (PSD) giving details of routing information to be maintained by each node in the network. The NTU group respecified part of the PSD in *me too* and found that the descriptions in it could be expressed more succinctly and unambiguously using *me too*. Further, the specification exercise revealed that many of the data structures were similar and could be combined. Other standards have also been specified in *me too*, namely parts of the Office Document Architecture standard being drawn up by ISO (Minkowitz and Henderson, 1985) and of the Graphics Kernel System (Minkowitz, 1985).

A further application of *me too* was in the development of a personal diary and scheduling package for ICL Applied Systems (AS), intended to explore the possible benefits of providing a computer-based personal planning system (A. Jones *et al.*, 1985). During the collaboration, it became clear that AS had primarily wanted to address issues concerning the user interface of the system rather than its functionality. After some time attempting to accommodate these needs, it was agreed that *me too* was more suited to specify the system's functionality and the work proceeded on that basis. The rapid iteration of the method made it possible to make radical changes to the design as a result of this and other decisions. The

* ExpertEase is a product marketed by Intelligent Terminals Ltd.

design which resulted was subsequently implemented by the *me too* project team (Bennett, 1986a).

Other areas where *me too* has been employed include retail business applications (Davies and Minkowitz, 1987), Petri net simulation (Minkowitz and Henderson, 1987), simulation of CSP (Henderson, 1986b), screen formatting (Rowles, 1986), a decision support system (Minkowitz, 1986), compilers (Bennett, 1986b) and process modeling (Rowles, 1987).

From this brief outline, we can see that *me too* has proved useful in a range of application areas. Given the power and expressiveness of mathematics, this is not surprising. The other side of the coin, though, is to note where it has been less successful or is less appropriate as a design method.

To start with, it should be recognized that the possibility of applying *me too* to a particular type of problem does not imply that *me too* is the best way to tackle it. The PARIS problem, for example, is essentially a problem of searching, of defining a predicate that says either there exist SKEs that match a set of symptoms or not. This kind of predicate may be more naturally expressed in Prolog. Similarly, the active object capability and inheritance features of object-oriented programming make this style more appropriate for particular kinds of problems. For example, such features may have been useful in amalgamating the objects in the domino case study in Chapter 12.

The experience with the AS group mentioned above highlighted the area of the user interface where *me too* has been less helpful. It seems that the term *prototype* can raise an expectation that the main area explored will be the user interface, which is one reason for preferring the term *model*. It is true, however, that in offering a prototyping capability, *me too* is often expected to produce models which can be demonstrated to potential users, customers or marketing staff. The notation given in this book would require such an audience to be tolerant of a presentation using function calls (invoking the operations) and displaying mathematical data (the objects). While this is better than having to read pages of mathematics, it is still not an ideal way of communicating the specification to such an audience. Designers are free to write a front-end program (in *me too*'s host language, Lisp) in order to present their *me too* prototype, but the fact remains that the executability of *me too* specifications is intended as an aid to designers rather than to analysts or users. This is the reason for locating *me too* in the system design phase rather than in system definition, with its necessity of referring back to users and marketing staff during requirements analysis.

It is worth pursing this issue further, since it reveals a more general point. What is it about the user interface that is hard to specify in *me too* or in its closest relatives, Z and VDM? Such languages can describe screen layouts, graphics primitives, menu and form handlers, and so on; the ExpertEase design, for example, includes specifications of menus and spreadsheets. They can specify the effects of individual interactions with the system, each of which may be complex and involve substantial manipulation of screen and application. What is difficult to express, however, is the possible sequences of events that may occur at any point in a user's dialog with the system. More generally, this same issue of ordering of events appears in other kinds of systems, notably real-time and concurrent systems. A valid inference from this is that it is hard to specify this aspect of such systems only using a language like *me too*. Notations like CSP (Hoare, 1985), CCS (Milner, 1985), Petri nets or state transition diagrams are more suitable for this.

Research work is continuing to investigate combining *me too* with other systems in order to extend its applicability. For specifying and prototyping concurrent and real-time systems, approaches which combine *me too* with CSP (Clark, 1988) and with statecharts (Harel, 1987; Naftalin, 1988) are being investigated. For user interface specification, *me too* has been linked with a subset of CSP (Alexander, 1987) and with a Prolog-based interface tool (Bennett, 1988).

Combining *me too* with performance modeling tools is also under consideration. Such tools require a fairly detailed description of the proposed system in order to model its performance; normally that is not available until implementation has begun. It may be that *me too* specifications offer sufficient detail in an appropriate language at a much earlier stage of development. As the development progresses and the specifications become more detailed, they can be used to provide more accurate performance estimates.

With the language as it stands, however, the main conclusion drawn from the experiences reported here is that *me too* can be applied to a wide variety of systems, as long as the primary purpose is to design or describe the functionality of those systems.

15.3 Comparisons with other methods

In general terms, we have to consider *me too* in comparison with methods which do not advocate formality, those which do, and methods which offer a prototyping capability. The following three sections describe these groups: the first examines the advantages and disadvantages of non-formal methods, the second discusses formal methods, while the third considers prototyping methods.

15.3.1 Non-formal methods

Recall that we have restricted our use of the term 'formal methods' to refer to mathematically based methods. As a result, all other methods are referred to here as 'non-formal'; such methods may involve defined notations, such as data flow diagrams, pseudo-code and structure diagrams. Individual non-formal methods are not described in great detail in this section since this is a large subject, covered by books on specific techniques, e.g. Downs *et al.* (1988), and books presenting comparative studies, e.g. Birrell and Ould (1985); Macro and Buxton (1987). Instead, we consider the advantages and disadvantages in general of non-formal methods over formal methods.

Some of the 'methods' often included in this non-formal category are actually basic philosophies or guidelines, such as top-down design, modularity and information hiding. Such considerations apply across a wide spectrum of design techniques, from informal to formal, and are not part of the discussion that follows.

Our starting point is to note that the purpose of system specification documents is to communicate the concepts of the system and its design, and to record agreement with them. A complication is that usually specifications are read by (at least) two disparate groups: those whose task is to see that the specification meets the requirements set for it, and those who have to implement the specification. The readers may also differ depending on the level of the specification, which may be architectural, functional, outline, detailed, etc.

Natural language has the singular advantage of being familiar to its readers, be they users, marketing staff or technical staff. However, it may or may not be comprehensible, depending on the lucidity of the author and the complexity of the subject. Specifications can be lengthy, and there is scope for ambiguity, contradiction and misunderstanding. The richness and ambiguity of natural language may be a literary strength but it can be a disadvantage when technical precision is required. Thus one reader's understanding may differ markedly from another, and in particular from what was intended by the original designer or designers. As pointed out in Part I, this difference of interpretation can be disastrous – when the product is not what the user expected or when the implementors have incorporated poor or wrong decisions in their code.

It is to address these problems that special notations, such as SADT and SSADM, have been devised. Symbols or text with particular meanings are less open to misinterpretation and can express concepts more succinctly. Of course, while such notations ensure that specifications can be reviewed and implemented by suitably trained technical staff, the specifications may not be so clear to the untrained staff and users who have to read and approve them.

It has to be said that many of the notations in current usage are not difficult to learn, especially when compared with both the perceived and actual intricacies of mathematics. Consequently, they are widely used, with the choice of technique depending on such issues as staff skills, tool availability and ease of document preparation and maintenance. Diagramming techniques, for example, have benefited a great deal from the advent of tools which maintain complex and inter-related diagrams.

The fact that non-formal notations can be read more easily than formal notations and permit a greater or lesser degree of vagueness, means that they are often used when addressing issues of requirements capture and analysis. In consequence, they are part of the earliest stages of system development. As can be seen in the section which follows, this is not a feature of formal methods, which are usually employed *after* requirements analysis.

To sum up in general terms, the less formal a notation is, the easier it is to read without training but the harder it is to agree a single interpretation of it. To pin down meaning with an informal language may require an extremely lengthy and complex description, which is then more likely to contain inconsistencies. Special notations bring the benefits of brevity and agreed meaning but require a readership educated in the chosen notation.

Because non-formal methods can address requirements issues and are more readily understandable than formal methods, the two approaches to system design may be seen as complementary. For example, non-formal methods may be used to elicit and document requirements on the system and to specify its top-level design. Formal notations can then be used to clarify, elaborate and make precise this specification.

15.3.2 Formal methods

By using mathematics, formal methods offer a language with a precise and agreed meaning. Mathematics provides a powerful language, enabling complex concepts to be expressed concisely. It can be used to define abstract ideas, allowing designers to concentrate on the issues of importance. However, mathematical languages suffer from the disadvantages of other specialized notations, even more so since trained mathematicians are a rare commodity amongst designers, implementors, analysts and users. A formal specification, however precise or brief, is likely to communicate very little to untrained readers.

Nevertheless, with suitably trained designers and implementors, formal specification of designs can overcome many of the problems of technical misinterpretation. There is also the possibility of checking consistency and correct usage throughout a specification. Moreover, writing formal specifications brings a clarification of ideas and concepts. This enhanced understanding can then be the basis of discussion with users, as a partial response to the problem of communicating via formal specifications. The formal specifications remain internal to the development group, while being used as the basis for producing non-formal descriptions comprehensible to a non-technical audience.

Valuable though these benefits may be, they are not the primary motivation behind many formal methods. Recognizing that unfulfilled requirements of one kind or another are a significant cause of system failure and non-acceptance, a major goal for users of these formal methods is to be able to *prove* that the specification of a design (and indeed its implementation) meets its requirements. For this to be achieved, it must be possible to state the user requirements formally; but this area is still very much a research issue. Consequently, it is more usual to prove that the specifications possess certain desirable properties or avoid undesirable properties (related to the system requirements), and then to prove that the implementation is consistent with its specification.

Often the term 'formal methods' is restricted to methods which not only employ a mathematical notation but also involve some means of proof-based verification. In contrast, *me too* is a formal method which verifies its formal specifications by testing them. Verification by testing relies, as with any testing, on a well-designed testing strategy and is less general than using proof techniques. For example, testing may show *liveness* properties – that the system can do X – but must neglect equally important *safety* properties – that the system cannot do Y. *me too* does not rule out the use of a more rigorous method, though. Often the hardest part of the proof process is knowing suitable theorems to be proved. Executing a *me too* model can provide ideas about suitable theorems. Also, the properties of a specification can be expressed by means of invariants and preconditions, albeit in a more constructive style than in other formal specification languages.

In general, attempting to prove that a given program satisfies its specification is an extremely difficult task, demanding a higher level of mathematical skill than is required to write the formal specification itself. This verification process can be made easier by using an approach such as VDM, which constructs a program step by step by deriving it from its high-level specification. At each step, the specification is made less abstract, by including more representation or algorithmic detail. At each step, too, the output of that step can be proved to be consistent with the output from the previous step. In the process, this demonstrates that the new specification preserves the properties of the original specification.

Methods such as VDM and Z, as well as algebraic methods, have this demonstration of program correctness (with respect to its specification) as a goal. Verification by testing is replaced by verification by proof. Since proof is more general than testing, these methods claim that the end-product should be a more reliable system, although this does rely on carrying out the proofs correctly, which is far from a trivial task.

With such desirable goals, we might ask why use of formal methods is not more widespread. A major reason is the shortage of trained staff and the cost of training them. A second is that the specifications produced are not comprehensible to users, non-technical or untrained staff, who are therefore reluctant to sign them off as an agreed statement of what the system will offer. For methods involving formal proofs, verification is both difficult and expensive, with or without theorem-proving tools. Nor does verification by proof render them immune to errors, either in the specification or in the proofs. Further, formal specification does not remove the possibility of producing a zero-defect system which does not do what the user actually wanted.

In other words, although there are benefits of formal specification and verification, they require developers to make a significant investment of time and effort, both in training and in the development process, and they do not guarantee an acceptable product. Few have been prepared to pay the price or run the risk of late delivery unless their systems are required to be extremely reliable, as in the defense, health and financial sectors, for example.

The rationale behind *me too* is that it can offer many of the undoubted benefits of formal methods for less investment and in a more palatable form for non-mathematical software engineers. There is a small amount of notation to learn, yet the expressive power of the language is still high. There are no proof techniques to acquire, so a lower level of mathematical skill is needed. As a result, a two-day intensive course is sufficient to train software engineers in the essentials of *me too*.

The ability to execute *me too* specifications is an empirical rather than analytic approach to verification that has the advantage of being familiar to software engineers. The fact that specifications can be rapidly constructed and tested means that designers can engage in several iterative cycles of improvements and corrections. The small level of investment in creating specifications means that it is feasible to discard designs and explore alternative options. These benefits are less evident when lengthy proof techniques are used. Some of these features of *me too* may be considered to be deficiencies as far as convinced formalists are concerned, but they are also the features which make *me too* acceptable to industrial development teams.

Our approach is due largely to the desire to make specifications executable; *me too* sacrifices the implicit style of some other formal methods in order to offer that capability. This has implications for the language since only executable constructs may be used. Further, the operations specified in *me too* have to be explicitly constructive in nature rather than implicit because they have to say more about how their results are constructed than would be necessary with a non-executable language. The explicit construction of results can bias a subsequent implementation of the operations; the implementors have to be aware of this tendency. It should be noted that no compromises are made in the mathematical nature of the specification, which could be used for verification by proof if desired.

Note also that *me too* does not enforce the specification of complete abstract data types which incorporate strict encapsulation, information hiding and error handling. The *me too* shell does not have a full type checker or library facility to enforce these features. In this respect, *me too* might be considered a weaker specification tool than, say, OBJ. There is nothing in the language, though, to prevent designers from structuring their specifications in this way. Indeed, designers are encouraged to do this, especially if the specifications are to be used as documentation for implementors. However, this concern may be ignored until after the design space has been sufficiently explored. It can be argued that the ability to delay modularization makes *me too* a more flexible tool for design exploration, certainly if we consider it in its prototyping rôle.

Perhaps, as with non-formal methods, it is more constructive to view *me too* and other formal methods as complementary rather than as competitors. They differ primarily in how the specifications are used but they share many of the same objectives and offer many of the same benefits.

15.3.3 Prototyping methods

The different reasons for, and approaches to, prototyping were introduced in Chapter 2. This section concentrates on the techniques by which prototyping of system functionality is undertaken.

There are three groups: techniques which are not based on using a machine at all, those which involve reuse of existing code and those which execute a description of the system prototype. The first group includes techniques such as pencil-and-paper exercises and screen mock-ups – they are often employed very early in the development process and do not exclude the use of more comprehensive prototypes later in the process. Techniques in the second group rely on using conventional tools (such as those provided by UNIX*) and/or reuse of existing software – again, these may be used in conjunction with other methods.

The third group includes *me too* and so is considered in more detail here. These methods involve supplying a machine-readable, executable description of the prototype to a prototyping tool. This executes the description, yielding the prototype. The differences between these methods may be characterized by the differences in the languages involved.

The method requiring least investment in new tools is to produce a prototype in the target programming language, achieving rapidity of production by omitting aspects of the system, ignoring quality issues, and so on. It is cheap and straightforward, but it has two main disadvantages: it still requires implementation-level detail and there is the risk that the hastily produced result is pressed into service as the actual system.

More powerful languages offer an alternative means of producing a system prototype. They allow greater abstraction from implementation details, they are more concise and they offer powerful data manipulation facilities. This group includes APL (Tavolato and Vincena, 1984), Prolog, SETL (Kennedy and Schwartz, 1975), Lisp and other functional languages. In particular, artificial intelligence environments such as KEE or ART offer powerful programming environments. Because fewer lines of code are needed to program the prototype, it can be produced more quickly. The disadvantages of this group of languages are that they are often inefficient or only suitable for specific kinds of prototype. For example,

* UNIX is a trademark of AT&T.

APL is suitable for, say, data processing applications but is less appropriate for expert systems where Prolog or Lisp would be a more obvious choice.

Executable specification languages such as OBJ and *me too* also allow a conciseness of description and powerful data modeling facilities with the added benefit that the prototype can be derived directly from the system specification without additional effort. The formal specification language of VDM also forms the basis of a sophisticated prototyping tool called EPROS (Hekmatpour and Ince, 1986), whose purpose is to provide a working version of the system from specification through to implementation. These languages may be less restricted in application than some of those in the previous group, but they share the same disadvantage of inefficiency in execution, coupled with the seeming reluctance of designers to acquire the necessary mathematics.

An alternative approach is to provide languages and tools which allow users and designers to describe the prototype in terms which they understand. Commonly referred to as *fourth-generation languages* and *application builders*, these are most often found in data processing applications. Application-building tools may allow systems to be described by filling in forms, drawing diagrams and adding text. From these descriptions, COBOL or other programs are generated which constitute the desired system.

Choosing between these language-based methods depends on the nature of the intended system, the availability of suitable tools and hardware, the skills of staff and the purpose of the prototyping exercise. Where the prototype is to be evolved into the final system, using the target programming language has obvious advantages. Where speed of construction is of the essence, a very high-level language may be more appropriate. Where developers wish to maintain close links between specification and prototype, executable specifications are a cost-effective way of achieving that end.

15.4 Summary

Formal methods, even when allied with prototyping (or despite that, perhaps), are not the cure for all the ills that beset software and systems development. It has been the contention of this book, though, that they do have considerable benefits to offer and that many of those benefits can be realized with *me too*.

me too resulted from the view that it is possible to make improvements in the development process by introducing formal specification along with the means to execute and test specifications. The aim is to make improvements now rather than wait for wider acceptance of methods involving formal verification. If the cost of verification by proof can be justified for a particular development, then it may be used. But if the development does not warrant the amount of effort and training required, or if the skills are not available, or if verification by proof is not an essential part of the method, or if some prototyping capability is needed, then *me too* may be more appropriate. Nor is investment in *me too* wasted; the notation is based on discrete mathematics, and an acquaintance with *me too* is a good introduction to other formal methods with a similar basis, such as VDM and Z.

Because of its mathematical notation, *me too* allows succinct and unambiguous statements about the design of a system, when compared with non-formal notations, leading to fewer errors in design and implementation. Because its notation is executable, it is more accessible and more acceptable to software engineers than formal methods which involve verification by proof rather than verification by testing. By combining mathematics and executability, *me too* occupies the middle ground between formalism and pragmatism, and thereby encourages designers and implementors to move towards the engineering practices necessary for the delivery of reliable, acceptable and effective systems.

You have endured worse things, God will grant an end even to these.
Virgil

Appendix 1

The *me too* language

A1.1 Summary of notation

Numbers

x + y	
x − y	
x * y	
x / y	
x mod y	remainder after integer division
x truncate y	x divided by y, truncated towards zero
is_number(n)	

Strings

is_string(e)

Booleans

true, false	constants
is_boolean(e)	
b_1 and b_2	
b_1 or b_2	
not(b)	
b_1 => b_2	implication
b_1 = b_2	equivalence

Relational Operators

x = y	equality – all types
x /= y	inequality – all types
x < y	less than – strings and numbers
x <= y	less than or equal – strings and numbers
x > y	greater than – strings and numbers
x >= y	greater than or equal – strings and numbers

Conditional expression

if b then e_1 else e_2

Local definition

let x_1 == e_1, . . ., x_k == e_k in e

Functions

f(p_1, . . ., p_n) == e ;	function definition
f(e_1, . . ., e_n)	function application
lambda(p_1, . . ., p_n) . e	lambda expression
is_lambda(e)	returns true for functions and lambda expressions
f reduce (u) s	reduction over sets and sequences

where f : T_1 x T_2 -> T_1, s ∈ set(T_2) or s ∈ seq(T_2), u ∈ T_1, and the result is of type T_1

Sets

{e_1, . . .,e_k}	enumerated set
{i, . . .,k}	set of integers from i to k
{}	empty set
is_set(e)	
s_1 union s_2	
s_1 inter s_2	intersection
s_1 diff s_2	difference
x member s	
s_1 subset s_2	
card(s)	cardinality
the(s)	where s is singleton set
dunion(ss)	distributed union
{e | x <- s}	
{e | x <- s; b}	
{e | (x_1, . . .,x_k) <- s}	
{e | (x_1, . . .,x_k) <- s; b}	
{e | g_1, . . ., g_k}	
all x in s . b	
all (x_1, . . .,x_k) in s . b	
exists x in s . b	
exists (x_1, . . .,x_k) in s . b	
exists1 x in s . b	
exists1 (x_1, . . .,x_k) in s . b	
f reduce (u) s	set reduction using f (see 'Functions')

Binary relations

{(e_1,e_2), . . .,(e_k,e_{k+1})}	
is_relation(e)	
dom(r)	domain
rng(r)	range
inverse(r)	
r dr s	domain restrict
r ds s	domain subtract
r im s	image

Maps (finite functions)

{e_1 -> e_2, . . . ,e_j -> e_k}	enumerated map
is_map(e)	
{ x : s -> e }	
{ x : s -> e; b }	
m[x]	map application
m[x,d]	map application with default
m_1 overwr m_2	

Records

rec-type :: f_1 . . . f_n ;	**This declaration is executable, and must not be part of the comments.** It declares a record type rec-type, composed of fields with names f_1, . . . ,f_n.
is_record(e)	
is_<rec-type>(e)	
inv_<rec-type>(e)	invariant for record type
mk_<rec-type>(e_1, . . . ,e_n)	
upd_<f_j>(e,e_j)	updates field f_j

cases e of
  mk_<rec-type$_1$>(e_{11}, . . . ,e_{1j}) -> e_1, . . . ,
  mk_<rec-type$_k$>(e_{k1}, . . . ,e_{kn}) -> e_k
end

Tuples

(e_1, . . . ,e_k)
is_tuple(e)
first(e) . . . fifth(e)
nth(i,e)

Sequences

[e_1, . . . ,e_k]	enumerated sequence
[i, . . . ,k]	sequence of integers from i to k
[]	empty sequence
is_sequence(e)	
asm(q)	convert to map representation
asq(m)	convert to sequence representation
q_1 conc q_2	
hd(q)	
tl(q)	
last(q)	returns singleton sequence with last element
butlast(q)	
len(q)	
rng(q)	set of elements in q
dom(q)	set of indices of q
q[i]	select ith element of q
q[i,d]	select ith element of q, default d

q overwr m	m must evaluate to a map with dom(m) ⊆ dom(q)
dconc(qq)	
[e | x <− q]	
[e | x <− q; b]	
[e | $(x_1, \ldots, x_k)$ <− q]	
[e | $(x_1, \ldots, x_k)$ <− q; b]	
[e | $g_1, \ldots, g_k$]	
f reduce (u) q	sequence reduction using f (see 'Functions')

Data objects

n == e ;	to define an object where name n is an alphabetic character followed by zero or more alphanumerics and/or underscores and e is a *me too* expression to
e ;	evaluate and print the value of an expression

A1.2 Type specification

The basic types are Boolean, Nat, Int (or Integer), Real and String. Types are specified as follows:

$T = T_1$	e.g. Name = String Age = Nat
$T = \{x_1, x_2, \ldots\}$	enumerated type e.g. Weekday = {"mon","tue","wed","thur", "fri"}
$T = T_1$ union T_2	union type e.g. Day = Weekday union {"sat","sun"}

Sets

$T = \text{set}(T_1)$	objects of type T are sets whose elements are of type T_1

Relations

$T = \text{rel}(T_1, T_2)$	objects of type T are binary relations where members of the domain are of type T_1, and members of the range are of type T_2. If $r \in T$, $\text{dom}(r) \subseteq T_1$ and $\text{rng}(r) \subseteq T_2$

Maps (finite functions)

$T = \text{map}(T_1, T_2)$	objects of type T are finite functions mapping objects of type T_1 to objects of type T_2.

	If $m \in T$, $dom(m) \subseteq T_1$ and $rng(m) \subseteq T_2$ and $card(dom(m)) = card(m)$

Tuples

$T = tuple\ (T_1,T_2,\ldots,T_n)$	objects of type T are *n*-tuples whose kth element is of type T_k, where $1 \leq k \leq n$.
$T = pair(T_1,T_2)$	pairs are a special case of tuples

Sequences

$T = seq(T_1)$	objects of type T are sequences whose elements are of type T_1

Functions

$f: T_1 \times T_2 \times \ldots \times T_n -> T$	function f applied to arguments of types $T_1,\ldots,T_n$ returns a result of type T, where $n \geq 0$.

Records

$T = record(f_1 : T_1,\ldots,f_n : T_n)$	objects of type T are records whose kth field is named f_k and is of type T_k, where $1 \leq k \leq n$.

Appendix 2

Full specifications of examples and case studies

The specifications of the examples and case studies discussed elsewhere in the book are shown in full below.

In a *me too* specification, only definitions of operations and record declarations are executable. If the other parts of the specification are typed into a *me too* file, each line should be preceded by the comment character, %.

A2.1 Telephone bills

A2.1.1 Version 1

SPECIFICATION OF PHONE_BILLS

DESCRIPTION

Calculation of cost of telephone bill from log of calls made, where currency is in gelds (G) and centigelds (c) (see Chapter 8)

MODEL

Objects

Log	log of phone calls
Call	duration of call in seconds (all long-distance calls made at peak rate)

Visible operations

cost : Log -> Real	cost in gelds, where unit cost is 5.06c

Hidden operations

units : Call -> Nat	number of time units used, where another unit is registered every 18 seconds

SPECIFY

Objects

```
Log = seq(Call)
Call = Nat
```

Operations

```
inv_Log(log) == all c in rng(log) . c > 0 ;

cost(log) == ((+ reduce (0) [units(c) | c <- log]) * 5.06)/100 ;

units(c) == 1 + (c truncate 18) ;
```

A2.1.2 Version 2

SPECIFICATION OF PHONE_BILLS

DESCRIPTION

Calculation of cost of telephone bill from log of calls made, where currency is in gelds and centigelds (see Chapter 8)

MODEL

Objects

Log	log of phone calls
Call	charge rate and duration of long-distance call in seconds
Rate	peak, standard or cheap

Visible operations

cost : Log -> Real	cost in gelds, where unit cost is 5.06c

Hidden operations

units : Call -> Nat	number of time units used, depending on duration and charge code

SPECIFY

Objects

```
Log  = seq(Call)
Call = pair(Rate,Nat)
Rate = {"peak","standard","cheap"}
```

Operations

```
inv_Log(log) ==
   all c in rng(log) .
         (first(c) member {"peak","standard","cheap"})
         and
         (second(c) > 0) ;

cost(log) == ((+ reduce (0) [units(c) | c <- log])* 5.06)/100 ;

units(c) ==
   let rate == first(c), dur == second(c)
   in  let timeunit == if     rate = "peak" then 18
                       else if     rate = "standard" then 24
                               else 45
       in 1 + (dur truncate timeunit) ;
```

A2.1.3 Version 3

SPECIFICATION OF PHONE_BILLS

DESCRIPTION

Calculation of cost of telephone bill from log of calls made, where currency is in gelds and centigelds (see Chapter 8)

MODEL

Objects

Log	log of phone calls
Call	charge rate and duration of call in seconds
Rate	peak, standard or cheap
Chargetable	table showing time per unit for different charge rates

Visible operations

cost : Log -> Real	cost in gelds, where unit cost is 5.06c

Hidden operations

units : Call -> Nat	number of time units used, depending on duration and charge code

SPECIFY

Objects

```
Log         = seq(Call)
Call        = pair(Rate,Nat)
Rate        = {"peak","standard","cheap"}
Chargetable = record(peak:Nat, standard:Nat, cheap:Nat)
```

Record declaration

```
Chargetable :: peak standard cheap ;
```

Operations

```
inv_Log(log) ==
  all c in rng(log) .
      (first(c) member {"peak","standard","cheap"})
      and
      (second(c) > 0) ;

inv_Chargetable(x) ==
  (peak(x) < standard(x)) and (standard(x) < cheap(x)) ;

cost(log,ct) ==
  ((+ reduce (0) [units(c,ct) | c <- log]) * 5.06)/100 ;
```

```
units(c,ct) ==
  let rate == first(c),
      dur == second(c)
  in let timeunit == if    rate = "peak"
                     then peak(ct)
                     else if   rate = "standard"
                          then standard(ct)
                          else cheap(ct)
     in 1 + (dur truncate timeunit) ;
```

A2.2 Frames

SPECIFICATION OF FRAMES

DESCRIPTION

Construction and query operations for frames systems

MODEL

Objects

Name	the name of a frame
Attr	the name of a slot
Val	the value stored in a slot
Frame	a frame
Db	a database of frames (a frames system)

Visible operations

```
emptydb : -> Db
putvalue : Name x Attr x Val x Db -> Db
getvalue : Name x Attr x Db -> Val
```

where

emptydb() constructs the empty database of frames

putvalue(n,a,v,db) constructs the new database derived from putting the value v into the slot labeled a in the frame named n in frames system db

getvalue(n,a,db) retrieves the value of attribute a from frame n in the frames system db, using inheritance if necessary

Hidden operations

```
inherit : Name x Attr x Db -> Val
supers : Name x Db -> set(Name)
```

where

inherit(n,a,db) searches for an inheritable value for attribute a for frame n in db

supers(n,db) returns the set of the names of frames which are superordinate in the kind hierarchy to n in db

SPECIFY

Objects

```
Name = String
Attr = String
Val  = String
```

```
Frame = map(Attr,Val)
Db    = map(Name,Frame)
```

Operations

```
inv_Db(db) ==
  (all f in rng(db) .
     ("kind" member dom(f)) => (f["kind"] member dom(db)))
  and
  (not(exists n in dom(db) . n member supers(n,db))) ;

emptydb() == {} ;

putvalue(n,a,v,db) ==
  let new == db overwr { n -> db[n,{}] overwr { a -> v}}
  in if inv_Db(new) then new else db ;

getvalue(n,a,db) ==
  if    n member dom(db)
  then db[n][a,inherit(n,a,db)]
  else "undefined" ;

inherit(n,a,db) ==
  if    "kind" member dom(db[n])
  then getvalue(db[n]["kind"],a,db)
  else "undefined" ;

supers(n,db) ==
  let parent == db[n,{}]["kind","undefined"]
  in if    parent = "undefined" then {}
     else {parent} union supers(parent, db ds {n}) ;
```

A2.3 A simple text processing package

SPECIFICATION OF TEXT_PROC

DESCRIPTION

Simple text analysis package – produces statistics, frequency tables, indexes and concordances of texts

IMPORTS

Objects

Position	from Sequence_Extensions

Operations

removedups, positions, delete	from Sequence_Extensions
minstring	from String_Extensions

MODEL

Objects

Text	
FreqTable	table showing all the word types in the text, and their frequencies
Index	a list of the words in the text, showing their positions
Concordance	like an index, but showing context for each instance of a word
Entry	one entry in a concordance
Type	a distinct word
Token	an instance of a word type

Visible operations

```
wordcount        : Text -> Nat
type_token_ratio : Text -> Real
freqtab          : Text -> FreqTable
index            : Text -> Index
concord          : Text x Nat -> Concordance
```

where

wordcount(t) returns the total number of word tokens in text t

type_token_ratio(t) gives the ratio of word types to tokens in the text t

freqtab(t) tabulates the frequency of each word type in text t

index(t) produces an alphabetical index of word types in text t

concord(t) gives a concordance of text t

Hidden operations

```
context    : Position x Nat x Text -> Text
```

```
freq        : Type x Text -> Nat
alphasort   : Text -> Text
```

where

context(p,n,t) gives the key word in pth position in text t, shown with n words of context before and after

freq(typ,t) gives the raw frequency of word type typ in text t

alphasort(t) sorts the text t alphabetically

SPECIFY

Objects

```
Text          = seq(Token)
FreqTable     = seq(pair(Type,Nat))
Index         = seq(pair(Type,seq(Position)))
Concordance   = seq(Entry)
Entry         = pair(Text,Position)
Type, Token   = String
```

Operations

```
wordcount(t) == len(t) ;

type_token_ratio(t) == wordcount(removedups(t)) / wordcount(t) ;

freqtab(t) ==
  [(typ,freq(typ,t)) | typ <- alphasort(removedups(t))] ;

index(t) ==
  [(typ,positions(typ,t)) | typ <- alphasort(removedups(t))] ;

concord(t,n) ==
  [(context(p,n,t),p) | typ <- alphasort(removedups(t)),
                        p   <- positions(typ,t) ] ;

context(p,n,t) ==
  if    p member dom(t)
  then [t[pos," "] | pos <- [p - n,...,p + n]]
  else [] ;

freq(typ,t) == wordcount([tok | tok <- t; tok = typ]) ;

alphasort(t) ==
  if    t = [] then []
  else let x == minstring reduce ("zzz") t
       in [x] conc alphasort(delete(t,hd(positions(x,t)))) ;
```

SPECIFICATION OF SEQUENCE_EXTENSIONS

DESCRIPTION

Extension to set of generic sequence operations

MODEL

Objects

Position the position of an element in a sequence

Operations

```
removedups  : seq(T) -> seq(T)
positions   : T x seq(T) -> seq(Position)
delete      : seq(T) x Position -> seq(T)
```

removedups(q) removes any duplicated items from a sequence, leaving only the last one

positions(x,q) gives a sequence of positive integers representing the positions (in ascending order) of item x in sequence q

delete(q,i) deletes the item in ith position from sequence q

SPECIFY

Objects

Position = Nat

Operations

```
removedups(q) ==
  if    q = [] then []
  else if     hd(q) member rng(tl(q))
        then removedups(tl(q))
        else [hd(q)] conc removedups(tl(q)) ;

positions(x,q) ==
  [ p | p <- [1,...,len(q)]; q[p] = x] ;

delete(q,i) ==
  if    i member dom(q)
  then asq({(if j < i then j else j - 1, x) | (j,x) <- asm(q);
                                                j /= i})
  else q;
```

SPECIFICATION OF STRING_EXTENSIONS

DESCRIPTION

Extension to set of predefined string operations

MODEL

Operations

```
minstring : String x String -> String
```

where

minstring(a,b) returns the string which is lower in an alphabetic sorting order

SPECIFY

Operations

```
minstring(a,b) == if a < b then a else b ;
```

A2.4 Automated teller machine

A2.4.1 Version 1

SPECIFICATION OF BANK

DESCRIPTION

Specifies the basic functionality for operating bank accounts

MODEL

Objects

BankDb	the bank database
Customer	customer identification
Account	
AccNo	account number
Amount	a sum of money

Visible operations

```
NewBankDb : -> BankDb
OpenAccount : BankDb x Customer x AccNo -> BankDb
CloseAccount : BankDb x AccNo -> BankDb
Deposit : BankDb x AccNo x Amount -> BankDb
Withdraw : BankDb x AccNo x Amount -> BankDb
Balance : BankDb x AccNo -> Amount union String
```

where

NewBankDb() creates a new bank database

OpenAccount(db,c) opens the account for customer c by adding an empty account to the database db

CloseAccount(db,n) closes account n by removing it from the database db

Deposit(db,n,m) credits the amount m to account n in database db

Withdraw(db,n,m) debits account n by amount m in database db

Balance(db,n) shows the balance of account n in database db

SPECIFY

Objects

```
BankDb    = map(AccNo,Account)
Account   = tuple(Customer,Amount)
AccNo     = Nat
Amount    = Integer
Customer  = String
```

Operations

```
NewBankDb() == {} ;
```

```
OpenAccount(bdb,c,acc) ==
  if   not(acc member dom(bdb))
  then bdb overwr {acc -> (c,0)}
  else bdb ;

CloseAccount(bdb,acc) ==
  if   (acc member dom(bdb)) and (second(bdb[acc,(" ",0)]) = 0)
  then bdb ds {acc}
  else bdb ;

Deposit(bdb,acc,amt) ==
  if   acc member dom(bdb)
  then let acct == bdb[acc]
       in  bdb overwr {acc -> (first(acct),second(acct) + amt)}
  else bdb ;

Withdraw(bdb,acc,amt) == Deposit(bdb,acc,-amt) ;

Balance(bdb,acc) == second(bdb[acc,(" ","no such account")]) ;
```

A2.4.2 Version 2

SPECIFICATION OF BANK

DESCRIPTION

Provides the staff banking operations, i.e. this module retains the functionality of the BANK module in the first iteration

MODEL

Objects

BankDb	the bank database
Account	
AccNo	account number
Amount	a sum of money
PIN	personal identification number
AtmCard	
CardNo	

Visible operations

NewBankDb : -> BankDb
OpenAccount : BankDb x AccNo -> BankDb
CloseAccount : BankDb x AccNo -> BankDb
Deposit : BankDb x AccNo x Amount -> BankDb
Withdraw : BankDb x AccNo x Amount -> BankDb
Balance : BankDb x AccNo -> Amount union String
CBooksOrdered : BankDb -> BankDb
StatementsOrdered : BankDb -> BankDb
IssueCard : BankDb x AtmCard -> BankDb
RetainCard : BankDb x AtmCard -> BankDb
ReleaseCard : BankDb x AtmCard -> BankDb
CardKnown : BankDb x AtmCard -> Boolean
CardLegal : BankDb x AtmCard -> Boolean
AcctKnown : BankDb x AccNo -> Boolean

where

NewBankDb() creates a new bank database

OpenAccount(db,n) opens account n by adding an empty account to the database db

CloseAccount(db,n) closes account n by removing it from the database db

Deposit(db,n,m) credits the amount m to account n in database db

Withdraw(db,n,m) debits account n by amount m in database db

Balance(db,n) shows the balance of account n in database db

CBooksOrdered() handles orders for check books

StatementsOrdered() handles orders for statements

IssueCard(db,c) associates a card with an account

RetainCard(db,c) renders card c unusable by adding it to list of illegal cards

ReleaseCard(db,c) removes card c from list of illegal cards

CardKnown(db,c) checks if card c and its account are in bank database db

CardLegal(db,c) checks if card c is in illegal list

AcctKnown(db,n) determines if account n is present in bank database db

SPECIFY

Objects

```
BankDb = record(accts:map(AccNo,Account),
                limit:Amount,
                illegal:set(AtmCard),
                statements:set(AccNo),
                cbooks:set(AccNo))
Account = tuple(set(AtmCard),Amount)
AtmCard = record(acc:AccNo, cid:CardNo, pin:PIN)
AccNo, CardNo, PIN = Nat
Amount = Integer
```

Record declarations

```
BankDb :: accts limit illegal statements cbooks ;

AtmCard :: acc cid pin ;
```

Operations

```
% invariant

  inv_BankDb(bdb) ==
    let all_cards == { c | a <- rng(accts(bdb)),
                           c <- first(a) }
    in let cids == { cid(c) | c <- all_cards },
           pins == { pin(c) | c <- all_cards }
       in (card(cids) = card(all_cards))
          and
          ((card(pins) = card(all_cards))
          and
          ((cids inter pins) = {})) ;

% account manipulation

  NewBankDb() == mk_BankDb({}, 0, {}, {}, {}) ; % zero limit

  OpenAccount(bdb,acc) ==
    if   AcctKnown(bdb,acc)
    then bdb
    else upd_accts(bdb,accts(bdb) overwr {acc -> ({},0)}) ;

  CloseAccount(bdb,acc) ==
    if   AcctKnown(bdb,acc) and (second(bdb[acc,("",0)]) = 0)
    then upd_accts(bdb,accts(bdb) ds {acc})
    else bdb ;
```

```
  Deposit(bdb,acc,amt) ==
    if    AcctKnown(bdb,acc)
    then let acct == accts(bdb)[acc]
         in upd_accts(bdb,accts(bdb) overwr
                          {acc -> (first(acct),second(acct)+amt)})
    else bdb ;

  Withdraw(bdb,acc,amt) == Deposit(bdb,acc,-amt) ;

  Balance(bdb,acc) ==
    if    AcctKnown(bdb,acc)
    then second(accts(bdb)[acc])
    else "no such account" ;

% card handling

  IssueCard(bdb,c) ==
    if    AcctKnown(bdb,acc(c))
    then let acct == accts(bdb)[acc(c)]
         in let new == upd_accts(bdb,accts(bdb) overwr
                          {acc(c) -> (first(acct) union {c},
                                      second(acct))})
            in if inv_BankDb(new) then new else bdb
    else bdb ;

  RetainCard(bdb,c) == upd_illegal(bdb,illegal(bdb) union {c}) ;

  ReleaseCard(bdb,c) == upd_illegal(bdb,illegal(bdb) diff {c}) ;

% order acknowledgement

  CBooksOrdered(bdb) == upd_cbooks(bdb,{}) ;

  StatementsOrdered(bdb) == upd_statements(bdb,{}) ;

% checking operations

  CardKnown(bdb,c) ==
    AcctKnown(bdb,acc(c)) and
    (c member first(accts(bdb)[acc(c),({},0)])) ;

  CardLegal(bdb,c) == not(c member illegal(bdb)) ;

  AcctKnown(bdb,acc) == acc member dom(accts(bdb)) ;
```

SPECIFICATION OF ATM_USER

DESCRIPTION

Introduces operations for ATM transactions and security

IMPORTS

Objects

BankDb	from BANK
AtmCard	from BANK

PIN	from BANK
Amount	from BANK

Operations

Balance	from BANK
Withdraw	from BANK
CardKnown	from BANK
CardLegal	from BANK

MODEL

Visible operations

```
atm_OrderCBook : BankDb x AtmCard x PIN -> BankDb
atm_OrderStatement : BankDb x AtmCard x PIN -> BankDb
atm_Balance : BankDb x AtmCard x PIN -> Amount union String
atm_Withdraw : BankDb x AtmCard x PIN x Amount -> BankDb
```

where

atm_OrderCBook(db,c,p) orders a check book for account in db named on card c

atm_OrderStatement(db,c,p) orders a statement for account in db named on card c

atm_Balance(db,c,p) enquires on balance of account in db named on card c

atm_Withdraw(db,c,p,amt) withdraws amt from account in db named on card c subject to ATM restrictions

Hidden operations

```
TransactionOK : BankDb x AtmCard x PIN -> Boolean
PINOK : Atmcard x PIN -> Boolean
AmountOK : BankDb x AtmCard x Amount -> Boolean
```

where

TransactionOK(db,c,p) checks account, card c and PIN p are valid

PINOK(c,p) matches PIN p against number on card c

AmountOK(db,c,m) enforces ATM restrictions on withdrawal

SPECIFY

Operations

```
atm_OrderCBook(bdb,c,p) ==
  if   TransactionOK(bdb,c,p)
  then upd_cbooks(bdb,cbooks(bdb) union {acc(c)})
  else bdb ;

atm_OrderStatement(bdb,c,p) ==
  if   TransactionOK(bdb,c,p)
  then upd_statements(bdb,statements(bdb) union {acc(c)})
  else bdb ;
```

```
atm_Balance(bdb,c,p) ==
  if     TransactionOK(bdb,c,p)
  then Balance(bdb,acc(c))
  else "transaction refused" ;

atm_Withdraw(bdb,c,p,amt) ==
  if     TransactionOK(bdb,c,p) and AmountOK(bdb,c,amt)
  then Withdraw(bdb,acc(c),amt)
  else bdb ;

TransactionOK(bdb,c,p) ==
  CardKnown(bdb,c) and (PINOK(c,p) and CardLegal(bdb,c) ;

PINOK(c,p) == pin(c) = p ;

AmountOK(bdb,c,amt) ==
  ((amt < limit(bdb)) and ((amt mod 5) = 0))
  and (amt <= second(accts(bdb)[acc(c),({},0)])) ;
```

A2.4.3 Version 3

SPECIFICATION OF BASIC_BANK

DESCRIPTION

Provides all the bank and ATM objects needed, together with operations to create, manipulate and interrogate them

MODEL

Objects

Bank	the bank
BankDb	the bank database
Atm	ATM-specific information
AtmId	ATM identifier
Account	
AccNo	account number
Amount	a sum of money
AtmCard	
PIN	personal identification number
CardNo	card number

Visible operations

NewBank : -> Bank
bdb : Bank -> BankDb
atms : Bank -> map(AtmId,Atm)
ReplaceAtm : Bank x AtmId x Atm -> Bank
ReplaceBankDb : Bank x BankDb -> Bank
CardKnown : BankDb x AtmCard -> Boolean
CardLegal : BankDb x AtmCard -> Boolean
AcctKnown : BankDb x AccNo -> Boolean
EnoughCash : Atm x Amount -> Boolean
AtmKnown : Bank x AtmId -> Boolean

where

NewBank() creates a new bank

bdb(b) extracts the bank database from a bank b

atms(b) extracts the ATMs in bank b

ReplaceAtm(b,i,a) constructs a new bank from b replacing ATM i by a

ReplaceBankDb(b,db) constructs a new bank from b replacing the bank database by db

CardKnown(db,c) checks if card c and its account are in bank database db

CardLegal(db,c) checks if card c is in illegal list

AcctKnown(db,n) determines if account n is present in bank database db

EnoughCash(a,m) checks that ATM a contains at least amount m

AtmKnown(b,i) checks that ATM named i is registered in bank b

SPECIFY

Objects

```
Bank = tuple(BankDb,map(AtmId,Atm))
BankDb = record(accts : map(AccNo,Account),
                limit : Amount,
                illegal : set(AtmCard),
                statements : set(AccNo),
                cbooks : set(AccNo))
Atm = Amount
AtmId = String
Account = tuple(set(AtmCard),Amount)
AtmCard = record(acc:AccNo, cid:CardNo, pin:PIN)
AccNo, CardNo, PIN = Nat
Amount = Integer
```

Record declarations

```
BankDb :: accts limit illegal statements cbooks ;

AtmCard :: acc cid pin ;
```

Operations

```
inv_BankDb(bdb) ==
  let all_cards == { c | a <- rng(accts(bdb)),
                         c <- first(a) }
  in let cids == { cid(c) | c <- all_cards },
         pins == { pin(c) | c <- all_cards }
     in (card(cids) = card(all_cards))
        and
        ((card(pins) = card(all_cards))
        and
        ((cids inter pins) = {})) ;

% constructors and selectors

  NewBank() == (mk_BankDb({}, 0, {}, {}, {}),{}) ;

  bdb(b) == first(b) ;

  atms(b) == second(b) ;

  ReplaceAtm(bank,aid,atm) ==
    (bdb(bank),atms(bank) overwr {aid -> atm}) ;

  ReplaceBankDb(bank,db) == (db,atms(bank)) ;

% checking operations

  CardKnown(bdb,c) ==
    AcctKnown(bdb,acc(c)) and
    (c member first(accts(bdb)[acc(c),({},0)])) ;
```

```
CardLegal(bdb,c) == not(c member illegal(bdb)) ;
AcctKnown(bdb,acc) == acc member dom(accts(bdb)) ;
EnoughCash(atm,amt) == atm >= amt ;
AtmKnown(bank,aid) == aid member dom(atms(bank)) ;
```

SPECIFICATION OF BANK_STAFF

DESCRIPTION

Provides the operations for bank staff

IMPORTS

Objects

Bank	from BASIC_BANK
AtmCard	from BASIC_BANK
AccNo	from BASIC_BANK
Amount	from BASIC_BANK
AtmId	from BASIC_BANK

Operations

bdb	from BASIC_BANK
atms	from BASIC_BANK
AcctKnown	from BASIC_BANK
ReplaceBankDb	from BASIC_BANK
ReplaceAtm	from BASIC_BANK

MODEL

Visible operations

```
OpenAccount : Bank x AccNo -> Bank
Deposit : Bank x AccNo x Amount -> Bank
Withdraw : Bank x AccNo x Amount -> Bank
Balance : Bank x AccNo -> Amount union String
CloseAccount : Bank x AccNo -> Bank
CBooksOrdered : Bank -> Bank
StatementsOrdered : Bank -> Bank
IssueCard : Bank x AtmCard -> Bank
RetainCard : Bank x AtmCard -> Bank
ReleaseCard : Bank x AtmCard -> Bank
AddCash : Bank x AtmId x Amount -> Bank
RemoveCash : Bank x AtmId x Amount -> Bank
```

where

OpenAccount(b,n) opens the account n by adding an empty account to the database in bank b

CloseAccount(b,n) closes account n by removing it from the database in bank b

Deposit(b,n,m) credits the amount m to account n in database in bank b

Withdraw(b,n,m) debits account n by amount m in database in bank b

Balance(b,n) shows the balance of account n in database in bank b

CBooksOrdered(b) handles orders for check books

StatementsOrdered(b) handles orders for statements

IssueCard(b,c) associates a card with an account

RetainCard(b,c) renders card c unusable by adding it to list of illegal cards

ReleaseCard(b,c) removes card c from list of illegal cards

AddCash(b,i,m) increases the amount of cash held in ATM i by m

RemoveCash(b,i,m) reduces the amount of cash held in ATM i by m

SPECIFY

Operations

```
OpenAccount(bank,acc) ==
  let db == bdb(bank)
  in if    AcctKnown(db,acc)
     then bank
     else ReplaceBankDb(bank,
                       upd_accts(db,accts(db) overwr {acc -> ({},0)})) ;

CloseAccount(bank,acc) ==
  let db == bdb(bank)
  in if    AcctKnown(db,acc)
           and (second(db[acc,(" ",0)]) = 0)
     then ReplaceBankDb(bank,upd_accts(db,accts(db) ds {acc}))
     else bank ;

Deposit(bank,acc,amt) ==
  let db == bdb(bank)
  in if    AcctKnown(db,acc)
     then let acct == accts(db)[acc]
          in ReplaceBankDb(bank,
               upd_accts(db,accts(db) overwr
                         {acc -> (first(acct),second(acct) + amt}))
     else bank ;

Withdraw(bank,acc,amt) == Deposit(bank,acc,-amt) ;

Balance(bank,acc) ==
  if    AcctKnown(bdb(bank),acc)
  then second(accts(bdb(bank))[acc])
  else "no such account" ;

% order management

  CBooksOrdered(bank) ==
    ReplaceBankDb(bank,upd_cbooks(bdb(bank),{})) ;

  StatementsOrdered(bank) ==
    ReplaceBankDb(bank,upd_statements(bdb(bank),{})) ;
```

```
% card handling

  IssueCard(bank,c) ==
    let db == bdb(bank)
    in if    AcctKnown(db,acc(c))
       then let acct == accts(db)[acc(c)]
            in let new == upd_accts(db,
                                        accts(db) overwr
                            {acc(c) -> (first(acct) union {c},second(acct))}))
               in if     inv_BankDb(new)
                  then ReplaceBankDb(bank,new) else new
       else bank ;

  RetainCard(bank,c) ==
    ReplaceBankDb(bank,
                  upd_illegal(bdb(bank),illegal(bdb(bank)) union {c})) ;

  ReleaseCard(bank,c) ==
    ReplaceBankDb(bank,
                  upd_illegal(bdb(bank),illegal(bdb(bank)) diff {c})) ;

% cash management for atms

  AddCash(bank,aid,amt) ==
    if     AtmKnown(bank,aid)
    then ReplaceAtm(bank,aid,atms(bank)[aid] + amt))
    else bank ;

  RemoveCash(bank,aid,amt) ==
    if     AtmKnown(bank,aid)
    then let atm == atms(bank)[aid]
         in if    atm < amt
            then ReplaceAtm(bank,aid,0)
            else ReplaceAtm(bank,aid,atm - amt)
    else bank ;
```

SPECIFICATION OF ATM_USER

DESCRIPTION

IMPORTS

Objects

Bank	from BASIC_BANK
AtmId	from BASIC_BANK
AtmCard	from BASIC_BANK
PIN	from BASIC_BANK
Amount	from BASIC_BANK

Operations

bdb	from BASIC_BANK
atms	from BASIC_BANK

CardKnown	from BASIC_BANK
CardLegal	from BASIC_BANK
EnoughCash	from BASIC_BANK
AtmKnown	from BASIC_BANK
Balance	from BANK_STAFF
Withdraw	from BANK_STAFF

MODEL

Visible operations

atm_OrderCBook : Bank x AtmId x AtmCard x PIN -> Bank
atm_OrderStatement : Bank x AtmId x AtmCard x PIN -> Bank
atm_Withdraw : Bank x AtmId x AtmCard x PIN x Amount -> Bank
atm_Balance : Bank x AtmId x AtmCard x PIN -> Amount union String

where

atm_OrderCBook(b,i,c,p) orders a check book for account in b named on card c using ATM i

atm_OrderStatement(b,i,c,p) orders a statement for account in b named on card c using ATM i

atm_Balance(b,i,c,p) enquires on balance of account in b named on card c using ATM i

atm_Withdraw(b,c,i,p,amt) withdraws amt from account in b named on card c subject to ATM restrictions, using ATM i

Hidden operations

TransactionOK : Bank x AtmId x AtmCard x PIN -> Boolean
PINOK : AtmCard x PIN -> Boolean
AmountOK : BankDb x AtmCard x Amount -> Boolean

where

TransactionOK(db,i,c,p) checks account, card c, PIN p and ATM i are valid

PINOK(c,p) matches PIN p against number on card c

AmountOK(db,c,m) enforces ATM restrictions on withdrawal

SPECIFY

Operations

```
atm_OrderCBook(bank,aid,c,p) ==
  let db == bdb(bank)
  in if   TransactionOK(bank,aid,c,p)
     then ReplaceBankDb(bank,
                        upd_cbooks(db,cbooks(db) union {acc(c)}))
     else bank ;
```

```
atm_OrderStatement(bank,aid,c,p) ==
  let db == bdb(bank)
  in if    TransactionOK(bank,aid,c,p)
     then ReplaceBankDb(bank,
                        upd_statements(db,statements(db) union {acc(c)}))
     else bank ;

atm_Withdraw(bank,aid,c,p,amt) ==
  if    TransactionOK(bank,aid,c,p)
        and AmountOK(bdb(bank),c,amt)
  then if    EnoughCash(atms(bank)[aid],amt) )
       then Withdraw(RemoveCash(bank,aid,amt),acc(c),amt)
       else bank
  else bank ;

atm_Balance(bank,aid,c,p) ==
  if    TransactionOK(bank,aid,c,p)
  then Balance(bank,acc(c))
  else "transaction refused" ;

TransactionOK(bank,aid,c,p) ==
  CardKnown(bdb(bank),c)
  and (PINOK(c,p)
  and (CardLegal(bdb(bank),c)
  and AtmKnown(bank,aid) )) ;

PINOK(c,p) == pin(c) = p ;

AmountOK(bdb,c,amt) ==
  ((amt < limit(bdb)) and ((amt mod 5) = 0))
  and (amt <= second(accts(bdb)[acc(c),({},0)])) ;
```

A2.5 The domino problem

A2.5.1 Version 1

SPECIFICATION OF DOMINO

DESCRIPTION

Specification as supplied by NTU design group

MODEL

Objects

Domino	
EndSystem	
Db	collection of dominoes
Route	names of dominoes needed for connection
TransType	transport-level attributes
Name	
AppType	application-level attributes
Protocol	
Attribute	

Visible operations

```
mk_Db : -> Db
add_domino : Db x Domino -> Db
del_domino : Db x Name -> Db
gateways : EndSystem x EndSystem x Db -> set(Route)
```

where

mk_Db() creates an empty collection of dominoes

add_domino(db,d) adds domino d to collection db

del_domino(db,d) removes domino d from collection db

gateways(e1,e2,db) attempts to find dominoes in db which will link e1 to e2

Hidden operations

```
fromES : EndSystem -> Domino
toES : EndSystem -> Domino
prot1 : Domino -> Protocol
prot2 : Domino -> Protocol
gender1 : Domino -> Attribute
gender2 : Domino -> Attribute
matches : Domino x Domino -> Boolean
gender_match : Domino x Domino -> Boolean
connectable : Attribute x Attribute -> Boolean
find_routes : Domino x Domino x Db -> set(Route)
successors : Domino x Db -> set(Domino)
find_shortest : set(Route) -> set(Route)
```

```
len_of_shortest : set(Route) -> Integer
min : Number x Number -> Number
```

where

fromES(e) converts end-system e to domino at start of chain

toES(e) converts end-system e to domino at end of chain

prot1(d) extracts first protocol from domino d

prot2(d) extracts second protocol from domino d

gender1(d) extracts first gender from domino d

gender2(d) extracts second gender from domino d

matches(d1,d2) sees if d2 can be placed beside d1

gender_match(d1,d2) sees if d1 and d2 match on protocol and attribute

connectable(a1,a2) sees if attributes a1 and a2 match

find_routes(d1,d2,db) finds all possible routes between d1 and d2

successors(d,db) finds all dominoes in db which can be placed beside d

find_shortest(rs) finds shortest route in routes in rs

len_of_shortest(rs) finds length of shortest route in rs

min(a,b) returns the smaller of a and b

SPECIFY

Objects

```
Domino                      = record(name:Name, upper:AppType,
                                       ttl:TransType, tt2:TransType )
EndSystem                   = record(top:AppType, bottom:TransType)
Db                          = set(Domino)
Route                       = seq(Name)
TransType                   = record(prot:Protocol, attr:Attribute) union
                              {"dummy"}
Name, AppType, Protocol     = String
Attribute                   = { "NULL", "+", "-" }
```

Record declarations

```
domino :: name upper tt1 tt2 ;

endsystem :: top bottom ;

transtype :: prot attr ;
```

Operations

```
% Domino and database manipulation:

mk_Db() == {} ;

add_domino(db,d) == db union {d} ;

del_domino(db,n) == { d | d <- db; name(d) /= n } ;
```

```
  fromES(e) == mk_Domino("ES1",top(e),"dummy",bottom(e)) ;

  toES(e) == mk_Domino("ES2",top(e),bottom(e),"dummy") ;

% Field selection:

  prot1(d) == prot(tt1(d)) ;

  prot2(d) == prot(tt2(d)) ;

  gender1(d) == attr(tt1(d)) ;

  gender2(d) == attr(tt2(d)) ;

% Matching operations:

  matches(d1,d2) == (upper(d1) = upper(d2)) and gender_match(d1,d2) ;

  gender_match(d1,d2) ==
    (prot2(d1) = prot1(d2))
    and
    connectable(gender2(d1),gender1(d2)) ;

  connectable(a1,a2) ==
    ((a1="NULL") and (a2="NULL"))
    or
    ( ((a1 = "+") and (a2 = "-"))
      or
      ((a1 = "-") and (a2 = "+")) ) ;

% Creating a route:

  gateways(e1,e2,db) ==
    find_shortest(find_routes(fromES(e1),toES(e2),db)) ;

  find_routes(d1,d2,db) ==
    if    matches(d1,d2)
    then { [] }
    else { [name(next)] conc r |
                next <- successors(d1,db),
                r <- find_routes(next,d2,
                                  del_domino(db,name(next))) } ;

  successors(d,db) == { d1 | d1 <- db; matches(d,d1) } ;

  find_shortest(rs) == { r | r <- rs; len(r) = len_of_shortest(rs) } ;

  len_of_shortest(rs) == min reduce (999) { len(r) | r <- rs } ;

  min(a,b) == if a < b then a else b ;
```

A2.5.2 Version 2

SPECIFICATION OF DOMINO

DESCRIPTION

Amalgamates EndSystem and Domino objects; allows 'flipping' of dominoes

MODEL

Objects

Domino	
EndSystem	
Connection	the transport-level side(s)
Db	collection of dominoes
Route	
TransType	transport-level attributes
Name	
AppType	application-level attributes
Protocol	
Attribute	

Visible operations

mk_Db : -> Db
add_domino : Db x Domino -> Db
del_domino : Db x Name -> Db
gateways : EndSystem x EndSystem x Db -> set(Route)

where

mk_Db() creates an empty collection of dominoes

add_domino(db,d) adds domino d to collection db

del_domino(db,d) removes domino d from collection db

gateways(e1,e2,db) attempts to find dominoes in db which will link e1 to e2

Hidden operations

is_EndSystem : Domino -> Boolean
flip : Domino -> Domino
prot1 : Domino -> Protocol
prot2 : Domino -> Protocol
gender1 : Domino -> Attribute
gender2 : Domino -> Attribute
tt1 : Domino -> TransType
tt2 : Domino -> TransType
matches : Domino x Domino -> Boolean
gender_match : Domino x Domino -> Boolean
connectable : Attribute x Attribute -> Boolean
find_routes : Domino x Domino x Db -> set(Route)
successors : Domino x Db -> set(Domino)

```
find_shortest : set(Route) -> set(Route)
len_of_shortest : set(Route) -> Integer
min : Number x Number -> Number
```

where

is_EndSystem(d) sees if domino d has only one 'side'

flip(d) flips domino d to other orientation

prot1(d) extracts first protocol from domino d

prot2(d) extracts second protocol from domino d

gender1(d) extracts first gender from domino d

gender2(d) extracts second gender from domino d

matches(d1,d2) sees if d2 can be placed beside d1

gender_match(d1,d2) sees if d1 and d2 match on protocol and attribute

connectable(a1,a2) sees if attributes a1 and a2 match

find_routes(d1,d2,db) finds all possible routes between d1 and d2

successors(d,db) finds all dominoes in db which can be placed beside d

find_shortest(rs) finds shortest route in routes in rs

len_of_shortest(rs) finds length of shortest route in rs

min(a,b) returns the smaller of a and b

SPECIFY

Objects

```
Domino                      = record(name:Name, upper:AppType,
                                     lower:Connection )
EndSystem                   = Domino
Connection                  = tuple(TransType,TransType) union TransType
Db                          = set(Domino)
Route                       = seq(Name)
TransType                   = record(prot:Protocol, attr:Attribute)
Name, AppType, Protocol = String
Attribute                   = { "NULL", "+", "−" }
```

Record declarations

```
domino :: name upper lower ;
transtype :: prot attr ;
```

Operations

```
% Domino and database manipulation:
  mk_Db() == {} ;
  add_domino(db,d) ==
       if flip(d) member db then db else db union {d} ;
  del_domino(db,n) == { d | d <- db; name (d) /= n } ;
  is_EndSystem(d) == is_TransType(lower(d)) ;
```

```
flip(d) ==
  if    is_EndSystem(d)
  then d
  else upd_lower(d,(tt2(d),tt1(d))) ;

% Field selection:

  prot1(d) == prot(tt1(d)) ;

  prot2(d) == prot(tt2(d)) ;

  gender1(d) == attr(tt1(d)) ;

  gender2(d) == attr(tt2(d)) ;

  tt1(d) ==
    if is_EndSystem(d) then lower(d) else first(lower(d)) ;

  tt2(d) ==
    if is_EndSystem(d) then lower(d) else second(lower(d)) ;

% Matching operations:

  matches(d1,d2) ==
    (upper(d1) = upper(d2)) and gender_match(d1,d2) ;

  gender_match(d1,d2) ==
    (prot2(d1) = prot1(d2))
    and
    connectable(gender2(d1),gender1(d2)) ;

  connectable(a1,a2) ==
    ((a1="NULL") and (a2="NULL"))
    or
    ( ((a1 = "+") and (a2 = "-"))
      or
      ((a1 = "-") and (a2 = "+")) ) ;

% Creating a route:

  gateways(e1,e2,db) == find_shortest(find_routes(e1,e2,db)) ;

  find_routes(d1,d2,db) ==
    if    matches(d1,d2)
    then { [] }
    else { [name(next)] conc r | next <- successors(d1,d2),
                                 r <- find_routes(next,d2,
                                          del_domino(db,name(next))) } ;

    successors(d,db) ==
      { d1 | d1 <- db; matches(d,d1) }
      union
      { flip(d1) | d1 <- db; matches(d,flip(d1)) } ;

    find_shortest(rs) ==
      { r | r <- rs; len(r) = len_of_shortest(rs) } ;

    len_of_shortest(rs) == min reduce (999) { len(r) | r <- rs } ;

    min(a,b) == if a < b then a else b ;
```

A2.6 Devolved PARIS

A2.6.1 Version 1

SPECIFICATION OF PARIS

DESCRIPTION

Based on GIS version

MODEL

Objects

SKEs:

SKEs	collection of SKEs
SKE	
Symptoms	symptom types and values
SKEid	SKE identifier
ProdGp	product group
EntryCl	entry class
SymType	symptom type
SymValue	symptom value

Standards:

Standards	standards at product-group level
ECstandard	standards at entry-class level
SKEstd	format for each valid symptom-type
Format	definition of valid symptom-type
ValType	flags if numeric or text symptom-type

Visible operations

SearchSKE : SKEs x Standards x ProdGp x EntryCl x Symptoms
-> set(SKEid)

where

SearchSKE(skes,stds,pg,ec,sy) checks that the product-group pg, entry-class ec and symptoms sy conform to the standards in std and searches for SKEs in SKEs that match the enquiry parameters pg, ec and sy.

Hidden operations

valid_symptoms : SKEstd x Symptoms -> Boolean
check_mand : set(SymType) x Symptoms -> Boolean
check_all : set(SymType) x Symptoms -> Boolean
check_num : set(SymType) x Symptoms -> Boolean
check_text : set(SymType) x Symptoms -> Boolean
check_single : set(SymType) x Symptoms -> Boolean
check_values : SKEstd x set(SymType) x Symptoms -> Boolean
SKEmatches : SKE x ProdGp x EntryCl x Symptoms -> Boolean

values_match : set(SymValue) x set(SymValue) -> Boolean

where

valid_symptoms(st,sy) checks that symptoms sy conform to standard st

check_mand(sts,sy) checks mandatory symptoms supplied in sy match sts

check_all(sts,sy) checks symptoms supplied in sy are present in sts

check_num(sts,sy) checks numeric symptoms supplied in sy match sts

check_text(sts,sy) checks text symptoms supplied in sy match sts

check_single(sts,sy) checks number of symptom values supplied in sy matches those allowed by sts

check_values(std,sts,sy) checks values of text symptoms supplied in sy are valid according to std

SKEmatches(ske,pg,ec,sy) checks for match between ske, product group pg, entry class ec and valid symptoms sy

values_match(sv1,sv2) checks values given sv1 against those in SKE sv2

SPECIFY

Objects

```
SKEs = set(SKE)
SKE = record(sid:SKEid, pg:ProdGp, ec:EntryCl, syms:Symptoms)
Symptoms = map(SymType,set(SymValue))

SKEid = Integer
SymType, ProdGp, EntryCl = String
SymValue = String union Number

Standards    = map(ProdGp,ECstandard)
ECstandard   = map(EntryCl,SKEstd)

SKEstd       = map(SymType,Format)

Format       = record(mand:Boolean, multi:Boolean,
                      type:ValType, maxv:Integer)
ValType      = {"Number", "Text"}
```

Record declarations

```
ske :: sid pg ec syms ;

format :: mand multi type maxv ;
```

Operations

```
% Search operation:

SearchSKE(skes,stds,pgroup,eclass,symp) ==
  if    valid_symptoms(stds[pgroup,{}][eclass,{}],symp)
  then { sid(ske) | ske <- skes;
                    SKEmatches(ske,pgroup,eclass,symp) }
  else {} ;
```

```
% Checking operations:

  valid_symptoms(std,symp) ==
    let mands == { st | (st,fmt) <- std; mand(fmt) },
        singles == { st | (st,fmt) <- std; not(multi(fmt)) },
        nums == { st | (st,fmt) <- std; type(fmt)="Number" },
        texts == { st | (st,fmt) <- std; type(fmt)="Text" }
    in
        check_mand(mands,symp)
        and (check_all(dom(std),symp)
        and (check_num(nums,symp)
        and (check_text(texts,symp)
        and (check_single(singles,symp)
        and check_values(std,texts,symp) )))) ;

  check_mand(mands,symp) ==
    (mands = {}) or ((symp dr mands) /= {}) ;

  check_all(alls,symp) == dom(symp) subset alls ;

  check_num(nums,symp) ==
    all sv in dunion(rng(symp dr nums)) . is_number(sv) ;

  check_text(texts,symp) ==
    all sv in dunion(rng(symp dr texts)) . is_string(sv) ;

  check_single(singles,symp) ==
    all svs in rng(symp dr singles) . card(svs) = 1 ;

  check_values(std,texts,symp) ==
    let sym_rel == { (st,sv) | (st,svs) <- symp dr texts, sv <- svs }
    in  all (st,sv) in sym_rel . stringlength(sv) <= maxv(std[st]) ;

% Matching operations:

  SKEmatches(ske,pgroup,eclass,symp) ==
    (pgroup = pg(ske))
    and ((eclass = ec(ske))
    and (all st in dom(symp) .
             values_match(symp[st],syms(ske)[st,{}]))) ;

  values_match(inpv,skev) ==
    (inpv = skev)
    or ((inpv subset skev)
    or (skev subset inpv)) ;
```

A2.6.2 Version 2

SPECIFICATION OF PARIS

DESCRIPTION

Less explicit version of GIS specification

MODEL

Objects

SKEs:

SKEs	collection of SKEs
SKE	
Symptoms	symptom types and values
SKEid	SKE identifier
ProdGp	product group
EntryCl	entry class
SymType	symptom type
SymValue	symptom value

Standards:

Standards	standards at product-group level
ECstandard	standards at entry-class level
SKEstd	format for each valid symptom-type
Format	definition of valid symptom-type
ValType	flags if numeric or text symptom-type

Visible operations

SearchSKE : SKEs x Standards x ProdGp x EntryCl x Symptoms -> set (SKEid)

where

SearchSKE(skes,stds,pg,ec,sy) checks that the product-group pg, entry-class ec and symptoms sy conform to the standards in stds and searches for SKEs in SKEs that match the enquiry parameters pg, ec and sy.

Hidden operations

valid_symptoms : SKEstd x Symptoms -> Boolean
has_mand_sym : SKEstd -> Boolean
contains_mand_sym : SKEstd x Symptoms -> Boolean
valid_format : Format x set(SymValue) -> Boolean
SKEmatches : SKE x ProdGP x EntryCl x Symptoms -> Boolean
values_match : set(SymValue) x set(SymValue) -> Boolean

where

valid_symptoms(st,sy) checks that symptoms sy conform to standard st

has_mand_sym(std) checks if mandatory symptom must be present

contains_mand_sym(std,sy) checks if mandatory symptom is present in sy valid_format(f,svs) checks symptom values svs against format f

SKEmatches(ske,pg,ec,sy) checks for match between ske, product group pg, entry class ec and valid symptoms sy

values_match(sv1,sv2) checks values given sv1 against those in SKE sv2

SPECIFY

Objects

```
SKEs = set(SKE)
SKE = record(sid:SKEid, pg:ProdGp, ec:EntryCl, syms:Symptoms)
Symptoms = map(SymType,set(SymValue))

SKEid = Integer
SymType, ProdGp, EntryCl = String
SymValue = String union Number

Standards = map(ProdGp,ECstandard)
ECstandard = map(EntryCl, SKEstd)
SKEstd = map(SymType,Format)

Format = record(mand:Boolean, multi:Boolean, type:ValType, maxv:Integer)
ValType = {"Number", "Text"}
```

Record declarations

```
ske :: sid pg ec syms ;

format :: mand multi type maxv ;
```

Operations

```
% Search operation:

  SearchSKE(skes, stds, pgroup,eclass,symp) ==
    if    valid_symptoms(stds[pgroup,{}][eclass,{}],symp)
    then { sid(ske) | ske <- skes; SKEmatches (ske,pgroup,eclass,symp) }
    else {} ;

% Checking operations:

  valid_symptoms(std,symp) ==
    if    dom(symp) subset dom(std)
    then (has_mand_sym(std) => contains_mand_sym(std,symp))
         and
         (all (st,v) in symp . valid_format(std[st],v))
    else false ;

  has_mand_sym(std) == exists fmt in rng(std) . mand(fmt) ;

  contains_mand_sym(std,symp) ==
    exists st in dom(symp) . mand(std[st]) ;

  valid_format(fmt,values) ==
    (not(multi(fmt)) => (card(values) = 1))
    and
    (((type(fmt) = "Text") =>
      (all v in values . is_string(v) and (stringlength(v) <= maxv(fmt))))
       and
       ((type(fmt) = "Number") => (all v in values . is_number(v)))) ;
```

```
% Matching operations:

  SKEmatches(ske,pgroup,eclass,symp) ==
    (pgroup = pg(ske))
    and ((eclass = ec(ske))
    and (all st in dom(symp) . values_match(symp[st],syms(ske)[st,{}]))) ;

  values_match(inpv,skev) ==
    (inpv = skev)
    or ((inpv subset skev)
    or (skev subset inpv)) ;
```

A2.7 The Fundamental Association Model

A2.7.1 Module FAM

SPECIFICATION OF FAM

DESCRIPTION

This module handles the basic association mechanisms

IMPORTS

Objects

Rating	from RATING

Operations

ConfirmConnect	from CONNECT
ReceiveConnect	from CONNECT
EmptyRating	from RATING

MODEL

Object

FedSystem	the federated system
Environment	system contains environments which contain servers
Server	some entity in the system which can offer or use a service
RouteInfo	routes between servers
Routes	from, to and names of routes
Where	identifier for server in its environment
What	route and server ids
Security	ratings for routes and servers
Tokens	token pool
Token	token id and body
TokenBody	
SI	service instance
Status	flag for connections
Id	
RouteId	
TokenId	

Visible operations

EmptySys : –> FedSystem
EmptyEnv : –> Environment
AddServer : FedSystem x Where x Server –> FedSystem
AddRatings : FedSystem x Id x Security –> FedSystem
AddRoutes : FedSystem x Id x Routes –> FedSystem

```
NewServer : FedSystem x Where -> FedSystem
GetServer : FedSystem x Where -> Server
Associated : FedSystem -> rel(Where,Where)
Connected : FedSystem -> rel(Where,Where)
EnvRating : FedSystem x Id x What -> Rating
RespToken : FedSystem x Where x TokenId -> Token
InitToken : FedSystem x Where x TokenId -> Token
TokenFor : FedSystem x Where x Where -> Token union {"NO_ASSOC"}
NewTokenI : FedSystem x Where x TokenId x TokenBody -> FedSystem
NewTokenR : FedSystem x Where x TokenId x TokenBody -> FedSystem
StartResp : FedSystem x Where x TokenId x Rating -> FedSystem
StartInit : FedSystem x Where x Token -> FedSystem
EndAssoc : FedSystem x Where x TokenId -> FedSystem
RespToInit1 : FedSystem x Where x Where x TokenId -> FedSystem
InitToResp : FedSystem x Where x Where x TokenId -> FedSystem
RespToInit2 : FedSystem x Where x Where x TokenId -> FedSystem
```

Hidden operations

```
NoWhere : -> Where
EmptyServer : -> Server
```

SPECIFY

Objects

All environments in the system are held in a single database, each with a name by which it may be accessed. This does NOT reflect the intended architecture of a federated system.

```
FedSystem = map(Id,Environment)
Environment = record(servers:map(Id,Server),
                     FAMdata:Security,
                     routeinfo:RouteInfo)
```

An individual server can only be located in conjunction with its containing environment

```
Where = record(envId:Id, servId:Id)
```

Routes are held between servers (rather than environments)

```
RouteInfo = set(Routes)
Routes = record(from_wh:Where, to_wh:Where, how:set(RouteId))
```

Each server has a pool of tokens which it (as initiator) has received from other servers, and a set of service instances which it (as responder) has offered elsewhere. One decision reflected in the representations chosen here is that only one token is associated with an SI, so an SI can be indexed by the id of its token. Servers no longer hold local ratings

```
Server = record(tokens:map(TokenId,TokenBody),
                SIs:map(TokenId,SI))
```

Ratings are local views of security levels, where a security level is expressed in terms of security factors which make it up

```
Rating = map(FactorName,Factor)
Factor = set(FactorValue)
```

Security information can refer to a server or to a route

```
What = RouteId union Where
Security = map(What,Rating)
```

A token has a name and a body. When held in a pool, each token can be extracted by its name. The body records the servers at each end of the association it is used for. It also contains the security level required or achieved for a particular connection across the association.

```
Token = record(tkid:TokenId, tkbody:TokenBody)
TokenBody = record(respr:Where, initr:Where,
                   conn:Status,
                   SL:Rating, route:RouteId)
```

A service instance contains the skeleton token which it sends out when offering its service to other servers

```
SI = record(skeleton:TokenBody, SIrat:Rating)

Status = {"REQU", "ACCPT", "NONE", "ACK"} ;
Id, FactorName, FactorValue, RouteId, TokenId = String
```

Record declarations

```
environment :: servers FAMdata routeinfo ;

where :: envId servId ;

server :: tokens SIs ;

routes :: from_wh to_wh how ;

token :: tkid tkbody ;

tokenbody :: respr initr conn SL route ;

SI :: skeleton SIrat ;
```

Operations

```
% creating and changing databases

  EmptySys() == {} ;

  EmptyEnv() == mk_Environment ({}, {}, {}) ;

  AddServer(sys,wh,s) ==
    let env == sys[envId(wh),EmptyEnv()]
    in sys overwr
       {envId(wh) -> upd_servers(env,servers(env)
        overwr {servId(wh) -> s})};

  AddRatings(sys,eid,sec) ==
    let env == sys[eid,EmptyEnv()]
    in sys overwr
       {eid -> upd_FAMdata(env, FAMdata(env) overwr sec) } ;

  AddRoutes(sys,eid,rs) ==
    sys overwr {eid -> upd_routeinfo(sys[eid,EmptyEnv()],rs)} ;

  NoWhere() == mk_Where("","");

% operations for servers

  EmptyServer() == mk_Server({},{}) ;
```

```
  NewServer(sys,wh) == AddServer(sys,wh,EmptyServer()) ;

  Get Server(sys,wh) ==
    let eid == envId(wh), sid == servId(wh)
    in  servers(sys[eid,EmptyEnv()])[sid,EmptyServer()] ;

% operations to enquire about the state of a system, for checking
% which associations and connections have been established. These
% are not part of FAM but are for validating the model

  Associated(sys) ==
    let I  == { (eid,sid,tid) | (eid,env) <- sys,
                                (sid,s) <- servers(env),
                                tid <- dom(tokens(s)) },
        R  == { (eid,sid,tid) | (eid,env) <- sys,
                                (sid,s) <- servers(env),
                                tid <- dom(SIs(s)) }
    in
       { (mk_Where(eid1,iid),mk_Where(eid2,rid)) |
                                        (eid1,iid,tid1) <- I,
                                        (eid2,rid,tid2) <- R; tidl = tid2 } ;

  Connected(sys) ==
    let I  == { (eid,sid,tid,conn(tb)) | (eid,env) <- sys,
                                         (sid,s) <- servers(env),
                                         (tid,tb) <- tokens(s) },
        R  == { (eid,sid,tid,conn(skeleton(SI)) | (eid,env) <- sys,
                                                  (sid,s) <- servers(env),
                                                  (tid,SI) <- domSIs(s) }
    in
       { (mk_Where(eid1,iid),mk_Where(eid2,rid)) |
                                          (eid1,iid,tid1,conn1) <- I,
                                         (eid2,rid,tid2,conn2) <- R;
         (tid1 = tid2) and ((conn1 = "ACK") and (conn2 = "ACCPT")) } ;

% looking up ratings in environments

  % always returns valid rating (empty if no env. or rating)
  EnvRating(sys,eid,wh) ==
    FAMdata(sys[eid,EmptyEnv()])[wh,EmptyRating()] ;

% operations to handle tokens and service instances in servers

  RespToken(sys,wh_r,tid) ==
    mk_Token(tid,skeleton(SIs(GetServer(sys,wh_r))[tid])) ;

  InitToken(sys,wh_i,tid) ==
    mk_Token(tid,tokens(GetServer(sys,wh_i))[tid]) ;

  % find token for association from initiator pool;
  % there cannot be more than one.
  TokenFor(sys,wh_i,wh_r) ==
    let toks == {mk_Token(tid,tb) |
                   (tid,tb) <- tokens(GetServer(sys,wh_i));
                   respr(tb) = wh_r }
    in  if card(toks) = 0 then "NO_ASSOC" else the(toks) ;
```

```
% change token body for token in initiator pool
NewTokenI(sys,wh_i,tid,tb) ==
  let s == GetServer(sys,wh_i)
  in  AddServer(sys,wh_i,
              mk_Server(tokens(s) overwr {tid -> tb}, SIs(s))) ;

% change token body for token in SI
NewTokenR(sys,wh_r,tid,tb) ==
  let s == GetServer(sys,wh_r)
  in  let si == SIs(s)[tid]
      in  AddServer(sys,wh_r,
                  mk_Server(tokens(s),
                          SIs(s) overwr {tid -> upd_skeleton(si,tb)})) ;

% operations to create and end associations between servers

  % assoc. created by responder. Some info given as parameters
  % here would presumably be generated from within responder
  % (which would also call this operation). Can give a rating to
  % tailor SI for anticipated use (only local rating).
  StartResp(sys,wh_r,tid,rat) ==
    let R == GetServer(sys,wh_r),
        tb == mk_TokenBody(wh_r,NoWhere(), "NONE",
                          EmptyRating(),"")
    in  AddServer(sys, wh_r,upd_SIs(R,
                  SIs(R) overwr {tid -> mk_SI(tb,rat)})) ;

  % initiator acquires token; accepting it into pool sets up the
  % association
  StartInit(sys,wh_i,tok) ==
    NewTokenI(sys,wh_i,tkid(tok),upd_initr(tkbody(tok),wh_i)) ;

  % either server can end association. If initiator, it just
  % removes token from its pool (so there may still be other
  % associations with the SI offering the service). If responder
  % it removes the SI, thus killing ALL its associations.
  EndAssoc(sys,wh,tid) ==
    let s == GetServer(sys,wh)
    in  AddServer(sys,wh,mk_Server(tokens(s) ds {tid},
                                  SIs(s) ds {tid})) ;

% operations to encapsulate token sending (for convenience only)

  % extract skeleton token from responder and hand to initiator
  RespToInit1(sys,wh_r,wh_i,tid) ==
    StartInit(sys,wh_i,RespToken(sys,wh_r,tid)) ;

  % extract token from initiator and send to responder
  InitToResp(sys,wh_i,wh_r,tid) ==
    ReceiveConnect(sys,wh_r,InitToken(sys,wh_i,tid)) ;

  % extract token from responder and send to initiator
  RespToInit2(sys,wh_r,wh_i,tid) ==
    ConfirmConnect(sys,wh_i,RespToken(sys,wh_r,tid)) ;
```

A2.7.2 Module RATINGS

SPECIFICATION OF RATINGS

DESCRIPTION

This module provides operations to create and manipulate ratings

MODEL

Objects

Rating	local view of a security level
Factor	one aspect of a rating
FactorName	
FactorValue	

Visible operations

EmptyRating : -> Rating
AddFactor : Rating x FactorName x Factor -> Rating
exact : Factor -> Boolean
inexact : Factor -> Boolean
trusted : Rating -> Boolean
untrusted : Rating -> Boolean
includes : Rating x Rating -> Boolean
filter_exact : Rating x Rating -> Rating
bind : Rating x Rating -> Rating

where

EmptyRating() creates a rating with no factors

AddFactor(r,n,f) adds factor values f for name n in rating r

exact(f) determines if factor f is exact

inexact(f) determines if factor f is inexact

trusted(r) determines if rating r is trusted

untrusted(r) determines if rating r is untrusted

includes(r1,r2) determines if rating r1 includes rating r2

filter_exact(m,r) filters factors from r which are exact in m

bind(r1,r2) binds ratings r1 and r2

Hidden operation

prohibited : Rating -> set(FactorName)

where

prohibited(r) returns names of prohibited factors in r

SPECIFY

Objects

```
Rating = map(FactorName,Factor)
Factor = set(FactorValue) union {"NULL"}
FactorName = String
FactorValue = String union Number
```

Operations

```
inv_Rating(r) == not ({} member rng(r)) ;

EmptyRating() == {} ;

AddFactor(r,fn,fv) == r overwr {fn -> (r[fn,{}]) union fv} ;

exact(f) == card(f) = 1 ;

inexact(f) == not(exact(f)) ;

trusted(r) == exists (fn,f) in r . inexact(f) ;

intrusted(r) == not(trusted(r)) ;

includes(r1,r2) == all (fn,f) in r1 . f subset r2[fn,{}] ;

filter_exact(mask,r) ==
  { (fn,f) | (fn,f) <- r; not(fn member dom(mask))
                          or inexact(mask[fn,{}]) } ;

prohibited(r) == { fn | (fn,f) <- r; f = "NULL" } ;
bind(r1,r2) ==
  let r1OK == r1 ds prohibited(r1),
      r2OK == r2 ds prohibited(r2)
  in
      if   ((prohibited(r1) inter dom(r2OK)) /= {})
           or ((prohibited(r2) inter dom(r1OK)) /= {})
      then "FAIL"
      else
           let R == r1 overwr (r2 overwr
                {(fn, r1[fn] inter r2[fn]) | fn <- (dom(r1OK) inter dom(r2OK))})
           in if inv_Rating(R) then R else "FAIL" ;
```

A2.7.3 Module SECURITY

SPECIFICATION OF SECURITY

DESCRIPTION

Encapsulates the rules for combining ratings at each stage of connection

IMPORTS

Objects

FedSystem	from FAM
Environment	from FAM
SI	from FAM
Where	from FAM
Security	from FAM
RouteId	from FAM
Rating	from RATING

Operations

EnvRating	from FAM
GetServer	from FAM
inv_Rating	from RATING
bind	from RATING

MODEL

Visible operations

```
setRSL : FedSystem x Where x Where x Rating -> Rating union {"FAIL"}
setLA2 : FedSystem x Where x Where x Rating -> Rating union {"FAIL"}
setLA3 : FedSystem x Where x Where x Rating ->
                              pair(RouteId,Rating) union {"FAIL"}
setLA5 : FedSystem x Where x Where x RouteId x Rating ->
                                      Rating union {"FAIL"}
setLA6 : FedSystem x Where x Where x TokenId x Rating ->
                                      Rating union {"FAIL"}
```

where

setRSL(s,I,R,r) sets required security level from rating r

setLA2(s,I,R,r) sets level achieved at stage 2, based on ratings held for servers I and R in system s and rating r supplied

setLA3(s,I,R,r) sets level achieved at stage 3, based on ratings held for servers I and R in system s and rating r supplied; also returns route to use

setLA5(s,I,R,t,r) sets level achieved at stage 5, based on ratings held for servers I and R and route t in system s and rating r supplied

setLA6(s,I,R,ti,r) sets level achieved at stage 6, based on rating held for service instance for token ti in R in system s and rating r supplied

Hidden operations

```
RouteRatings : FedSystem x Where x Where x Rating -> Security
choose : Security -> pair(RouteId,Rating)
```

where

RouteRatings(s,I,R,r) returns route and rating, based on ratings held for servers I and R in system s and rating r supplied

choose(sec) chooses a single route and its rating from those supplied in sec

SPECIFY

Operations

```
% operations at the initiator end

  setRSL(sys,wh_i,wh_r,QOS) == QOS ;

  setLA2(sys,wh_i,wh_r,RSL) ==
    let r1 == EnvRating(sys,envId(wh_i),wh_i),
        r2 == EnvRating(sys,envId(wh_i),wh_r)
    in
        if   RSL = "FAIL" then "FAIL"
        else bind(bind(RSL,r1),r2) ;

  setLA3(sys,wh_i,wh_r,LA2) ==
    if   LA2 = "FAIL" then "FAIL"
    else let routes == RouteRatings(sys,wh_i,wh_r,LA2)
         in if   routes = {}
            then "FAIL"
            else choose(routes) ;

% operations at the responder end

  setLA5(sys,wh_i,wh_r,rid,LA3) ==
    if   LA3 = "FAIL" then "FAIL"
    else let r4 == EnvRating(sys,envId(wh_r),wh_i),
             r5 == EnvRating(sys,envId(wh_r),wh_r),
             r6 == EnvRating(sys,envId(wh_r),rid)
         in
             bind(bind(bind(LA3,r4),r5),r6) ;

  setLA6(sys,wh_i,wh_r,tid,LA5) ==
    if   LA5 = "FAIL" then "FAIL"
    else bind(LA5,SIrat(SIs(GetServer(sys,wh_r))[tid])) ;

% route-finding operations

  RouteRatings(sys,wh_i,wh_r,LA2) ==
    let eid == envId(wh_i)
    in let % bind LA2 with rating for each possible route
           all_r == { (rid,bind(LA2,EnvRating(sys,eid,rid))) |
                                              ri <- routeinfo(sys[eid,EmptyEnv()] ;
                                              ((from_wh(ri) = wh_i)
                                              and (to_wh(ri) = wh_r)),
                                              rid <- how(ri) }
```

```
        in  % keep all routes with valid rating
            { (rid,r) | (rid,r) <- all_r;
                        ((r /= "FAIL") and inv_Rating(r)) } ;

% this operation selects a route from those which are
% possible. No algorithm was defined originally as it is not
% relevant at this abstract level of the model, so a fairly
% arbitrary decision is made among the routes. The
% specification of that choice is omitted here.
choose(sec) ==
   – returns a route and rating from those supplied –
```

A2.7.4 Module CONNECT

SPECIFICATION OF CONNECT

DESCRIPTION

Operations to create and delete connections across associations

IMPORTS

Objects

FedSystem from FAM
Server from FAM
SI from FAM
Token from FAM
TokenId from FAM
TokenBody from FAM
Where from FAM
RouteId from FAM
Rating from RATING

Operations

NewTokenI from FAM
NewTokenR from FAM
TokenFor from FAM
GetServer from FAM
AddServer from FAM
EnvRating from FAM
setRSL from SECURITY
setLA2 from SECURITY
setLA3 from SECURITY
setLA5 from SECURITY
setLA6 from SECURITY
EmptyRating from RATING
untrusted from RATING
filter_exact from RATING

MODEL

Visible operations

StartConnect : FedSystem x Where x Where x Rating -> Fedsystem
ReceiveConnect : FedSystem x Where x Token -> FedSystem
ConfirmConnect : FedSystem x Where x Token -> FedSystem
EndConnect : FedSystem x Where x TokenId -> FedSystem

where

StartConnect(s,I,R,r) requests connection in system s between I and R, with QOS rating r

ReceiveConnect(s,R,t) pass token t to responder R in system s asking for connection

ConfirmConnect(s,I,t) pass token t back to initiator I in system s confirming connection

EndConnect(s,S,i) end connections involving token named i in server S

Hidden operations

```
SetupConnect : FedSystem x Where x Where x Rating -> FedSystem
RequestConnect : FedSystem x Where x Where x Rating x RouteId
                                                        -> FedSystem
AcceptConnect : FedSystem x Where x Where x TokenId x Rating
                                              x RouteId -> FedSystem
AckConnect : FedSystem x Where x Where x TokenId x Rating
                                              x RouteId -> FedSystem
```

where

SetupConnect(s,I,R,r) for connection between I and R in system s, bind all ratings (including r) at initiator end and choose a route

RequestConnect(s,I,R,r,i) for connection between I and R in system s using route i, set up token to send to responder r

AcceptConnect(s,I,R,t,r,i) for connection between I and R in system s using route i and token t, bind ratings at responder end (including r) and set up final rating for connection

AckConnect(s,I,R,t,r,i) for connection between I and R in system s using route i and token t, set up token to send acknowledgement back to initiator

SPECIFY

Operations

```
% operations to start connections – located in initiator

  % in initiator, set up token to send to responder (if various
  % checks on security succeed)
  StartConnect(sys,wh_i,wh_r,QOS) ==
    let tok == (TokenFor(sys,wh_i,wh_r)
    in if    (tok = "NO_ASSOC")
             or (conn(tkbody(tok)) /= "NONE")
       then sys
       else SetupConnect(sys,wh_i,wh_r,QOS) ;

  SetupConnect(sys,wh_i,wh_r,QOS) ==
    let routeLA3 == setLA3(sys,wh_i,wh_r,
                          setLA2(sys,wh_i,wh_r,
                                 setRSL(sys,wh_i,wh_r,QOS)))
    in let rt == first(routeLA3),
           LA3 == second(routeLA3)
       in if    LA3 = "FAIL"
          then sys
          else RequestConnect(sys,wh_i,wh_r,LA3,rt) ;
```

```
  % all checks succeeded so initiator sets up its token
  RequestConnect(sys,wh_i,wh_r,LA3,rid) ==
    let tid == tkid(TokenFor(sys,wh_i,wh_r)),
        R2 == EnvRating(sys,envId(wh_i),wh_r)),
    in let r == if    untrusted(R2) then EmptyRating()
                 else filter_exact(R2,LA3)
       in NewTokenI (sys,wh_i,tid,
                        mk_TokenBody(wh_r,wh_i,"REQU",r,rid)) ;

% operations to accept connections - located in responder

  ReceiveConnect(sys,wh_r,tok) ==
    let resp == GetServer(sys,wh_r),
        tid == tkid(tok), tb == tkbody(tok)
    in if   not((tid member dom(SIs(resp)))
                or (conn(tb) = "REQU"))
       then sys
       else AcceptConnect(sys,initr(tb),wh_r,tid,SL(tb), route(tb)) ;

  AcceptConnect(sys,wh_i,wh_r,tid,LA3,rid) ==
    let LA6 == setLA6(sys,wh_i,wh_r,tid,
                         setLA5(sys,wh_i,wh_r,rid,LA3))
    in if   LA6 = "FAIL"
       then sys
       else AckConnect(sys,wh_i,wh_r,tid,
                        if   LA3 = EmptyRating()
                        then EmptyRating()
                        else LA6,
                        rid) ;

  % all checks succeeded so set up token for acknowledgement
  AckConnect(sys,wh_i,wh_r,tid,SLA,rid) ==
    NewTokenR(sys,wh_r,tid,
                 mk_TokenBody(wh_r,wh_i,"ACCPT",SLA,rid)) ;

% complete the connection - located in initiator

  % initiator receives its token back with SLA
  ConfirmConnect(sys,wh_i,tok) ==
    NewTokenI(sys,wh_i,tkid(tok),upd_conn(tkbody(tok),"ACK")) ;

% end the connection - can occur at either end

  EndConnect(sys,wh,tid) ==
    let s = GetServer(sys,wh)
    in if   tid member dom(tokens(s))
       then NewTokenI(sys,wh,tid,
                        upd_conn(tokens(s)[tid],"NONE"))
       else if tid member dom(SIs(s))
       then NewTokenR(sys,wh,tid,
                        upd_conn(skeleton(SIs(s)[tid]),"NONE"))
       else sys ;
```

Solutions to exercises

Exercises 5.6

(i) (b) should be bracketed

```
(3 + 2) + n
```

or

```
3 + (2 + n)
```

(e) "Hamlet needs a closing quote

(f) "x" is a string constant. The + operator requires a number.

(ii) (c) applies a logical operator to a number

(e) requires bracketing:

```
(true and false) or true
```

or

```
true and (false or true)
```

(iii) (c) has no terminating semicolon

(d) is a valid boolean expression, but not a variable definition – it has = for ==

(e) "queen" is a string constant, not an identifier

(iv) (a)
```
square : Integer -> Integer
square(n) == power(n,2) ;
```

(b)
```
square(n) == n * n ;
```

(c)
```
odd : Integer -> Boolean
odd(n) == not(even(n)) ;
```

(d)
```
odd(n) == (n mod 2) = 1 ;
```

(e)
```
oddoreven : Integer -> String
oddoreven(n) == if odd(n) then "odd" else "even" ;
```

(f) oddoreven is now defined for any type T
```
oddoreven : T -> String
oddoreven(e) ==
  if    not(is_number(e))
  then "type error"
  else if    odd(e)
       then "odd"
       else "even" ;
```

(v) (a)
```
rnd(x) ==
  let remainder == x mod 1,
      whole == x truncate 1
  in if    remainder = 0 then x
     else if    remainder < 0.5 then whole
          else whole + 1 ;
```

(b) ac == ("Terry",123,15) ;
    third(ac)
or nth(3,ac)

Exercises 6.4

(i) (a) s1 == {13,14,15,16,17,18,19} ;
    or
    s1 == {13,...,19} ;
(b) {6,9,12,13,14,15,16,17,18,19}
(c) {15,16,18}
(d) {13,14,17,19}
(e) {6,9,12}
(f) false
(g) true
(h) 13
(j) 10
(k) the(s1) is not a valid expression, since s1 is not a singleton set
(l) "aargh"
(m) true

(ii) (a) { n * 10 | n <- digits }
(b) { n | n <- digits; (n mod 3) = 0 }
(c) { a | (n,a,b) <- dodgybank }
(d)

```
robinhood : Bank -> Bank
robinhood(b) ==
  {(name,acno,bal - 100) | (name,acno,bal) <- b; bal > 1000 }
    union
  {(name,acno,bal + 100) | (name,acno,bal) <- b; bal <= 1000 } ;
```

Alternative definition:

```
robinhood(b) ==
  {(name,acno, if bal > 1000 then bal - 100 else bal + 100)
                                          | (name,acno,bal) <- b} ;
```

(e) {("Terry",123,115),("Arthur",124,2900)}

(iii) (a) all x in s2 . even(x) = false
(b) exists (n,a,b) in dodgybank . b < 50 = true
(c) exists1 (n,a,b) in dodgybank . b >= 0 = false

(iv) (a) 20
(b) true
(c) A first attempt might be

```
minset : set(Nat) -> Nat
minset(s) ==
  if   s = {} then 0
  else min reduce (1000000) s ;
```

where some arbitrary large number has been chosen as the unit. This is unsatisfactory, since the definition is correct only for part of the domain, i.e. those sets of natural numbers which have at least one member smaller than 1000001. To avoid this problem, we will use max to discover the largest number in the set, and use this number as the unit:

```
minset(s) ==
  min reduce (max reduce (0) s) s ;
```

Exercises 7.4

(i) (a) rel(String,Nat)
(b) {"a","b"}
(c) {1,2,5}
(d) {("b",5)}
(e) {("a",1),("a",2)}

(ii) (a) map(String,set(Nat))
(b) {1,2}
(c) false
(d) {}
(e) {"a" -> {3}, "b" -> {5}, "c" -> {10}}
(f) {1 -> 2, 4 -> 8, 9 -> 18}

(iii) (a)
```
lessons : Student x Register x Timetable -> set(Lesson)
lessons(stu,r,t) ==
  dunion({ t[sub,{}] | sub <- r[stu,{}] }) ;
```
(b)
```
attends : Lesson x Register x Timetable -> set(Student)
attends(les,r,t) ==
  { stu | stu <- dom(r), (sub,sles) <- t;
        (sub member r[stu]) and (les member sles)} ;
```
(c)
```
no_clashes : Register x Timetable -> Boolean
no_clashes(r,t) ==
  all (stu,sles) in r .
    all les1 in sles .
      all les2 in (sles diff {les1}) .
        (t[les1,{}] inter t[les2,{}]) = {} ;
```

Exercises 8.4

(i) (a) ["seek","simplicity","and","distrust","it"]
(A quote from Alfred North Whitehead)
(b) [(1,2),(2,4),(3,6),(4,8)]
(c) [(1,"a"),(1,"b"),(2,"a"),(2,"b"),(3,"a"),(3,"b")]

(ii) (a) {1,2,3,4,5,6,7}
(b) {1 -> "fair", 2 -> "is", 3 -> "foul", 4 -> "and",
5 -> "foul", 6 -> "is", 7 -> "fair"}
(c) "fair"
(d) "error"
(e) len(macbeth)
(f) card(rng(macbeth))
(g) len([w | w <- macbeth; w = "foul"])
(h) { p | (p,w) <- asm(macbeth); w = "foul"}

(iii) (a) [1,4,3,2,9]
(b) 4
(c) [2]

(iv) (a) vehicle :: reg year manuf model ;
(b) car1 ==
mk_vehicle("ME 2", 1953, "Chevrolet","Corvette") ;
(c) model(car1)
(d) car1 == upd_year(car1,1989) ;

References

Alexander, H. (1987) *Formally-based Tools and Techniques for Human–Computer Dialogues*, Ellis Horwood, Chichester, UK.

Alexander, H. (1988) 'Comments on "Formal specification of user interfaces"', *IEEE Trans. on Software Engineering*, **SE-14** (4), 438–9.

Alexander, H. and D.G. McVitie (1988) *Security Aspects of the Fundamental Association Model*, Technical Report SETC/IN/229, STC Technology Ltd, Newcastle-under-Lyme, UK, also *ICL Technical Journal*, Nov. 1989.

Alexander, H. and B.F. Potter (1987) 'Case study: the use of formal specification and rapid prototyping to establish product feasibility', *Information and Software Technology*, **29** (7), 388–94.

Bailey, R. (1987) 'An introduction to Hope', in *Functional Programming: languages, tools and architectures*, pp. 21–43, ed. S. Eisenbach, Ellis Horwood, Chichester, UK.

Bennett, S.M. (1986a) *A PS-algol Implementation of the Personal Planner from its me too Specification*, Technical Report SETC/IN/210, STC Technology Ltd, Newcastle-under-Lyme, UK.

Bennett, S.M. (1986b) *A me too Model of a Compiler*, Technical Report SETC/IN/221, STC Technology Ltd, Newcastle-under-Lyme, UK.

Bennett, S.M. (1988) *me too and PCE – The User Guide*, Technical Report SETC/IN/231, STC Technology Ltd, Newcastle-under-Lyme, UK.

Bennett, S.M., V.M. Jones, C.J. Minkowitz and J. Rowles (1989) *me too Reference Manual*, Technical Report SETC/IN/209, STC Technology Ltd, Newcastle-under-Lyme, UK.

Bird, R. and P. Wadler (1988) *Introduction to Functional Programming*, Prentice Hall, Hemel Hempstead, UK.

Birrell, N.D. and M.A. Ould (1985) *A Practical Handbook for Software Development*, Cambridge University Press, Cambridge, UK.

Blum, B.I. (1983) 'Still more about rapid prototyping', *ACM SIGSOFT Software Engineering Notes*, **8** (3), 9–11.

Boehm, B.W. (1981) *Software Engineering Economics*, Prentice Hall, Englewood Cliffs, N.J.

Boehm, B.W., T.E. Gray and T. Seewaldt (1984) 'Prototyping vs. specifying: a multi-project experiment', *IEEE Trans. on Software Engineering*, **SE-10** (3), 290–303.

Bonet, R. and A. Kung (1984) 'Structuring into subsystems: the experience of a prototyping approach', *ACM SIGSOFT Software Engineering Notes*, **9** (5), 23–7.

Boyer, R.S. and J.S. Moore (1981) *The Correctness Problem in Computer Science*, Academic Press, London, UK.

Brooks, F.P. (1975) *The Mythical Man-Month*, Addison-Wesley, Reading, MA.

Bruce, E. (1986) *A Formal Specification of a 'Prospector'-type Expert System Shell*, Technical Report SETC/IN/213, STC Technology Ltd, Newcastle-under-Lyme, UK.

Budde, R., K. Kuhlenkamp, L. Mathiassen and H. Zullighoven (eds) (1984) *Approaches to Prototyping*, Springer-Verlag, Berlin.

Carey, T.T. and R.E.A. Mason (1983) 'Information systems prototyping: techniques, tools and methodologies', *INFOR*, **21** (3), 177–91.

Clark, R.G. (1986) *Ada programs from me too specifications*, Technical Report TR17, Dept of Computing Science, University of Stirling, Scotland.

Clark, R.G. (1988) 'The design and development of Ada real-time embedded systems', *Proceedings BCS-FACS Workshop on Specification and Verification of Concurrent Systems*, University of Stirling, July.

Clocksin, W.F. and C.S. Mellish (1985) *Programming in Prolog*, Springer-Verlag, Berlin.

Codd, E.F. (1970) 'A relational model of data for large shared data banks', *Communications of the ACM*, **13**, 377–87.

Codd, E.F. (1972) 'Relational completeness of Data Base Sublanguages', *Data Base Systems*, Courant Comp. Sci. Symposia Series, Vol. 6, Prentice Hall, Englewood Cliffs, N.J.

Codd, E.F. (1979) 'Extending the database relational model to capture more meaning', *ACM Trans. on Database Systems*, **4**, 397–434.

Cohen, B., W. Harwood and M.I. Jackson (1986) *The Specification of Complex Systems*, Addison-Wesley, Wokingham, UK.

Cottam, I. (1984) 'The rigorous development of a system version control program', *IEEE Trans. on Software Engineering*, **SE-10** (2), 143–54.

Davies, K. and C.J. Minkowitz (1987) *Warehouse Planning Using an Object-oriented Simulation Tool Based on Petri Nets*, Technical Report TR38, Dept of Computing Science, University of Stirling, Scotland.

Denny, J. (1987) *Introduction to PARIS*, Internal ICL Report, ICL Bracknell, UK.

Denvir, B., W.T. Harwood, M.I. Jackson and M.J. Wray (eds) (1985) *The Analysis of Concurrent Systems*, Springer-Verlag, Berlin.

Diaz, M. (1982) 'Modeling and analysis of communication and cooperation protocols using Petri net based models', *Computer Networks*, **6** (6), 419–41.

Downs, E., P. Clare and I. Coe (1988) *Structured Systems Analysis and Design Method: Application and Context*, Prentice Hall, Hemel Hempstead, UK.

Ehrig, H. and B. Mahr (1985) *Fundamentals of Algebraic Specification I: Equations and Initial Semantics*, Springer-Verlag, Berlin.

Floyd, C. (1984) 'A systematic look at prototyping', in Budde *et al.* (1984), pp. 1–17.

Gane, C. and T. Sarson (1979) *Structured Systems Analysis: Tools and Techniques*, Prentice Hall, Englewood Cliffs, N.J.

Glaser, H., C. Hankin and D. Till (1984) *Principles of Functional Programming*, Prentice Hall, Hemel Hempstead, UK.

Goguen, J.A. and J. Meseguer (1982) 'Rapid prototyping in the OBJ executable specification language', in Squires (1982), pp. 75–84.

Goldberg, A. and D. Robson (1983) *Smalltalk-80 – the Language and its Implementation*, Addison-Wesley, Reading, MA.

Gomaa, H. (1983) 'The impact of rapid prototyping on specifying user requirements', *ACM SIGSOFT Software Engineering Notes*, **8** (2), 17–28.

Gray, P. (1984) *Logic, Algebra and Databases*, Ellis Horwood, Chichester, UK.

Guttag, J.V. and J.J. Horning (1978) 'The algebraic specification of abstract data types', *Acta Informatica*, **10** (1), 27–52.

Guttag, J.V., J.J. Horning and J. Wing (1982) 'Some notes on putting formal specifications to productive use', *Science of Computer Programming*, **2** (1), 53–8.

Harary, F. (1969) *Graph Theory*, Addison-Wesley, Reading, MA.

Harel, D.H. (1987) 'Statecharts: a visual formalism for complex systems', *Science of Computer Programming*, **8** (3), 231–74.

Hayes, I. (ed.) (1986) *Specification Case Studies*, Prentice Hall, Hemel Hempstead, UK.

Hekmatpour, S. and D.C. Ince (1986) 'A formal specification-based prototyping system', in *Proceedings Software Engineering '86*, 317–35, ed. D. Barnes, P. Brown, Peter Peregrinus, London, UK.

Henderson, P. (1980) *Functional Programming: Application and Implementation*, Prentice Hall, Hemel Hempstead, UK.

Henderson, P. (1985) *me too: a Language for Software Specification and Model Building (Preliminary Report)*, Internal Report FPN-9, Dept of Computing Science, University of Stirling, Scotland.

Henderson, P. (1986a) 'Functional programming, formal specification and rapid prototyping', *IEEE Trans. on Software Engineering*, **SE-12** (2), 241–50

Henderson, P. (1986b) Private communication.

Henderson, P., G. Jones and S.B. Jones (1983) *The LispKit Manual*, Technical Monograph PRG-32, Oxford University Computing Laboratory, Oxford, UK.

Henderson, P. and V.M. Jones (1988) *Software Architecture Modelling: Course Manual*, Centre for Software Engineering Technology, University of Stirling, Scotland.

Henderson, P. and C.J. Minkowitz (1986) 'The *me too* method of software design', *ICL Technical Journal*, **5** (1), 64–95.

Hoare, C.A.R. (1982) *Programming is an Engineering Profession*, Technical Monograph PRG-27, Oxford University Computing Laboratory, Oxford, UK.

Hoare, C.A.R. (1985) *Communicating Sequential Processes*, Prentice Hall, Hemel Hempstead, UK.

Hoare, C.A.R. and J.C. Shepherdson (1985) *Mathematical Logic and Programming Languages*, Prentice Hall, Hemel Hempstead, UK.

Hockey, S. and I. Marriott (1980) *Oxford Concordance Program Version 1.0: Users' Manual*, Oxford University Computing Service, Oxford, UK.

Hodges, W. (1977) *Logic*, Penguin, Harmondsworth, UK.

Hollingdale, S. and G. Tootill (1970) *Electronic Computers*, Penguin, Harmondsworth, UK.

Ince, D.C. and S. Hekmatpour (1987) 'Software prototyping – progress and prospects', *Information and Software Technology*, **29** (1), 8–14.

Ince, D.C. and S. Hekmatpour (1988) *Software Prototyping, Formal Methods and VDM*, Addison-Wesley, Wokingham, UK.

ISO (1985) *Estelle – a Formal Description Technique Based on an Extended State Transition Model*, Technical Report, ISO TC97/SC21/WG16-1.

Jackson, M.A. (1983) *System Development*, Prentice Hall, Hemel Hempstead, UK.

Jones, A., J.S. Rowles and E. Bruce (1985) *A Formal Specification of a Personal Planner*, Technical Report SETC/IN/206, STC Technology Ltd, Newcastle-under-Lyme, UK.

Jones, C.B. (1986) *Systematic Software Development Using VDM*, Prentice Hall, Hemel Hempstead, UK.

Jones, V.M. (1984) *A Resource Management and Planning System*, Technical Report TR17, Dept of Computing Science, University of Stirling, Scotland.

Jones, V.M., S.B. Jones and C.J. Minkowitz (1985) *A Formal Specification of an Expert System Shell*, Technical Report TR20, Dept of Computing Science,

University of Stirling, Scotland.

Kennedy, K. and J. Schwartz (1975) 'An introduction to the set theoretical language SETL', *Computation and Mathematics with Applications*, **1**, 97–119.

Kowalski, R. (1985) 'The relation between logic programming and logic specification', in Hoare and Shepherdson (1985), pp. 11–24.

Liskov, B. and S. Zilles (1975) 'Specification techniques for data abstractions', *IEEE Trans. on Software Engineering*, **SE-1** (1), 7–19.

McCarthy, J. (1960) 'Recursion functions of symbolic expressions and their computation by machine', *Communications of the ACM*, **3** (4), 184–95.

Macro, A. and J. Buxton (1987) *The Craft of Software Engineering*, Addison-Wesley, Wokingham, UK.

McVitie, D.G. (1987a) *Interworking Architecture*, Internal Report MSD 37, International Computers Ltd, West Gorton, UK.

McVitie, D.G. (1987b) *Quality of Service Parameters for Security Control Across Connections*, Discussion paper, International Computers Ltd, West Gorton, UK.

Manna, Z. and A. Pneuli (1981) 'Verification of concurrent programs: the temporal framework', in Boyer and Moore (1981), 215–73.

Milner, R. (1985) 'Using algebra for concurrency: some approaches', in *The Analysis of Concurrent Systems*, pp. 7–25, Springer-Verlag, Berlin.

Minkowitz, C.J. (1985) *Specification to Prototype – a Comparison of Two Methods of Software Design*, Technical Report TR18, Dept of Computing Science, University of Stirling, Scotland.

Minkowitz, C.J. (1986) *A Formal Design of a Decision Analysis System*, Technical Report TR27, Dept of Computing Science, University of Stirling, Scotland.

Minkowitz, C.J. and P. Henderson (1985) *An Example of the Use of me too to Describe Formally a Simplification of the ODA Layout Process*, Internal Report RGP-20, Dept of Computing Science, University of Stirling, Scotland.

Minkowitz, C.J. and P. Henderson (1987) 'An application of object-oriented programming to Petri net models of discrete event-driven simulation', *Proceedings AFCET European Conference on Object-Oriented Programming*, 187–92.

Minsky, M. (1975) 'A framework for representing knowledge', in *The Psychology of Computer Vision*, ed. P. Winston, McGraw Hill, New York.

Moszkowski, B. (1986) *Executing Temporal Logic Programs*, Cambridge University Press, Cambridge, UK.

Naftalin, M. (1988) *Report on the Combination of StateMate and me too*, Descartes ESPRIT Report D3-6-1, available from Dept of Computing Science, University of Stirling, Scotland.

Naur, P. (1982) 'Formalization in program development', *BIT*, **22** (4), 437–53.

NCC (1987) *The STARTS Guide* (2nd edn), NCC Publications, Manchester, UK.

Neumann, P.G. and contributors (1987a) 'Risks to the public', *ACM SIGSOFT Software Engineering Notes*, **12** (2), 4–22.

Neumann, P.G. and contributors (1987b) 'Risks to the public', *ACM SIGSOFT Software Engineering Notes*, **12** (3), 2–16.

Ould, M.A. and C. Unwin (eds) (1986) *Testing in Software Development*, Cambridge University Press, Cambridge, UK.

Peters, L.J. (1981) *Software Design: Methods and Techniques*, Yourdon Press, New York, US.

Rowles, J. (1986) *Describing Screen Layouts in a Purely Functional Style*, Technical Report SETC/IN/217, STC Technology Ltd, Newcastle-under-Lyme, UK.

Rowles, J. (1987) *Process Modelling in me too*, Technical Report SETC/IN/224, STC Technology Ltd, Newcastle-under-Lyme, UK.

Squires, S.L. (ed.) (1982) *ACM SIGSOFT Software Engineering Notes* (Special issue on rapid prototyping), **7** (5).

Tavendale, R. (1985) 'A technique for prototyping directly from a specification', in *Proceedings 8th Int. Conference on Software Engineering*, 224–9, London, UK.

Tavolato, P. and K. Vincena (1984) 'A prototyping methodology and its tools', in Budde *et al.* (1984), 434–46.

Till, D. and B.F. Potter (1987) 'The specification in Z of gateway functions within a communications network', in *Proceedings IFIP WG10.3 Conference*, North-Holland, Amsterdam.

Turner, D.A. (1982) 'Recursion equations as a programming language' in *Functional Programming and its Applications: an advanced course*, eds J. Darlington, P. Henderson, D.A. Turner, pp. 1–28, Cambridge University Press, Cambridge, UK.

Turner, D.A. (1985) 'Functional programs as executable specifications', in Hoare and Shepherdson (1985), pp. 1–10.

Turner, D.A. (1986) 'An overview of Miranda', *ACM SIGPLAN Notices*, **21** (12), 158–66.

Turner, K.J. (1987) 'LOTOS – a practical formal description technique for OSI', in *Proceedings Int. Conference on Open Systems Interconnection*, 265–80, Online International, UK.

Wikström, Å. (1987) *Functional Programming using Standard ML*, Prentice Hall, Hemel Hempstead, UK.

Index

Note: Primary references are shown in bold; references to figures or tables are shown in italics.